ACRONYM SOUP

ACRONYM SOUP

A Stirring Guide to Our
Newest Word Form

Gilda and Phil Feldman

William Morrow and Company, Inc.
New York

It is the policy of William Morrow and Company, Inc., and its imprints and affiliates, recognizing the importance of preserving what has been written, to print the books we publish on acid-free paper, and we exert out best efforts to that end.

Library of Congress Cataloging-in-Publication Data

Feldman, Gilda.
    Acronym soup : a stirring guide to our newest word form / by Gilda and Phil Feldman.
        p.   cm.
    Includes bibliographical references and index.
    ISBN 0-688-12160-8
    1. English language—Etymology. 2. Acronyms. I. Feldman, Phil.
II. Title.
PE1574.F46   1994
422—dc20   93-34440
                                                        CIP

Printed in the United States of America

First Edition

1 2 3 4 5 6 7 8 9 10

For Elmo and Paco Montalbin,
dear and valued friends,
before whose warm hearth,
in the deep green room,
one of the four of us
mused out loud, "Acronyms?
I wonder if there's a book in it."

Acknowledgments

THOUGH WE WEAR the big white chef's hats, many exceedingly helpful people have contributed key ingredients to *Acronym Soup*. We are very grateful for their help.

David "Bro" Feldman inspired us with his vast and imponderable knowledge about everything under the sun, encouraged us by reading, editing, and appreciating several early chapters of *Soup*, taught us nifty research tricks, and introduced us to . . .

Jim Trupin, our indefatigable agent, who found a home for *Soup* and whose caustic irrepressible wit is reason enough to tie up his phone (a fault to which we confess).

Randy Ladenheim-Gil, editor at William Morrow, believed in *Soup* from the beginning and was wonderfully patient with all our undoubtedly naive questions.

Bob Shuman, editor at William Morrow, was exceedingly warm and welcoming from the first moment we spoke together. His enthusiasm, creative suggestions, and willingness to laugh at our jokes made the editing process as painless as it could possibly be.

Joan Amico, copy editor at William Morrow, did the clearest, most thorough job of pruning sentences and catching errors that we've ever encountered in all our years of writing (and we've written more than thirty books between the two of us).

The enormously hardworking and unflappable staff at the Santa Monica Library in Los Angeles did their dogged best to find the answers to our cascades of odd questions and offered welcoming smiles to boot.

Tom Rugg plied us with acronyms he'd found, served as a technical consultant for the computer chapter, and even searched a database of the *Los Angeles Times* to find acronyms for *Soup* and thereby provided us with some of our best entries.

John Blees sent us a copy of JUG XI—Jargon Understanding Glossary—which was chock-full of official acronyms.

Dr. Phil Schwartzman told us about emergency-room slang and sent us to the right book for more.

Bob Gramcko told us acronyms and other lore about the big computer net.

Jeannette Shelburne found a book about teenage slang that was rich in acronyms.

Adolf Solis, the city clerk of Azusa, California, regaled us with a wonderful history of his city.

The Oregon Historical Society in Portland solved one of our biggest puzzles.

Leslie M. Kantor, the director of community advocacy at SIECUS, was kind enough to spend a good deal of time helping us chase down organizations.

Other people who were helpful include C. Amor Kramer of ASH, Cecile Starr of WIFE, Bill Morris of GASP, Michelle Scott of Kids F.A.C.E., Monica A. Depin of Hasbro, Inc., Lucy Skjelstad, director of the Horner Museum in Corvallis, Dawne Marshall of the New England Confectionery Company, and Captain Rodger K. Coombs of the Los Angeles Police Department.

Without the love and support of our family and dear friends, *Acronym Soup* would undoubtedly be a far weaker concoction. Thank you, Michael Leo and Nettie and Mary and Grampie and Snaz. You're somewhere on every page.

Contents

10 / CONTENTS

Introduction

Girls just want to have fun, according to Cyndi Lauper. Hey, so do boys. In fact, can you think of any activity that doesn't include some element of play? Funerals? Whole-body casts? The grimmer the subject, the more vivid the jokes. And look at our passion for sports. Look at the busy kaleidoscope of fashion. Look at language, that ever-changing soup we cook semiconsciously. We chop up sounds and concepts recklessly, stir with a giggle, and fish out new words whenever we need them.

Perhaps the most consciously crafted words in the pot are the acronyms. We combine the first letter from each word of a phrase and, *voilà*, we've got WIN (**W**hip **I**nflation **N**ow) or Scuba (**S**elf-**C**ontained **U**nderwater **B**reathing **A**pparatus). But often we've also got instant entertainment.

Why else would a service that arranges hotel accommodations for conventioneers call itself GRAB (**G**roup **R**ooms **A**vailable **B**ank)? Why else would a political action group of New Yorkers fed up with scraping dog poop off their shoes name their organization SCOOP (**S**top **C**rapping **O**n **O**ur **P**remises)? And why else would a scientific think tank coin the acronym ABRACADABRA (**AB**breviations and **R**elated **AC**ronyms **A**sso-ciated with **D**efense, **A**stronautics, **B**usiness, and **RA**dio-elec-

11

tronics) in a tongue-in-cheek effort to abolish acronyms themselves?

Certainly there are times when the humor in acronyms does serve a purpose beyond sheer entertainment. Let's say you live in a suburb whose main claim to fame is pristine white beaches. Some petroleum conglomerate starts drilling offshore and soon that glorious sand is stained and glopped with oil. You get together with your neighbors and form a political action committee called CACC (**C**oncerned **A**mericans for a **C**leaner **C**oastline) or, wait a minute, wouldn't GOO* (**G**et **O**il **O**ut!) be better? Media coverage would triple. These days we almost expect that a political action group will choose an attention-grabbing acronym for its name. And many nonpolitical groups have followed suit.

A Few Useful Terms

There are those who will argue that acronyms have popped up like mushrooms in late-twentieth-century English because they save time for ever-more-harried English speakers. It's faster to say ACCESS than **A**utomatic **C**omputer-**C**ontrolled **E**lectronic **S**canning **S**ystem. Undoubtedly true. But why not pick a shorter title to start with, say, Automatic Scanning, and be called AS?

Actually that often happens. Most people refer to terms like BLT or IRS, where we say the name of each letter, as abbreviations or even acronyms. Technically speaking, they're *initialisms*, only one part of the abbreviations family.

Another member of the family is the *acronym*. Webster's dictionary defines an acronym as a pronounceable word formed from the initial letter or letters of the successive (or major) parts of a compound term. SWAT (**S**pecial **W**eapons **A**nd **T**actics) is a well-known example. So is AIDS (**A**cquired **I**mmune **D**eficiency **S**yndrome).

AIDS, which uses the first letter of every word of its compound term, is what we might call a "pure" acronym. There are also many acronyms that fudge here or there, leaving out

---

*An actual group from Santa Barbara, California, in the early 1970s.

a letter or two, sometimes adding an extra letter or two. As a pure acronym, the airline industry's **A**utomatic **S**ystem for **P**assenger **R**eservation by **N**otation becomes ASPRN (boring). But borrow two I's and you have ASPIRIN (funny).

Acronym Soup focuses on acronyms, of course, but also includes portmanteau words like "sitcom," made from blending parts of two different words—situation + comedy. We choose the wider scope partly because some words straddle the line between acronyms and portmanteaus. (Consider AMESLAN—**AME**rican **S**ign **LAN**guage—or COMSTRIK-FORSOUTH—**COM**mander, Naval **STRIK**ing and **FOR**ces Support, **SOUTH**ern Europe). However, portmanteaus have also won their place in the book because, like their cousins the acronyms, they tickle our fancy, stir our feelings, and excite our admiration at their cleverness.

SOUP INGREDIENTS

Any acronym that has become prominent in its field will appear in this book. It would be hard to talk about the space program without mentioning NASA, for example. (See Chapter 12: From Lasers to Quasars.) Or the NASDAQ index in financial matters. (See Chapter 8: Money Makes the World Go 'Round.)

Perhaps the most charming kind of acronym is the sort where people start with a longish word like CAUTION and work backward until they've picked out the words to match the letters (**C**itizens **A**gainst **U**nnecessary **T**ax **I**ncreases and **O**ther **N**onsense). Aristotle, Socrates, Plato, Euclid, and Solomon have all had their names taken in vain in this manner, as is demonstrated in Chapter 16: How Clever Can You Get?

We also present a group of terms that are used as initialisms (pronounced letter by letter) but would be considerably more captivating, in one way or another, if pronounced as acronyms. The Society for American Philosophy's abbreviation, for example, is SAP. And the Navy Advisory Group is NAG. (For many more, see Chapter 17: Did They Realize?)

There are some exacting souls who claim that only fourteen acronyms are truly words, since only those have earned an uncapitalized dictionary entry. (Scuba and laser are examples.) On the other hand, there are those who believe that NEWS is an acronym for North, East, West, and South. Or that COP stands for Constable On Patrol. At times, acronymic research is a virtual minefield of controversy. Chapter 18: Oddities, Records, and Other Irresistible Miscellanea explores these and other such burning questions.

HAVE THERE ALWAYS BEEN ACRONYMS?

The first well-known acronym was created in Rome by the early Christians somewhere during the first century. It was a time of great persecution for the small Christian sect and they used ICHTHUS, a Greek word meaning fish, as a secret sign to identify themselves to each other. It stands for the Greek phrase "**I**esous **CH**ristos **T**heou **HU**ios **S**oter" meaning Jesus Christ, Son of God, Savior.

One of the earliest of what we might call proto-acronyms comes to us from the Middle Ages in the courts of law. If the accused claimed he or she was innocent, the clerk would write "culpable: prest" which was a shortened form of "culpable: prest d'averrer nostre bille." (He is guilty and I'm ready to prove our charge.) A further shortening led to "cul. prest," sometimes spelled "cul. prit." The Earl of Pembroke, being tried for murder in 1678, was the first prisoner actually called a "culprit."

In like fashion, the word "algebra" comes from foreshortening the ancient phrase "ilm al-jebr wa'l-muq-ab alah," meaning in Arabic "reduction and comparison by equations." The Italians were kind enough to telescope it, using parts of several syllables, in the middle of the seventeenth century.

A similar telescoping has gone to make some of our most common words: "God be with you" has contracted down to "Good-bye"; "Fiddle-dee-dee" (Scarlett O'Hara's favorite light oath) comes from the Italian "Fedidio, Fe di Dio" meaning "by the faith of God"; and the British epithet "Bloody" (somewhat stronger than the American "Damn") is made from bits of the pious phrase "By Our Lady."

One could even argue that "doff" and "don," stemming in

turn from the two North English phrases "do off" and "do on," were portmanteau words waiting for Mr. Carroll to christen them.

However, acronyms as we know them came into their own during World War I, with such terms as ANZAC (**A**ustralia–**N**ew **Z**ealand **A**rmy **C**orp) and WAAC (**W**omen's **A**rmy **A**uxiliary **C**orps). More popped up during the Great Depression, fueled by FDR's alphabet soup of helping agencies, like his Bureau of Personnel, called BUPERS. During World War II, acronyms multiplied like rabbits. Radar (**RA**dio **D**etection **A**nd **R**anging), Snafu (**S**ituation **N**ormal, **A**ll **F**ouled **U**p) and Gestapo (from **GE**heime **STA**ats**PO**lizei, German for "Secret State Police") all appeared during the 1940s.

As did the term "acronym" itself, in 1943. Taking as a model such well-accepted linguistic terms as "homonym," "synonym," and "eponym," the Greek root "akros," meaning "tip" or "extreme edge," was combined with "nym" from the Greek "nomos," meaning "name." As is typical with such terms, there were hordes of acronyms coined before anyone cooked up a word to describe them.

And we've never looked back. The acronym is the single fastest-growing type of word in post–World War II English. We laypeople may complain of impenetrable forests of jargon growing up around the simplest government activity. Language mavens may bemoan the FOG (**F**requency **O**f **G**obbledygook) beclouding Pentagon, Wall Street, and hospital corridors. But every morning, masses of Yuppies (**Y**oung **U**rban **P**rofessionals), both WASPs (**W**hite **A**nglo-**S**axon **P**rotestants) and JAPs (**J**ewish-**A**merican **P**rincesses), don their Adidas (named for Adi Dassler), kiss their POSSLQ (**P**erson of **O**pposite **S**ex **S**haring **L**iving **Q**uarters—pronounced "Posselcue"), and jog out into the dramedies (drama + comedies) of their lives. There's nowhere else to run.

CHAPTER 1

They're in the Air We Breathe

WHETHER YOU'RE a Yuppie or a Biddy (**B**aby boomer **I**n **D**ebt), a Moss (**M**iddle-aged, **O**verstressed, **S**emi-affluent **S**uburbanite) or a Skotie (**S**poiled **K**id **O**f **T**he **E**ighties), you're bombarded with acronyms every time you open a magazine or turn on the news. Some you know far too well. Like AIDS. Some you may not know much about, but you lose some of your paycheck to them every month (FICA) or trust your diagnosis to them (CAT scan).

They feed you (Nabisco) and shave you (TRAC II), fly you (Qantas) and drive you (Datsun), and even wrap up your leftovers (Alcoa). And they'll even save you money (IRA) as long as you're careful with the punctuation. (The I.R.A. or Irish Republican Army would certainly be happy to accept any contributions you might make, but don't expect either the cash back at retirement or much of a tax break.)

Let's begin with a fascinating group of words: the names of popular products and companies. Some originate with the inventor's name (Wrigley's gum); some dramatize an important quality of the product (Jell-O); some are simplifications of a complex scientific term (Teflon). Some are created mysteriously by the technical staff of a research and development wing of a large company and we'll probably never know how those terms were made. Some are actually created by computer programs that combine attractive-sounding syllables. And some, of course, are acronyms or portmanteaus.

Datsun
son of Dat

The original car was called a Dat. DAT comes from the initials of the three investors who provided the start-up money for the company, Den, Aoyama, and Takeuchi. The second model in the line was first called Datson, or "son of DAT." But when "son" is pronounced in Japanese, it sounds like an expression for losing money. So "son" became "sun," which worked in both Japanese and English.

Corvair
Corvette + Bel Air

This was the sporty little Chevrolet from the early '60s that was featured in Ralph Nader's 1965 best-seller *Unsafe at Any Speed*. He blamed many "one-car accidents" on the Corvair's tendency to fishtail and even turn over when cornering. General Motors added extra rear suspension support to its 1965 model, after the extremely popular car had been out for four years.

Nader reminds us that the comedian Ernie Kovacs died in a one-car accident in a Corvair.

Sentra
sentry + central

This was one of those intuitive, imagery-driven choices for a car name. The manufacturers apparently hoped that buyers would feel safe from both burglars and idiosyncrasy.

FIAT
Fabrica **I**taliana **A**utomobili, **T**orino

Toshiba
Tokyo + Shibaura (electrical company)

A company created in 1939 by a merger between the Shibaura Engineering Company and General Electric. What was GE doing in Japan before World War II? Trying to use its manufacturing expertise to create a new consumer market. Through an unlucky break, GE lost its power in the company after the Korean War. Toshiba, of course, considered itself lucky to run its burgeoning electronics firm alone. Today Toshiba manufactures everything from computers to televisions to microwave ovens.

Sanka
sans + caffeine
     Actually developed in 1903, Sanka was not well known until the 1930s, when General Foods began promoting the product. Okay, so it should be "Sanca."

Yuban
Yuletide + banquet or a scrambled version of "**A**rbuckle **B**rothers **N**ew **Y**ork"
     The name of this popular brand of coffee has mysterious origins. Two histories, each one plausible, have appeared. Story number one: As a special Christmas present for his business friends, a coffee merchant whipped up this special combination of beans around the turn of the century. He named it after the holiday. Story number two: The merchant's company was called Arbuckle Brothers and it operated out of New York. So the sacks of coffee beans designated for the company had ABNY printed on them. When working on a name for the coffee itself, employees tried different combinations of the four letters and the one they liked best was YBAN. Even that was rather odd, but a timely U solved the problem.

CANOLA oil
CANada **O**il **L**ow **A**cid
     The variety of the rapeseed from which Canola oil is extracted is Canada's second-largest cash crop. (Wheat's first.) There are two good reasons. One, the oil is low in heart-damaging erucic acid, making Canola the healthiest oil on the market. Two, American competition is minimal because the U.S. government does not subsidize American farmers for planting rapeseed. So the Canadian seed-oil industry, which developed the plant and named it in 1978, still has a clear field.

QANTAS
Queensland **A**nd **N**orthern **T**erritories **A**erial **S**ervices

AVIANCA
Aero**VIA**s **N**acionales de **C**olombi**A**

Noxema
knocks out eczema
  Dr. Bunting was a genial former school principal turned pharmacist who loved doodling in his lab around the turn of the century. His original name for the cooling white goo in its little blue bottles was Doctor Bunting's Sunburn Remedy, but he kept searching for a better name. One day, a customer came in and said, "Doc, you know your sunburn cream sure knocked out my eczema." A star was born.

MAALOX
MAgnesium **AL**uminum Hydr**OX**ide
  A commercial antacid.

ATRA
Automatic **T**racking **R**azor Action

TRAC II
Tandem **R**azor **A**nd **C**artridge II

Velcro
velours + croché
  French for "hooked velvet," this trademark was created in 1960 for a reusable fastener invented by George de Mestral.

Swatch
Swiss + watch
  Fifty years ago, Swiss watches were synonymous with excellence. The country's newest offering has a different appeal. Instead of touting precision and fine quality, the Swatch team promotes innovative design and cheap prices. Their first watch from 1984, called "The Jellyfish," recently sold at auction for over $17,000. (It originally cost $30.) And every season

we can expect a new batch, painted with knock-'em-in-the-eye colors and edged with everything from lace to faux mink.

ALCOA
ALuminum **C**ompany **O**f **A**merica

AMEX
AMerican **EX**press
     and
AMerican Stock **EX**change

TEXACO
The **TEXA**s **CO**mpany

ARCO
Atlantic **R**ichfield **CO**mpany

AMOCO
AMerican **O**il **CO**mpany
     Of Persian Gulf fame.

CONOCO
CONtinental **O**il **CO**mpany

Leica
Leitz + camera
     Leitz is a renowned manufacturer of lenses.
     Konica and Fujica are other camera companies that modeled their trademarks on Leica's.

NABISCO
NAtional **BIS**cuit **CO**mpany
     In 1899, Adolphus W. Green had a controversial idea. Instead of offering the public crackers out of barrels, how about putting crackers in packages? That way the crackers wouldn't break or get stale. And just consider the merchandising possibilities. A package offers a golden opportunity for hitting the shopper with an appealing name, a dramatic picture, vivid colors, etc.

Thus was born the first Nabisco product, the Uneeda Biscuit.

Today Nabisco's Ritz cracker is the single best-selling cracker in the country. And its Chips Ahoy! cookies are the number-one chocolate-chip cookie. Oreos, Fig (and other) Newtons, and Wheat Thins are also leaders in their respective snack fields.

In fact, Adolphus W. Green's brainchild is the largest cookie and cracker manufacturer in the United States (even if it has merged with a tobacco company—RJ Reynolds).

Beyond the world of buying and selling, acronyms pop up with amazing frequency, on everything from envelopes to highways, television shows to the skyline of Tel Aviv.

M*A*S*H
Mobile **A**rmy **S**urgical **H**ospital

The best-known, best-crafted acronymic television series of all time, *M*A*S*H* was a seventies (1972–1983) hit with a sixties antiwar sensibility about a fifties war in Korea. There really were MASH units in wartime Korea, makeshift hospitals struggling to save a flood of wounded soldiers. (The same type of units appeared in Vietnam too, but were called MUSTs—**M**edical **U**nit, **S**elf-contained **T**ransportation.) The last show about these acerbic doctors aired on February 28, 1983. It was the most-watched single episode in the history of television.

Also ending in 1983 after a six-year run, *CHIPs* (**C**alifornia **HI**ghway **P**atrol) was an hour-long crime drama on NBC that followed the rolling adventures of a pair of genial young policemen, Jon Baker and Francis "Ponch" Poncherello.

Another crime-busting dramatic show, airing on ABC in 1975 and '76, was called *S.W.A.T.* (**S**pecial **W**eapons **A**nd **T**actics). Steve Forrest starred as Lieutenant Hondo Harrelson, the leader of a special unit that came to the aid of beleaguered policemen. Its level of violence was high, even for the seventies. The show is long gone but real SWAT teams, of course, are still with us.

A more recent acronymic show is *ALF* (**A**lien **L**ife **F**orm). Originally a technical term for the intelligences we might encounter someday in the far reaches of outer space, in 1986 ALF metamorphosed into a 233-year-old, wisecracking, nozzle-nosed television creature who snacked on cats and who made NBC a bundle of money.

Most recent, and shortest-lived, is a TV series from 1990 called *E.A.R.T.H. Force* (**E**arth **A**lert **R**esearch **T**actical **H**eadquarters). This was a sixty-minute show about a crack team of professionals out to right ecological wrongs.

What's coming to the tube next? How about recycling the old sci-fi term BEM (**B**ug-**E**yed **M**onster)? Or yet another movie spin-off: CHUD (**C**annibalistic **H**umanoid **U**nderground **D**weller)? Nah. We'll just have to wait until next season.

PAC
Political **A**ction **C**ommittee

In 1982, the average wannabe United States senator had to spend approximately $600,000 to finance his campaign for a seat in Congress. By 1988, while general inflation had risen maybe 25 percent, the price for that same senator to run his race had shot up 570 percent to $4 million.

During those six years, thousands of PACs had swung into action. A PAC works like this. Some wealthy businessmen or labor moguls form a coalition. They pool their money and their fund-raising expertise, and gather a sizable chunk of capital. Then they examine the voting records of various lawmakers until one is found who votes the way the PAC prefers on a single group of issues. Maybe they pick a legislator who's conservative on abortion or one who's liberal on TAPS (**T**he **A**laska **P**ipeline **S**ystem). Then they contribute the whole caboodle to this candidate.

Easy to see how inflation hit three figures on Capitol Hill. Also easy to see that PACs tend to support the incumbents (whose voting record is there to peruse) and keep Congress from getting new blood.

Alarmed observers of both parties have introduced legislation to control the power of PACs. So far there's been only limited success. Expect to see this acronym in the media for some time to come.

ZIP code
Zone **I**mprovement **P**lan

In the early '70s, the Post Office introduced a new wrinkle in addressing envelopes: that five-digit code designed to speed your mail on its way. It must have worked. As of April 1990, there were 42,500 designated zips listed by the United States Postal Service.

Ever wondered what the numbers mean?

The first number refers to one of ten large geographical areas, consisting of several states each, that has a designated sectional central post office. Generally the number gets larger the farther west you go—it's 0 on the East Coast and 9 on the West Coast.

The next two numbers refer either to a large city within that area or to a specific section of the area.

The last two numbers designate a particular post office within that large city or a postal delivery system in the specific section.

Now you know.

AWOL
Absent **WithO**ut **L**eave

This one's been around since World War I. A soldier who didn't answer roll call but hadn't been gone long enough to be called a deserter was designated A.W.O.L. In 1935, the Armed Forces dropped the periods. During World War II, a particularly worrisome deserter was the KAWOL, where the K stood for Knowledgeable. This was the soldier who could conceivably give his classified information over to the enemy.

Recently the acronym, minus the K, has acquired a new meaning: **A W**olf **O**n the **L**oose.

CAT scan
Computerized **A**xial **T**omography

A little more than a decade ago, the best an X ray could do was produce a two-dimensional picture of your innards. Today, thanks to the ever-increasing complexity of the computer and the brilliance of Nobel Prize–winning scientists Allen M. Cormack and Sir Godfrey N. Hounsfield, your doctor can look at full three-dimensional "slices" of both your bones and softer tissues.

You lie absolutely motionless inside what looks like a hollowed-out box. The tomography consists of a large series of X rays which are shot of a particular area of your body by a special rotating machine. Each picture is taken from a slightly different angle (or axis—hence "axial"). Then the computer goes to work, transforming all of these two-dimensional pictures into one three-dimensional portrait of your pancreas, aorta, or whatnot.

It's wonderful stuff and exorbitantly expensive at present. Just as high priced and equally fascinating is a relative called the PETT (**P**ositron **E**mission **T**ransaxial **T**omography). Invented a couple of years after the CAT, the PETT is even safer since it doesn't require using X rays. A trace amount of radioactive isotope is injected into the area to be explored and the PETT records the gamma rays that come shooting back. Then the computer goes to work and, *voilà*—without any exploratory surgery, your doctor knows where a clot is blocking blood flow or a tumor is tiptoeing through your personal tulips. Tomography has revolutionized medical diagnosis and is opening exciting new doorways for research.

AIDS
Acquired **I**mmune **D**eficiency **S**yndrome

An ironic acronym for a tragic disease. ARC (**A**IDS-**R**elated **C**omplex) is the combination of symptoms that doctors look for when they suspect AIDS: weight loss, fever, fatigue, night sweats, diarrhea, and testing HIV-positive. (HIV is an initialism for **H**uman **I**mmunodeficiency **V**irus.)

Probably the most visible support group for AIDS victims is the political organization started by playwright Larry Kramer called ACT UP (**A**IDS **C**oalition **T**o **U**nleash **P**ower). The group effectively uses "zaps," confrontational demonstrations that stress homosexuality, to agitate for more government involvement in AIDS research.

CAIN (**C**omputerized **A**IDS **I**nformation **N**etwork) is a support group working out of Hollywood. PAWS LA (**P**ets **A**re **W**onderful **S**upport for people with AIDS/ARC) is another Los Angeles organization, which puts on art shows. The money raised is used to provide AIDS victims with pets. And AM FAR (**AM**erican **F**oundation for **A**IDS **R**esearch) has national scope.

We'd like to see LEAF—**L**et's **E**liminate **A**IDS **F**orever.

ASCAP
American **S**ociety of **C**omposers, **A**uthors, and **P**ublishers

Look at the copyright of any piece of music in this country and you'll find it's protected by either ASCAP or B.M.I. (an initialism for **B**roadcast **M**usic **I**ncorporated).

If Country Bob and the Toads record, let's say, "Rocky Mountain High" without the permission of its writer, John Denver, Mr. Denver can call on ASCAP or B.M.I. to prove that he wrote the song. And any court in the land will make Bob and his Toads croak up a punishing amount of money to pay for their larceny.

ASAP
As **S**oon **A**s **P**ossible

People say this either way: "Ay-sap" (acronym) or "Ay-Es-Ay-Pee" (initialism). In both cases they mean, "The day before yesterday."

SASE
Self-**A**ddressed **S**tamped **E**nvelope

Another two-faced term: "Sassy" or "Es-Ay-Es-Ee." This is what you send when you really want a newspaper columnist or a company to reply to your letter of complaint. It's also the part of the package an aspiring author sends to a publisher and hopes never to see again. If the envelope returns home, it's carrying a rejected manuscript.

Sitcom
situation + comedy

This term, coined by *Variety* magazine, refers to a large percentage of the shows on television. Sitcoms make us laugh by following the adventures of a single group of people, often but not always a family. Some examples—*Leave It to Beaver, Cheers, The Bill Cosby Show*. A subset of the sitcom is the warmedy (warm + comedy), which focuses on a warm-hearted, traditional family whose members are wholesome, very nice people. (*Eight Is Enough* is a good example.) There's also the skitcom (skit + comedy—word form modeled on sitcom), where a single person stars in several comedy skits. Carol Burnett has done several of these.

A dramedy (drama + comedy) is a recent form that adds a significant amount of humor to a dramatic show. Examples are *Doogie Howser M.D.* and *thirtysomething*. Another genre-blurring show type is the docudrama (documentary + drama), where a story based on an actual occurrence is presented dramatically. Remember Farrah Fawcett as a wife-beater's victim in *The Burning Bed*? Or *Blind Ambition*, the post-Watergate depiction of the rise and fall of John Dean, Richard Nixon's legal adviser? A different method of turning real life into drama has been labeled infotainment (information + entertainment). Oprah Winfrey, Geraldo Rivera, Phil Donahue, and a host of other interviewers present us with the bizarre, the tantalizing, the shocking, and, sometimes, the downright unbelievable.

Both radio and television use the chatcom (chatter + comedy) format for light entertainment. Johnny Carson was the seemingly effortless master of this form. For somewhat heavier entertainment, there's confrotalk (confrontation + talk), where politically conservative hosts like Morton Downey, Jr., deliberately pick left-wing guests to demolish.

Finally there's the current combination usually found on very late-night local stations and on the more obscure cable stations—the infomercial (information + commercial). Michael E. Marcovsky, a cable-TV consultant, says he coined this term for a nonprogram segment of his radio show in the early 1980s. Now found mostly on television, the infomercial is a three-minute or ten-minute or even hour-long chat about muscle building or vegetable slicing that turns out to be subtly promoting a specific product.

EPCOT Center
Experimental **P**rototype **C**ommunity **O**f **T**omorrow

In 1982 in Orlando, Florida, Walt Disney World opened a permanent World's Fair called the Epcot Center. This is where you go to see what your house, car, and grocery shopping might look like in two hundred years. Half of the joy of viewing the futuristic technological exhibits is the optimistic assumptions about the future that underlie the clean soaring lines and ingenious concepts: We'll solve the big problems of over-population and ecological damage and burgeoning under-classes and treat each other very well indeed when tomorrow arrives.

PATRIOT Missile
Phased **A**rray **TR**acking to **I**ntercept **O**f **T**arget

In the Persian Gulf War of 1991, some of the major names seemed unusually appropriate. The bad guy's missile was an old Soviet weapon that NATO nicknamed the Scud. Brings to mind scuttling things, and scuz, and the scum of the earth, right? And the anti-missile missiles we sent to Israel to protect innocent civilian populations against the evil Scuds were red, white, and blue Patriots. Even the news commentators had the right monikers. Remember CNN's Wolf Blitzer?

IRA
Individual **R**etirement **A**ccount

The IRA was first established in 1974 for those people working without an employer-sponsored retirement fund. At that time, the employee was allowed to save, tax-free, $1,500 each year for retirement.

In 1982, Congress broadened the law to allow all people who worked to tuck away up to $2,000 per year in an IRA and not pay taxes on the money until retirement, when their income would likely be considerably lower.

But in 1986, the law was amended. Today the earnings of an IRA are tax-free only if the employee has no other retirement plan and if his or her income is below $50,000 annually.

Oh, well. It was great while it lasted.

PIN
Personal **I**dentification **N**umber

In the early 1980s, banks began assigning us these individual codes and warning us *not* to write them down but to memorize them. Then, if anyone stole our bankbooks and tried to withdraw cash from our accounts, the bank would send the would-be thief away empty-handed because the corresponding PIN wasn't logged in. PINs are also essential for withdrawing money from ATMs (**A**utomatic **T**eller **M**achines) and other cash machines.

FICA

Federal **I**nsurance **C**ontribution **A**ct

Every month of your adult life that you work for someone else, a percentage of your pay is extracted by the federal government and saved for you. This involuntary retirement system is called Social Security. It is not affected by your marital state or number of dependents, or even if you are over sixty-five and receiving a Social Security check every month. In 1990, FICA withholding tax was 7.65 percent of your salary, bonuses, commissions, vacation pay, sick leave pay, and contributions to pension plans or tax-sheltered annuities.

Will Social Security provide you with a comfortable retirement? Today the question is hotly debated.

VASCAR

Visual **A**verage **S**peed **C**omputer **A**nd **R**ecorder

You probably don't recognize this acronym. But the chances are good that if you've been hit with a speeding ticket, this is the device that busted you. Marketed in 1966, VASCAR electronically measures how long it takes your car to move between two reference points. Wherever the signs say SPEED CHECKED BY RADAR, you know VASCAR is watching you.

CHAPTER 2

All About Us

WE LOVE TO LABEL ourselves. Define and redefine ourselves. We subdivide ourselves by everything from salary level to preference in beverages. We are bleeding-heart liberals and born-again Christians, Rotarians and Libertarians, Deadheads and Skinheads. And we call ourselves DINKs, WASPs, swingles, and buffarillas as well.

Let's begin with an acronym that has more spin-offs than any other: Yuppie or **Y**oung **U**rban **P**rofessional. What *is* it about those baby boomers? The story starts with the '60s term Hippie (itself a derisive name coined by '50s beatniks for an upstart group of would-be hipsters). Then Abbie Hoffman changed the first letter, calling his band of absurdist activists the Yippies. (See Chapter 4 for a fuller discussion of Yippies.)

In 1982, in an analytic article about the writer John Irving, Joseph Epstein spoke of Yuppies as a socioeconomic group coming up in the world yet still clutching their hippie past. Newspaper writer Bob Greene fleshed out more details and discussed their elitist preoccupations in a column about Yuppies in 1983. Others in these early months called the same group Yumpies, **Y**oung **U**pwardly **M**obile **P**rofessionals, but this variant soon died. In early '84, C. E. Crimmins's book named them YAPs or **Y**oung **A**spiring **P**rofessionals. And later in '84, Marissa Piesman and Marilee Hartley published *The Yuppie Handbook*, a playful how-to-be-a-yuppie description that subdivided yuppiedom into groups like Puppies (**Preg**nant **U**rban **P**rofessionals) and Guppies (**G**ay **U**rban **P**rofessionals).

In December of '84, America's preoccupation with these thirtyish, networking, Perrier-swigging consumers had reached such massive proportions that *Newsweek* devoted its cover story to this social class of young, ambition-driven professionals who are dedicated to transcendental acquisition (BMWs, Rolex watches, glossy condos, fern-hung restaurants-of-the-week, hundred-dollar running shoes) and the narcissistic perfecting of their bodies.

And we've never looked back. What follows is a list of no fewer than thirty-four hippie/yuppie variants. Most of these terms appeared in print only once or twice, often coined by an anonymous journalist seeking to spice up his or her copy. Though ephemeral as dragonflies, for the week or two of their existence, these acronyms were a delight to behold.

Yuppies come in many nationalities and ethnicities:

CHUPPIE —**CH**icano **U**rban **P**rofessional
JUPPIE —**J**apanese **U**rban **P**rofessional
YUCA —**Y**oung **U**pwardly mobile **C**uban **A**merican
BUPPIE —**B**ritish **U**rban **P**rofessional and **B**lack **U**rban **P**rofessional

And belief systems:

YUKKIE —**Y**oung **U**pwardly mobile **C**ommunist
FRUMPIE —**F**ormerly **R**adical **U**pwardly **M**obile **Per**son
HUPPIE —hippie + yuppie (upwardly mobile but in denial—maintains hippie life-style)
GUPPIE —green + yuppie (a yuppie involved in environmental issues)
MUPPIE —**M**ennonite **U**rban **P**rofessional
FRUPPIE —fromm + yuppie (*Fromm* is a Yiddish word meaning "religious.") Fruppies are

Jewish baby boomers returning to their roots after trying other life-styles.

And ages:

SKOTIE —**S**poiled **K**id **O**f **T**he **E**ighties (the offspring of yuppies)

SKIPPIE —**S**chool **K**id with **I**ncome and **P**urchasing **P**ower (a marketing term from 1987)

PUP —**P**re-**U**rban **P**rofessional (coined by *TeenAge* magazine to describe its readers)

GRUMPIE —**GR**own-**U**p **M**ature **P**erson

ZUPPIE —**Z**estful **U**pscale **P**eople in their **P**rime

WOOPIE —**W**ell-**O**ff **O**lder **P**erson

GLAM —**G**raying **L**eisured **A**ffluent **M**iddle-aged

MAFFIE —**M**iddle-aged **A**ffluent **F**olk

YEEPIE —**Y**outhful **E**nergetic **E**lderly **P**erson **I**nvolved in **E**verything

GUPPIE —**G**eriatrically **U**seless **P**erson **P**assing **I**nto **E**ternity

There is also the:

YUMMIE —**Y**oung **U**pwardly **M**obile **M**ommie

GUPPIE —**G**ay **U**pwardly mobile **P**rofessional

PIPPIE —**P**erson **I**nheriting **P**arents' **P**roperty (yuppies who inherit the houses their folks bought in the post–World War II housing boom)

TAFFY —**T**echnologically **A**dvanced **F**amily (always has a computer in the home and very possibly centrally controlled lighting)

TRUPPIE —trucker + yuppie (An upscale trucker whose truck cab pulls the very expensive living quarters occupied by his or her family. Husband and wife teams can share the driving, thus covering double the distance of the normal truck in the same amount of time.)

RUBBIE —**R**ich **U**rban **B**iker

RUMPIE   —**R**ural **U**pwardly **M**obile **P**rofessional

Then we have those who for various reasons stand in marked contrast to the affluent Yuppie:

YUFFIE   —**Y**oung **U**rban **F**ailure (Patty Friedmann used this term about brilliant under-achievers in her humorous book *Too Smart to Be Rich: On Being a Yuffie.*)

BIDDIE   —**B**aby boomer **I**n **D**ebt

DUMPIE   —**D**ownwardly mobile **M**iddle-aged **P**rofessional

DOMO   —**DO**wnwardly **MO**bile professional (a former yuppie who opts for more personally meaningful work and more quality time in his or her life—often has wealthy spouse)

PUPPIE   —**P**oor **U**rban **P**rofessional

DROPPIES   —**D**isillusioned **R**elatively **O**rdinary **P**rofessional **P**referring **I**ndependent **E**mployment **S**ituations (a mock-sociological category coined in Britain in 1986)

As if the yuppie menagerie weren't sufficient, in late 1986, the first member of a whole other group of single-syllable acronyms appeared. The actual initiator of these labels is unknown, but the terms are used to refer to demographically significant family groupings. Whoever the perpetrator was, he or she was probably an advertising executive, a real estate agent, or maybe a politico working on a campaign. Once the form was created, journalists once again started inventing variants to tickle our fancy.

First, the wealthiest group:

DINK   —**D**ouble (or **D**ual) **I**ncome, **N**o **K**ids

DINC   —   "   "   "   " **C**hildren

DINKY   —**D**ouble **I**ncome, **N**o **K**ids **Y**et

SWELL   —**S**ingle **W**oman **E**arning **L**ots of **L**olly (from Britain)

OINK　　—**O**ne **I**ncome, **N**o **K**ids (another British term)

Now a somewhat less wealthy bunch:

DIK　　　—**D**ouble **I**ncome, **K**ids
DEWK　　—**D**ual **E**mployed **W**ith **K**ids
TICKS　　—**T**wo **I**ncome **C**ouple with **K**ids in **S**chool
SIK　　　—**S**ingle **I**ncome, **K**ids
OIK　　　—**O**ne **I**ncome, **K**ids (British version)
TINKIE　—**T**wo **I**ncomes, **N**anny, and **K**ids (British again)

Have you found yourself yet? If not, try these:

DIMP　　—**D**ouble **I**ncome, **M**oney **P**roblems
LIPS　　　—**L**ow **I**ncome, **P**arents **S**upporting
TIPS　　　—**T**iny **I**ncome, **P**arents **S**upporting
NILKIE　—**N**o **I**ncome, **L**ots of **K**ids
SITCOM　—**S**ingle **I**ncome, **T**wo **C**hildren, **O**utrageous **M**ortgage
RAIDS　　—**R**ecently **A**cquired **I**ncome **D**eficiency **S**yndrome
MISHAP　—**M**uch **I**ncreased **S**alary, **H**ardly **A**ny **P**ension
DILS　　　—**D**ouble **I**ncome, **L**ittle **S**ex
DINS　　　—**D**ouble **I**ncome, **N**o **S**ex (These last two terms were coined by psychotherapist Jackie Singer, who counsels yuppies who put in so many extra hours at work that they're too tired for each other when they finally get home.)

Or if you're monied and a bit older:

WOOP　　—**W**ell-**O**ff **O**lder **P**eople (parents of yuppies)
LUMPS　—**L**ife-giving **U**nselfish **M**iddle-class **P**arent **S**urvivors (Erma Bombeck's version of a yuppie's parents)

Of course, there were life-style designations way before the yuppies jogged onto the scene. Thirty-odd years ago, the

WASPs (**W**hite **A**nglo-**S**axon **P**rotestants) received their somewhat derisive label. (It has been pointed out that this enormous group should really be called ASPs since few, if any, Anglo-Saxons of color have shown up.) And JAPs (**J**ewish **A**merican **P**rincesses) were identified in the same era. WUMPs (**W**hite **U**rban **M**iddle-class **P**rotestants) are a WASP subclass. The Israelis have their own version of WASPs—**W**hite **A**shkenazi **S**abras with **P**ull. And more recently, Jack Smith playfully offered us the acronym MASH (**M**ale **A**nglo-**S**axon **H**eterosexual). He was hoping that his own social grouping could gain some of the same sympathy as other oppressed minorities, but he reported his efforts were stymied because the term had already been taken by another special-interest group.

Our English-speaking cousins across the water have invented two more wonderful groups. In the late '80s, British yuppies coined LOMBARD (**L**oads **O**f **M**oney **B**ut **A** **R**eal **D**ickhead) (or **D**olt, if you prefer). What's especially apt about this designation is that Lombard Street is the home of many banks and insurance companies in London. Then there are the CORGIs (a **C**ouple **O**f **R**eally **G**hastly **I**ndividuals), jokingly created as a play on the DINK/OINK family in the late '80s as well.

Some other British people-defining acronyms:

RHINO
Really **H**ere **I**n **N**ame **O**nly
The sort of student who finds a seat farthest from the front of the class and then disappears mentally into his or her private landscape.

MIF
Milk **I**n **F**irst
A term used by class-conscious snobs, it refers to the way one adds milk to one's tea. The MIF, characteristically from the lower classes, pours milk into his or her teacup before pouring in the tea itself. A well-bred person from the upper class in England supposedly knows that the tea must go in first.

LIG
Least **I**mportant **G**uest
   When you lig, or are a ligger, you attend receptions and parties thrown by record companies in the rock and pop world in order to freeload. Liggers include music journalists, groupies, and other hangers-on. Coined in the early 1970s. (The origin of this word is not certain—it also may be a portmanteau made from linger + gig. It has even been suggested that lig stems from the Anglo-Saxon word "liegan" meaning "to lie.")

   We turn now to a group with a particularly free and irreverent way with wordplay—teenagers. Some acronymic and blending slang:

TAN
Tough **A**s **N**ails
   Meaning aggressively masculine, this term and the two that follow were collected by Professor Connie Eble at the University of North Carolina at Chapel Hill between 1972 and 1989.

PHAT
Pretty **H**ips **A**nd **T**highs
   Having a shapely female body

Spadet
space + cadet
   A student preoccupied with studying

Clydesdale
Clyde + Dale
   Combining two WASP names, this late '80s term refers to an attractive male. The earlier Clydesdale is a large handsome horse that is hardworking and strong and worth a lot of money. The word turns up in Valtalk in Southern California and in the preppie subculture.

Buffarilla
buffalo + gorilla
   An ugly young woman—an American slang term from the mid-twentieth century.

Twimp

twerp + wimp

A late '80s American high school term for a foolish and/or insignificant person.

TWIRP

The Woman Is Required to Pay

A young man too poor to pay his date's way. Reportedly, the term has also been used to describe a certain kind of school dance.

Biftad

Bif + Tad

A preppy—comes from combining two prep names as in "Say, Bif?" "Yes, Tad."

Teens grow up, put on three-piece suits, take up positions of responsibility, and in their newfound maturity, give up their incessant preoccupation with sex. Right? If these acronyms are any indication, wrong.

MAMMA

Men Against the Maxi-Midi Atrocity

That is, men for the miniskirt. There's also OGLE—**Or**ganization for **G**etting **L**egs **E**xposed, PEEK—**P**eople for the **E**njoyment of **E**yeballing **K**nees, and WHIM—**W**omen **H**appy **I**n **M**inis. This last group is from Boise, Idaho, and strenuously opposed the below-the-knee fashions introduced in the '70s.

SNOFF

Saturday **N**ight **O**nly, **F**riend, **F**emale

This is a very early social acronym—from 1949. It refers to a man's weekend heartthrob as opposed to one's steady. In this category of singles socializing, there's the LIL—**L**ive-**I**n **L**over, the Swingle—swinging + single (from 1967), the FAST—**F**ree **A**nd **S**ingle **T**ourist, and finally (and exhaustedly), the WOW—**W**orn-**O**ut **W**olf. What do these guys and gals have in common? They're all RAW—**R**eady **A**nd **W**illing.

LADIES
Life **A**fter **D**ivorce **I**s **E**ventually **S**ane

In 1983, in Beverly Hills, California, Marion Segal (George Segal's ex), Jacky Joseph (Ken Berry's ex), Patti Lewis (Jerry Lewis's ex), and twelve other famous men's former wives formed a support group to discuss the issues arising from their shared experiences. The idea actually emerged during a USA cable TV show called *Are You Anybody?* LADIES later extended the organization by adding a sister group called LADIES TOO which welcomed divorced women of noncelebrities.

ADAM
American **D**ivorce **A**ssociation for **M**en

Founded in 1970, this Illinois organization with 12,000 members works for reform in the divorce laws. It provides counseling, mediation, and lawyer referral lists and also maintains a women's council.

LOW
Loners **O**n **W**heels

Poplar Bluffs, Missouri, is the home of this social group for singles, especially retirees, who own and travel in recreational vehicles. If you're one of the 3,400 members, you can get invitations from other members to visit and park, information on local camp-outs, even tips on RV maintainance, and all from people who promise to respect your desire to be alone. Should you happen to marry anyway, you can become instead a member of EX-LOW.

Apparently these folks are quite serious about their aloneness. When we called LOW to find out why their members want to be alone, no one ever answered the phone.

WORMS
World **O**rganization to **R**estore **M**ale **S**upremacy

Having found no references to this group's origin throughout our usual sources, we surmise this is a tongue-in-cheek creation. And we like it very much.

The final set of terms ranges widely from rich to poor, young to old, angry to cool.

Anecdotard
anecdote + dotard

If you've explored the far ranges of your extended family, you've almost certainly run into one of these: a very old and feeble person who spends most of his or her waking hours spinning tales. A living, wheezing history book.

It's one of the oldest blended words around—the *Oxford English Dictionary* reports 1894 as the date of its first appearance.

Weenybopper
weeny (very small) + teenybopper

Kids sure grow up earlier these days. Or try to. Things the baby boomers did at thirteen, today's adolescents get into at eleven. Even at nine and ten, they're practicing rap and Paula Abdul moves. This phenomenon of a preadolescent "practice" mini-generation earned its own name in 1973. Weenybopper replaced the earlier term "bubblegum," used to characterize the kind of music eight- to twelve-year-olds bounced around to, like the Jackson Five and the Osmonds.

KAOS
Kids **A**gainst **O**ur **S**ociety

A street gang from West Los Angeles. They modeled their name on Maxwell Smart's nemesis from the '60s TV show *Get Smart*.

(big) MAC
Mellow at **A**ll **C**osts

A '70s term for someone who never loses his or her cool, no matter what the circumstances. (For another acronym based on this double-decker hamburger, see page 80.) There's also MEAT—**M**e **A**t **A**ll **T**imes—which has a definite '80s flavor.

FRUMPs of America
Frugal, **R**esponsible, **U**npretentious, **M**ature **P**ersons

This is an organization founded in 1965 that is dedicated to the idea that ordinary people can be extraordinary. It's a grass-roots association that celebrates the joy of mundane things. Its 2,500 members receive a monthly FRUMP newsletter that contains, among other things, money-saving ideas and unusual recipes. Practically militantly average.

Glitterati
glitter + literati (the learned or literate class)

This term was created in *Time* magazine in 1956 as another way to refer to the jet set or the Beautiful People. In the late '70s and early '80s, when expensive glitter was de rigueur for the celebrities of fashionable society, those attending cultural events fit the term perfectly. Glitterati in the late '80s and early '90s has widened to include any famous/wealthy/ successful people, even business and political figures. So if you've got spangles on your hips and gold cards in your hip pocket, you too can wear the big G.

Or you might be called an Affluential—affluent + influential—a term coined in the second half of the '70s. And you'd certainly want to be sure that you spoke the Acrolect of English. Acrolect is a term created in 1964 by American linguist William A. Stewart, combining "acro" meaning the tip (same as in acronym) and "lect" coming from dialect. The acrolect of a language is the way the upper classes speak. It is commonly accepted as the standard form of the language and has the most prestige. Stewart also invented the term Basilect, where "bas" means low. This is the dialect of the lower classes and carries the least prestige. All the glitter in the world won't win you the respect of the hoi polloi if you call your hostess "pretty mama."

CHAPTER 3

Arts and Entertainment

BET YOU CAN'T THINK of more than one movie whose title is an acronym. How about a rock album? Can you come up with four pop-music genres whose names are portmanteaus? Read on, read on.

Let's begin with life in the land of the celluloid jungle.

D.A.R.Y.L.
Data **A**nalyzing **R**obot **Y**outh **L**ifeform

There was a moment back in the mid '80s when it seemed Hollywood had noticed a whole new truth about its summer audience—over half of all sunburned moviegoers were teenagers. Summer of '85 saw a spate of science-fiction movies aimed straight at those adolescent pocketbooks: *Back to the Future, My Science Project*, and an odd story about a mysterious abandoned child called *D.A.R.Y.L.* Adopted by a childless couple despite his strange memory loss, complete lack of social skills, and overly exact speech patterns, Daryl learns slowly how to be a caring son even as he amazes his adopted parents with his genius. When the secret Pentagon team that created him as an experimental super soldier wants him back to destroy him, his parents refuse. Having learned that Daryl is a robot doesn't lessen their love for him.

F.I.S.T.
Federation of Inter**S**tate **T**ruckers
In 1978, Norman Jewison did a biopic (biography + picture) of Jimmy Hoffa's rise through the ranks to the leadership of the Teamsters. Sylvester Stallone toughs his way through a blizzard of physical intimidation, blackmail, and other assorted challenges as the powerful labor leader.

C.H.O.M.P.S.
Canine **HOM**e **P**rotection **S**ystem
An early cross between *Beethoven* and *Honey, I Shrunk the Kids*, this 1979 Warner Bros. movie has a sympathetic young security systems engineer who invents a computer-controlled robot dog. There's lots of slapstick action as the dog outwits various neighborhood burglars and helps Our Hero get the Girl.

H.E.A.L.T.H.
Happiness, **E**nergy **A**nd **L**ongevity **T**hrough **H**ealth
A Robert Altman film from 1980 with Lauren Bacall, Glenda Jackson, and Dick Cavett (playing himself) telling the story of political infighting at a Florida health-food convention.

B.O.R.N.
Body **O**rgan **R**eplacement **N**etwork
Just another horror/sci-fi flick about hesitant organ donors. Oh, you know, where the beautiful young girls disappear into that murky medical center where aberrant doctors cut them up into highly lucrative bits and then the hero has to put an end to the evil system before they get *him*. It's a Prism film from 1989.

H.O.T.S.
Help **O**ut **T**he **S**eals
Animal House was a hit in 1978 so it spawned lots of imitations. This '79 one again lands us in the Greek subculture

of the campus world and there's lots of skin, excretory, and particularly seal jokes. (The plot has to do with a couple of rival sororities playing practical jokes on each other. One of the sororities has a pet seal which it allows to run wild.)

Gidget
girl + midget

Sandra Dee's portrayal of the perky, very diminutive (hence "midget"), and unbelievably wholesome California teenager with a crush on a surfer named Moondoggie became the role model for a whole generation of girls in the late '50s and early '60s. The 1959 movie (adapted from a book of the same name by Frederick Kohner) was such a big hit that there were two sequels—*Gidget Goes Hawaiian* in 1961 and *Gidget Goes to Rome* in 1963—and a TV series starring Sally Field.

SPILL
Society of **P**etroleum **I**ndustry **L**eaders
SMOKE
Society for **MO**re **C**oal **E**nergy (Yes, yes, it should be
SMOCE)
KABOOM
Key **A**tomic **B**enefits **O**ffice **O**f **M**ankind

Three fictitious but plausible energy organizations that are introduced in the first scene of *Naked Gun 2½*. Along with "Barbara Bush" taking a great pratfall and Lieutenant Frank Drebin being honored for killing his one thousandth drug dealer, the president introduces representatives of SPILL, SMOKE, and KABOOM, nasties all. As the story unfolds, the groups live up to their acronyms.

Z.O.W.I.E.
Zonal **O**rganization on **W**orld **I**ntelligence **E**spionage

In 1966, after James Bond had dominated the screen and bookshelf for fourteen years, Hollywood decided to have some fun with the superspy concept. James Coburn played Derek Flint in two save-the-earth scenarios: *Our Man Flint* and sequel *In Like Flint* (1967). Flicking his eighty-three-function cigarette lighter, key ZOWIE spy Derek Flint stopped an evil gang from controlling all the weather on earth and then turned around and foiled the nefarious world-dominion plans of a secret society of female villains.

HAL 9000
is *not* intended to refer to IBM (one letter away)

In Stanley Kubrick's 1968 movie *2001*, the spacemen call the near-human robot that runs their ship "Hal" (from his designation "Hal 9000"). He seems less human when his programming goes awry and he tries to kill them. Is this amok computer a symbol for IBM, the biggest computer company in the '60s when the film was created? Is the movie warning against our excessive dependence on bits and bytes?

Here's Jeremy Bernstein in a movie review of *2001* written for *The New Yorker* issue of September 21, 1968: "Kubrick, incidentally, was stunned himself when it was pointed out to him that if the letters of the name he had chosen, Hal, are shifted by one to the right the result read IBM."

Cinerama
cinematic + panorama

Fred Waller, a Paramount special-effects technician, invented this wide-screen process that gives watchers the effect of three-dimensional film. Cinerama requires that each scene be shot with three different cameras: one facing straight ahead and the other two slightly to the left and the right of the middle camera. Then three synchronized projectors shoot the different versions at the same time onto a curved screen.

The earliest version was shown in 1939 at the New York World's Fair. *This Is Cinerama* and other early films in the '50s were travelogues, taking viewers on wild roller-coaster rides and tilting flights over the Grand Canyon. Unlike 3D films, which survived only until 1955, Cinerama gleaned special status from the fact that only a theater with specialized equipment could show it. In 1962, in fact, a full-length feature film, *How the West Was Won*, was shot with this technique.

By the early 1970s, however, Cinerama was abandoned by Hollywood. It was so difficult to keep the three projectors synchronous that the technology was simplified. Only one huge image was projected. And the Cinerama movies made in this form didn't attract a big enough crowd to pay for themselves. You can still find the films shown in expositions and in some amusement parks.

Sensurround
sense + surround

Remember *Rollercoaster*? *Earthquake*? The sound was unusually real in those films because of a special effect. Low-frequency sounds were added to the soundtrack and amplified by ten to twenty large speakers in special theaters. The audience could actually feel tremors and vibrations as the earth shook on screen or the roller coaster swayed high in the sky. This technique was trademarked in 1974.

Claymation
clay + animation

A trademark for a new process of making cartoons. Instead of drawing figures in slightly different poses to simulate movement, clay models are formed, photographed on a single frame of film, adjusted slightly, and then photographed on the next frame. With enough tiny adjustments, a palm tree made of clay can look as if it's swaying in the breeze.

FLIC
Film **L**ibrary **I**nformation **C**ouncil

FLIC was originally formed to collect 16-millimeter films. In 1984 it was absorbed by the American Film and Video Association. This larger organization, in which FLIC functions as an information library, gives film and video awards annually at the American Film and Video Festival.

WIFE
Women's **I**ndependent **F**ilm **E**xchange

Founded in 1977, this small New York–based group works to establish recognition of women who have not been given creative credit for their films. For example, members of WIFE learned and published new information about the famous documentary *Nanook of the North*. This seminal exploration of Eskimo life was not created by Bob Flaherty alone (as is commonly claimed) but by himself and his wife, Frances Flaherty. WIFE also promotes recognition of women's contribution to the film industry. The group supplies biographical information about such women as Mary Ellen Bute, the first American to make abstract films (nonrepresentational images set to music) and the first person to use electronically generated images in film.

Free-lance filmmakers, teachers, writers, and distributors are welcome.

GLAAD
Gay and **Lesbian Alliance Against Defamation**

In order to help shape more positive attitudes toward gay men and women, this watchdog organization evaluates television shows, rock songs, movies, and other popular entertainment that deals with homosexual themes and/or has gay characters. Sometimes, for example, advocates will ask to examine a screenplay before it is filmed. If a film goes out to the public that GLAAD feels depicts gay life unfairly, the group will picket theaters that screen the movie. A recent film that received GLAAD adverse publicity was *Basic Instinct*, where Sharon Stone portrayed a lesbian who was a psychopathic killer.

WASP
Woody Allen's Spring Picture
and
WAFP
Woody Allen's Fall Picture

Woody Allen must drive distributors crazy. In an industry that starts promoting major pictures three or four months before release, he refuses to give out even the title, let alone the concept or, heaven forbid, a coming attraction. He's a filmmaker who treasures spontaneity when he's directing a movie, keeping rehearsals to a minimum and rewriting as he goes.

These two film industry acronyms are a rueful nod to his idiosyncrasy.

On to the small screen that connects us all in universal boob-tubery, shooting canned laughter into every room of the house if desired, with 58 or 102 channels that always seem to be beaming down *I Dream of Jeannie* reruns.

T.H.E. Cat
Thomas **H**ewitt **E**dward Cat

If some heavy gang member had threatened to kill you, would you hire an ex-circus aerialist/cat burglar who never carries weapons to save your life with his agility? Fat chance. NBC gave it a whirl and the half-hour series lasted one season—fall 1966. The Cat was played by Robert Loggia.

The C.A.T. Squad
The **C**ounter **A**ssault **T**actical Squad

(Is there something about felines and acronyms?) This one's another NBC action series that ran starting in July 1986. The squad, based on a true-life organization, protected American citizens against international terrorism. The writers of the series tried for a John Le Carré tone, where members of the team constantly questioned their own and their country's motives, exploring complicated moral and ethical questions. The show had a very short run.

Tom of T.H.U.M.B.
Tiny **H**umans **U**nderground **M**ilitary **B**ureau

Secret agent Tom and his Oriental assistant, Swinging Jack, work for a secret U.S. government agency that sends them on special missions infiltrating hostile foreign agencies and undermining their nefarious plans. This ABC Saturday morning cartoon used up the last bit of the half-hour slot mostly filled by a children's sci-fi/fantasy show called *King Kong* from September 1966 to August 1969. This pint-sized *Mission Impossible* was one of the first Rankin-Bass TV productions. The company went on to supply much of the Saturday morning animated fare.

The Man from U.N.C.L.E.
United **N**etwork **C**ommand for **L**aw **E**nforcement

The cat-acronym connection might be subtle, but the link between acronyms and spy networks, both good and evil, is plain as the nose on your face. This long-running hour-long series (September 1964 to January 1968) was NBC's answer to James Bond and SPECTRE (more on SPECTRE later). Robert Vaughn as ultra-smooth Napoleon Solo and David McCallum as tow-headed, introverted Illya Kuryakin disappeared weekly into a New York City dry-cleaning store and reappeared somewhere else in the world as the major deterrent to the wicked machinations of THRUSH (**T**echnological **H**ierarchy for the **R**emoval of **U**ndesirables and the **S**ubjugation of **H**umanity).

Spin-offs included another series, *The Girl from U.N.C.L.E.* (1966–1967), and a single long show, *The Return of the Man from U.N.C.L.E.: The 15 Years Later Affair*.

Mr. Atoz
Mr. A to Z

Yeah, this one's not exactly an acronym and not exactly a portmanteau either, but it's in the family. We could call it a halfcronym maybe? Mr. Atoz was the bald druidic fellow in the dark patterned robes who presided over an enormous library in the *Star Trek* episode "All Our Yesterdays." That doughty trio, Kirk, Spock, and McCoy, beam down to the surface of the planet Sarpeidon just before it is about to be engulfed by the explosion of its sun. They find the entire planet deserted but for the solemn Mr. Atoz, mysteriously guarding a machine called The Atavachron. He explains that each member of the entire citizenry of Sarpeidon has chosen an era in the past of their planet and has walked into this time device which transports them forever to their chosen time. After our three heroes have some adventures in the planet's past (Spock even falls in love during an ice age), they all make it back to the library in time to watch Mr. Atoz leap through the portal into his own chosen era as the planet explodes. Scottie manages to beam them up in the nick of time. Whew.

Dalek
Da to Lek

England's answer to action-adventure on the final frontier is the BBC's *Dr. Who*, with considerably more thriller-chiller action and less moral philosophy than *Star Trek*. The doctor has been escaping death by the skin of his teeth for close to thirty years, if you count the countless reruns. One of the endless series of bad guys is the Dalek, a robot with a rasping, monotonous voice. The name was coined in 1965, apparently by a script writer whose eye happened to catch volume Da to Lek of an encyclopedia as he was casting about for an evil android name. In England, the word has been used attributively when describing bureaucrats, politicians, and military personnel who seem robotlike.

Kidult
kid + adult

Used first in the late '50s to describe a special type of adventure series aimed at kids but also designed to achieve cult status among some adults. *Batman*, with its action written out across the screen in grunt words like "BIF!" and "POW!!," is an example. In the next two decades, reviewers used the adjective somewhat derisively, and in the '80s, a kidult could also be a person with immature taste in shows. Today the word is media slang for a TV show or movie created with the whole family in mind.

RALPH
Royal **A**ssociation for the **L**ongevity and **P**reservation of the **H**oneymooners

This fan club, organized in 1982, has 12,000 members. The name, of course, refers to the role played by Jackie Gleason—that irascible bus driver Ralph Kramden. The club works to secure original prints of the thirty-nine episodes of the CBS 1955–1956 television show. One of its proudest acquisitions is Gleason's big-bellied bus driver's uniform.

HINT
Happy **I**diot **N**ews **T**alk (or **T**eam)

In the '70s it became quite the fashion for TV news teams to wear identical blazers and shoot inconsequential banter back and forth between serious news items. Sometimes it got so bad that a report of a tragedy would be immediately followed by clowning around and giggles. The informal ensemble approach began at local stations low in the ratings as a way to get viewer attention. It was so successful that the style, sometimes called "action news" or "eyewitness news," was taken up by major networks across the country. There's still some HINT around today, but thankfully it's shrunk to an occasional exchange.

Popular music, from rock to country to soul, contributes more than a handful of acronyms to the collection.

Motown
motor + town

A slang term for the city of Detroit. The musical history of the word began in 1962 when it became the trademark of Berry Gordy's brainchild—a record company that has given us such stellar groups as the Supremes and the Four Tops. Motown has since come to refer to a particular musical style: lush strings (Gordy used members of the Detroit Symphony Orchestra), elements of gospel singing like call-and-response (where part of a singing group sings the first half of a line and the other part of the group answers with the second half, imitating the two parts of a church choir), the use of tambourines (also borrowed from gospel style), and horns with a rhythm and blues push. The genre became so popular that in 1966, for example, 75 percent of Motown songs made the national pop charts. The Supremes alone had three monster hits that single year: "You Can't Hurry Love" (one of the year's top ten), "My World Is Empty Without You," and "Love Is Like an Aching in My Heart."

Rockabilly
rock and roll + hillbilly

Another music genre, probably most famous as the rock and roll/country music style of young Elvis Presley. Other stars who sing in this blues-and-bluegrass manner: Roy Orbison, Johnnie Cash, Jerry Lee Lewis. (The term appeared in 1956.)

Soca (or Soka)
soul + calypso

In 1977, a record appeared called "Sokah, Soul of Calypso" by Lord Shorty, one of the founders of this musical mélange. The music added elements of soul, American funk, and British rock to the classic music of Trinidad. Though Soca began in the Caribbean, by the end of the '70s it was enjoyed as far away as the British Isles. It's a pop style of calypso, with a highly danceable beat and good-time energy. Popular Soca performers include David Rudder, Tambu, Mighty Sparrow, and Arrow.

Wunk
wasp + funk

A slang term for the mainstream teen hits of the '60s, which recently have returned to the pop charts—a new generation finds baby-boomer music mildly entertaining. Michael Bolton's versions of "Dock of the Bay" and "When a Man Loves a Woman" are recent examples.

SNFU
Several Neurons Fry Utterly

A thrash-rock band from Canada whose name is a play on the army acronym "snafu." Members of the band characterize their music as not really hard-core punk, but a reviewer felt that the combination of extraordinary volume and words screamed to the point of unintelligibility made SNFU live up to their name, at least in the case of his brain.

Rockumentary
rock + documentary

A term invented by Boston critic Ernie Santosuosso in 1977 to describe a film documenting the history of rock and roll or the life of rock stars. Movies like *Woodstock* and *Gimme Shelter*, both from 1970, made this subgenre very popular in the '70s. Elvis, Jimi, Janis, Dylan, the Beatles, all were rockumentaried. But it wasn't until 1984 that Rob Reiner captured the essence of the genre in his parody *This Is Spinal Tap*, which traces an amazingly long-lived (though apocryphal) rock group from their early '60s beginning as clean-cut folk-rockers through a mop-top Beatles stage, a Carpenters mellow stage, then heavy metal and punk, ending with their current David Bowie-like bizarre and fantastical stage show (where one device unfortunately refuses to open and disgorge the guitar player). The movie is almost a rockumentary of rock itself.

DAISY
DA **I**nner **S**ound, **Y'**all

This is the name of the crew and production company of a rap group called De La Soul. "It was just our way of saying the music is something real, something from our heart."

SHLOCK
Society to **H**onor **LO**unge **C**abaret

A San Francisco-based group trying to revive the lounge style of small nightclub entertainment that was popular in the '50s—their act is a mixture of standards and songs they write themselves.

Dobro
Dopera + brothers

The Dobro is a guitar with raised strings and a resonator cone inside that causes it to produce a whining sound similar to that of a Hawaiian guitar. It was invented by the aforementioned brothers and introduced to the world of country music in 1955 by Flatt and Scruggs and their Foggy Mountain Boys Band.

Satchmo
satchel + mouth

Louis Henry Armstrong (1900–1971) was the quintessential trumpeter of jazz. His extraordinary ability to improvise, his wonderful showmanship, his inimitable gravely voice, made him a legend worldwide. He was given his nickname by friends because of his unusually wide mouth.

Cassingle
cassette + single

Remember the first time you strolled down a record-store aisle and were greatly pleased and mildly puzzled to find a cassette priced at less than two bucks? It even had a hot singer on the cover. And then you realized. You were paying for two songs. A little math eliminated any remaining trace of elation: at the rate of a buck a song, you'd have to pay twelve dollars or so for a full album's worth. Today, with cassingles at three bucks a crack, that price has gone up to eighteen dollars.

But the cassingle did well (until the advent of CD singles) for the same reason those old '45s did—we the public are hit-driven. Cassingle was even trademarked by IRS Records in 1982.

BOF
Best **OF**

Another easy moneymaker for the record companies, this is the album of a single artist's big hits collected from his or her previous albums. The word is also probably connected to the show-biz term "boffo." To gather the easy pickings of a BOF album, a record company needs to go HIP (**H**igh-**I**ntent **P**riority) on an artist's earlier efforts, launching all-out promotional, publicity, and advertising campaigns in order to get RAP (**R**adio **A**ir **P**lay). If a record company decides instead, as they do with the majority of releases, to go NOPE (**NO P**romotion) on an album, the music will seldom get RAPPED unless a particular DeeJay falls in love with it. Thank goodness that happens from time to time. It would be sad to think that our musical choices are completely dictated by record executives.

From music it's a short lamp (choreographic terminology for leap + stamp) to dance.

ISO (and the Bobs)
I'm **S**o **O**ptimistic

A modern dance troupe that combines acrobatics, modern dance techniques, and very imaginative choreography.

BAD
Boys' **A**thletic **D**ancing

Dance was one of the few professions where the female was clearly the star and males mostly decorative and/or supportive. In an effort to attract more men to the dance stage, BAD was formed. It's a boys-only dance training and performance program—girls need not apply.

LEGACY
LEaders **GA**thered for **C**ommitment and **Y**ak

This 285-member square-dance organization from Oconomowoc, Wisconsin, was founded in 1973. It periodically gathers together dancers, callers, record producers, and editors in the field in order to reestablish the "three C's": coordination, cooperation, and continuity. Members focus on such issues as square-dance heritage, standardization, and ethics.

On to the world of print.

PORGIE
Paperback **ORIG**inal

An award given for the best books in a given year that first saw shelf life in soft cover. Almost all romantic fiction enters the market this way, so most of the annual RITA awards (**R**omance **I**s **T**reasured **Al**ways) go to paperbacks. The RITA is bestowed by Romantic Writers of America and honors cofounder Rita Clay Estrada. Nora Roberts is a frequent winner.

Plot boiler
plot + pot boiler

Actually this term is an example of what we affectionately call a repetitious redundancy—like "past history" or "utterly unique." Pot boiler is a slang term for a story that keeps the reader's attention all steamed up by overheating the plot (like the glitz novels of Jackie Collins). A plot boiler's the same thing. But it's cute.

S.H.E.R.L.O.C.K.
Sherlock **H**olmes **E**nthusiastic **R**eaders **L**eague **O**f **C**riminal **K**nowledge

Talk about fan clubs! There are over 150 local and regional Sherlock Holmes societies throughout the United States. This is the only acronymic one we discovered, but the names are wonderful, everything from The Creeping Men of Cleveland to Doctor Watson's Neglected Patients to The Five Orange Pips of Westchester County to The Noble and Most Singular Order of the Blue Carbuncle.

Smersh
smiert + shpionam (Russian for "death to spies")

Part of the immense attraction of the James Bond books was their wonderful combination of high-blown heroic fantasy and gritty realism. Much of the realism stemmed from the fact that their author, Ian Fleming, actually participated in secret service activities during World War II. In his first few books, the Russian counterpart to Bond's spy organization was given the name of the Soviet Union's actual secret service. Then Fleming changed Bond's nemesis to SPECTRE (**SP**ecial **E**xecutive for **C**ounterintelligence, **T**errorism, **R**evenge and **E**xtortion) in *Thunderball* and so it remained for the rest of the best-selling series.

SCUM Manifesto
Society for **C**utting **U**p **M**en

Written in the late '60s by Valerie Solanis, this was a violent diatribe against the male sex. (Bet you suspected that.) She wrote it to justify her shooting and wounding of Andy Warhol in June of '68. Ms. Solanis was an actress in one of his pop art films—*I, a Man*—and afterward wanted more of his attention than he was willing to give. Warhol developed a cult of noninvolvement that apparently had destructive effects on several of his followers.

SACs
SAcred **C**ows

Haven't we all wondered why JFK's sexual peccadilloes were never even hinted about in the press while he was president? He was a SAC, a person who was revered so highly by the readers of this country's newspapers that journalists hesitated to question any aspect of his personal life. An institution can also be a SAC, though today there are fewer and fewer people and groups immune from journalistic scrutiny.

MUGG
Marries, **U**nusual, **G**orgeous or **G**one

Newspapers maintain thick files of these mugg shots, photographs of celebrities that can be pulled out and used to accompany an article on someone famous getting married or dying. They're also used when something bizarre enough to be newsworthy happens or simply when the editor feels a bit of cheesecake will liven an otherwise dull page.

OP-ED page
OPposite **ED**itorial page

It has become a journalistic tradition, since personal columns became popular, to place a page of them facing the editor's page of commentary. In some cases, a single columnist will contribute an article daily while other columns are written by various experts invited to comment by the newspaper.

The arts have several major professional organizations with acronymic appellations.

SAG
Screen **A**ctors' **G**uild

Funny name for a group (70,000 strong at present) whose members finger every wrinkle with dismay. This is the AFL-CIO labor union for the performing arts. Founded in 1933, the union deals with such issues as agent relations, casting, creative rights, and legislation affecting actors, stunt people, and other such performers. AFTRA (**A**merican **F**ederation of **T**elevision and **R**adio **A**rtists) is the analogous union for TV and radio. It was founded even earlier, in 1919.

ACT
American **C**onservatory **T**heater

This foundation, formed in 1965, functions as a repertory theater and accredited acting school. Every year, the 150-member staff holds auditions in major American cities for potential students. ACT also has outreach programs to schools and an 8,000-volume library of plays, and sponsors in-theater discussions between the audience and the actors. It is based in San Francisco.

PEN
International Association of **P**oets, Playwrights, **E**ditors, Essayists and **N**ovelists

This venerable (founded in 1921) organization of writers had as its first president British novelist John Galsworthy. There are chapters in many countries, from Bangladesh to Belgium, Vietnam to South Africa, Latvia to Lebanon. In America, both New York City and Los Angeles have groups.

PEN encourages translation, bestows awards, and maintains an emergency fund for families of impoverished writers. The organization also works to combat the suppression of free expression and fights against censorship throughout the world.

What follows is a potpourri of acronyms from other arts and entertainments.

Ice Capades
ice + escapades
In 1950, Walter Brom and John H. Harris met to come up with a new, public-rousing name for a theatrical ice show. And they did.

Coleco Industries Inc.
Connecticut + Leather + Company
The toy company that brought us Cabbage Patch Kids actually started out as a supplier of leather to shoe-repair shops. It was founded by Russian immigrant Maurice Greenberg in 1932 and only entered the margins of the toy business in the '50s when it began manufacturing Mickey Mouse and Davy Crockett moccasin-making kits. It hit its first big-time toyland success in the late '70s and early '80s with hand-held electronic games and ColecoVision games for the TV. But the company had a bad habit of turning booms into busts. Even after its ugly charmers from the cabbage patch caused toy-store riots during the 1983 Christmas season, the company went belly-up in 1989 due to poor marketing judgment and was brought up by . . .

Hasbro, Inc.
Hassenfeld + brothers
The largest toy company in the United States was begun in 1923 when Herman, Harry, and Hillel Hassenfeld, three Polish immigrant brothers, bought up felt scraps from textile mills and made liners for hats with the cloth. The second generation of brothers, Merrill and Harold, took the company into the toy business during World War II. But it wasn't until 1952, during the reign of the third generation of Hassenfeld

brothers, Stephen and Alan, that the company's first star toy, Mr. Potato Head, appeared. Since then, Hasbro has been responsible for such toy hits as G.I. Joe (a doll for boys who can't bring themselves to play with Barbie), My Little Pony (a plastic horse with mane and tail made of Barbie dolllike hair), and Transformers (robots that can be changed through a series of steps into weapons). The financially healthy company has bought up many other toy manufacturers, among them Milton Bradley, the longtime purveyer of such games as Monopoly, Candy Land, and the acronymic THINGS—**T**otally **H**ilarious **I**ncredibly **N**eat **G**ames of **S**kill.

LEGO
LEg **GO**dt (Danish for "play well")

Perhaps the best-known maker of building blocks in the Western world. Parents find these tiny interlocking pieces everywhere: deep beneath the most surprising pieces of furniture, in bowls of cereal, and even in bowls of toilets. The Danish toy company has recently announced plans to build a theme park in Carlsbad, California, an upper-middle-class suburb of San Diego. If the Lego Family Park turns out anything like its sister park in Billund, Denmark, millions of little Lego bricks will be used to create replicas of such famous sites as the Parthenon, Mount Rushmore, and the Statue of Liberty. But there's a rub.

A group of Carlsbad homeowners have formed NAIL, **N**eighbors **A**gainst the **I**nvasion of **L**ego, to protest what they fear will be the "Disneylandization" of their tranquil seaside town. Given the state of California's economy and Lego's promise of 650 jobs and $76 million a year in revenues, we'd venture to predict that NAIL will not prevail.

MEGO
Mine **E**yes **G**laze **O**ver

When a theater reviewer calls a play MEGO, he or she doesn't have to say much more. The term is also used on Capitol Hill, where many a speech must earn that nonaccolade. In fact, former president Bush is reported to have described Vice President Gore's book on ecology, *Earth in the Balance*, as "MEGO City."

Animatronics
animation + electronics

If you've been to Disneyland, you've probably stared at Abraham Lincoln, looming large as life, as he spoke to you in a theater on Main Street. His lifelike robot is a product of a process developed by Walt Disney in the '60s that was first used at the World's Fair. The Lincoln animatron and others like it are programmed to perform very realistic movements, accompanied by a prerecorded soundtrack.

SHAZAM
Solomon's wisdom, **H**ercules' strength, **A**chilles' courage, **Z**eus' powers, **A**tlas' stamina, **M**ercury's speed

Shazam is the magic word that turns homeless orphaned boy Billy Bateson into the superhero Captain Marvel, a comic-book character whose exploits were followed worldwide in the 1940s. (The barest whisper of the same word also turns him back to Billy—a transformational method considerably easier than searching out a phone booth.)

Billy's female counterpart, Mary Marvel, had the same magic word, but in her case the letters stood for: **S**elena's grace, **H**ippolyta's strength, **A**riadne's skill, **Z**ephyrus' speed, **A**urora's beauty, **M**inerva's wisdom.

CHAPTER 4

Like a Fly in Amber

LANGUAGE IS AN extraordinary preservative. There are certain words that seem to contain a whole chunk of history. You hear one of these words and Bingo!—you're transported back in time to an era you actually lived in or one you know from your parents' stories, from movies or from books. Try it. Watch what comes to mind when you pick one from this list: WACs, CONELRAD, napalm, palimony, Contragate.

If you chose WACs (**W**omen's **A**rmy **C**orps), you got back to the '40s—World War II, women in the army and in the factories, the whole tough, can-do American ethos. CONELRAD (**CON**trol of **EL**ectromagnetic **RAD**iation) evokes the '50s—the beginning of the Cold War and the fear-filled plans Americans made in case of a nuclear attack. Napalm (**NA**phthene **PALM**itate)—Vietnam and students protesting the Dow Chemical Company—classic '60s. Palimony (pal + alimony) evokes the whole sexual revolution that came to fruition in the '70s. And if you picked Contragate (Contra + Watergate), you were back in the '80s watching Oliver North and company protect the president from an enormous international scandal.

Like the sticky prehistoric tree sap that trapped insects and later hardened to amber, the acronyms and portmanteaus in this chapter have preserved facets of history and can present them to us as fresh as the day the acronym was coined.

* * *

The following terms come from the era of World War I; they all come from England and have to do with women.

DORA
Defense **O**f the **R**ealm **A**ct

A set of laws passed in England in 1914 that required the civilian population to adhere to many wartime restrictions. DORA was visualized as a stern, disapproving older woman— the very personification of the spirit of restriction.

FANY
First **A**id **N**ursing **Y**eomanry

Just prior to World War I, in 1909, the British created this women's organization to serve with the army and do general medical work. In 1916, FANY was changed to the Women's Transport Service and its members were the first women to run ambulance convoys.

WRNS ("Wrens")
Women's **R**oyal **N**aval **S**ervice

A section of the British Navy for women that was created in 1917, toward the end of World War I. It was disbanded after the war and re-created in 1939.

During World War II, acronyms began multiplying like rabbits. And what better place to find them than the military world? One astounding acronymic explosion occurred in the newly created women's branches of the armed forces.

WAACs
Women's **A**rmy **A**uxiliary **C**orps

"I'd Rather Be with Them—Than Waiting for Them."
"Speed Them Back! Join the WAAC."

Recruiting signs like these appeared all over America in 1942. By 1943, more than 100,000 women had joined up. By taking over the army's clerical and truck transport work, these women freed up men to go into combat. In 1943, in recognition of their powerful contribution to the war effort, the army dropped "Auxiliary" out of the title and the WACs became members of the U.S. Army. Women remained segregated in their own units, however, until 1978.

WAVES (1942)
Women **A**ccepted for **V**olunteer **E**mergency **S**ervice

The U.S. Navy's version of the WACs. By 1945, there were 86,000 women serving. Today women are part of the regular navy service but they cannot serve on combat vessels.

SPARs
"**S**emper **P**aratus: **A**lways **R**eady"

The women's auxiliary for the Coast Guard. SPAR comes from the Coast Guard motto. One recruiting poster showed a spare tire with these words printed across it: "Don't be a Spare. Be a Spar."

WAFS
Women's **A**uxiliary **F**errying **S**quadron

Established by the air force in 1939 to help ferry planes from defense plants to military bases both in America and abroad. In 1940, the group's function was broadened to include women doing clerical work as well. The air force kept the acronym but changed what it stood for: **W**omen in the **A**ir **F**orce. Women were not allowed to fly military aircraft until 1977.

WASPs
Women's **A**ir Force **S**ervice **P**ilots

A civilian unit which flew noncombat aircraft. Its founder and organizer was the famous aviatrix Jacqueline Cochran, the first woman who ever flew a plane faster than the speed of sound. In many ways, she personified the independent spirit of the American woman in the '40s.

Femarines
female + marines

The marines didn't have a specifically named women's group. If a woman wanted to join the marines, she signed up for the Women's Reserve of the Marine Corps. However, there were lots of nicknames like "Jungle Juliets" and "Leather-nectarines."

WIRES
Women **I**n **R**adio and **E**lectrical **S**ervice

All over the country, army posts made use of young women to send and receive messages. At one post in the South, the women came up with this name for themselves in imitation of their older sisters serving in official armed services groups like the WAC and the WAVES.

WINS
Women **I**n **N**ational **S**ervice

In the March 1943 issue of *Ladies' Home Journal*, a writer coined this term, speaking of the twenty million American housewives and their teenaged daughters as "the greatest reserve strength of America." By "manning" the factories, saving important resources like tin and aluminum, and sending optimistic letters to their fighting men, women made their contribution to the war effort. There were also WINKs—**W**omen **I**n **N**umerous **K**itchens.

WOWs
Women **O**rdnance **W**orkers

Founded in 1942, an organization of women who worked at an electric company in Chicago. It became a national organization with 33,000 members only a year later.

CWACs ("Quacks")
Canadian **W**omen's **A**rmy **C**orps

A nod to the "Wrens" perhaps?

WAPS
Women of the **A**merican **P**ress **S**ervice

In World War II, women who were accredited war correspondents belonged to this group.

The rest of these acronyms from the '40s are also concerned with the war effort.

Grumlins
gremlin + grumble

Air Force pilots blamed mysterious glitches in their air-crafts' instrumentation on a mythical little mischief-maker called the gremlin. In 1943, Sam Rayburn, the Speaker of the House, created a new variation, saying, "The Grumlin does the same job of sabotage on the home front as the gremlin does to the airplanes of our pilots fighting the Axis."

Gyrene
G.I. + marine

This term was actually used at Annapolis in 1925 but it became popular slang for a marine in 1940 and was used throughout the Pacific Theater.

C.B.s ("Seabees")
Construction **B**attalion

This started out as an initialism but it was transformed into a quasi-acronym because the Seabees were part of the navy: "C" became "Sea." Originally the men were civilian engi-neers who would land on a South Pacific island like Guam or Wake right after the marines. On each embattled island, Seabees built the parts of a secret naval base: a dock, an airstrip, fortifications, barracks, and a hospital. But the work was both dangerous and secret so the navy decided to draft the men, providing them with combat training and secrecy briefings. Seabees made the bulldozer glamorous.

Amtrac
amphibian + tractor

In the '30s, inventor Donald Roebling created a swamp buggy called the Alligator that was used to rescue hurricane victims and aviators who had crashed in the Everglades. Dur-ing the war, the marines renamed the Alligator and used it for assaults on hostile beaches in the Pacific. The amtrac became a universal beast of burden, carrying troops from naval vessels across coral reefs to shore, transporting cargo, and evacuating the wounded. Some buggies were changed into armored cars with mounted machine guns, and some versions that carried radio equipment even served as command posts in battle.

Fighting squads scattered over the field sent their reports in and received their orders from the officers riding the command amtrac.

STEN gun
Sheppard **T**urpin **EN**gland

The British Army needed enormous numbers of light submachine guns and the Sten gun could be produced quickly and inexpensively. Because it was mass-produced, the gun (named for its two inventors and their country) was considered a cheap piece of junk but in fact it did the job.

Blimp
B + limp

The first blimp was called a dirigible balloon in World War I and was used in England for coastal patrols, keeping a lookout for enemy submarines. The Germans used it to bomb British cities. There were two classifications: A-rigid—where the gas bag was supported by a rigid framework—and B-limp—where the gas bag was supported only by its internal gas pressure. In World War II, the second kind was eventually called a blimp.

FIDO
Fog **I**nvestigation and **D**ispersal **O**peration

England is famous for its impenetrable pea-soup fogs. During the war, especially in winter, such weather made airplane landings nearly impossible. Fifteen of the major British airfields were kept open by an ingenious contraption. Pipes were set up along both sides of a landing strip and gasoline was forced through them. Then members of a FIDO team would run alongside the strip with torches and ignite the fuel. The intense heat from the wall of flaming gasoline burned off the fog, enabling exhausted RAF pilots returning from bombing missions to land their planes.

HFDF ("huff-duff")
High **F**requency, **D**irection **F**amiliar

In the Battle of the Atlantic, a British battleship surrounded by a hunter-killer pack of German submarines was a goner. To safeguard their ships, the British used the huff-duff, a device that listened to the high-frequency radio broadcasts emitted by a group of enemy subs and then located the source of the sounds.

COSSAC
Chief **O**f **S**taff to **S**upreme **A**llied **C**ommander (Europe)

In 1943, the Allies began planning Operation Overload, their code name for the Normandy invasion. Lieutenant General Sir Frederick E. Morgan was appointed COSSAC, a high military position in the British Armed Forces. The name of his office became the code name for the headquarters of the staff planning the invasion.

SHAEF
Supreme **H**eadquarters, **A**llied **E**xpeditionary **F**orce

When the fight to take back the continent of Europe actually began, in June of 1944, COSSAC was changed to SHAEF. General Dwight D. Eisenhower led this multinational army. France, of course, was the first country to be liberated from the Germans, and much of the SHAEF staff requisitioned quarters in classy Parisian hotels. Some of the hoteliers, irritated by this arrangement, claimed that SHAEF actually stood for **S**ociété des **H**oteliers **A**méricains **E**n **F**rance (Society of American Hotel keepers in France). They were no doubt relieved when SHAEF disbanded after Germany surrendered in 1945.

FUSAG
First **U**nited **S**tates **A**rmy **G**roup

A completely fictitious invasion force invented by the Allied intelligence organization in 1943 to confuse the Axis powers about when and where and with which forces the retaking of Europe would begin. It was part of an elaborate screen of disinformation used to keep the Axis off balance.

AMGOT
Allied **M**ilitary **G**overnment of **O**ccupied **T**erritories

After SHAEF liberated countries from the Nazis, an interim military government was set up in each country and administered jointly by the Americans and the British. The first one, structured so that similarly patterned organizations could be used in subsequent countries, was called AMGOT, and in Sicily it worked well. One month later, when it was used in Turkey, its name was hastily changed to AMG. Apparently AMGOT was an unprintable word in Turkish.

SEAC
South **E**ast **A**sia **C**ommand

The Allied command for the Burma-Malaysia-Thailand-Singapore Theater with headquarters in India. It was established in 1943 with Admiral Mountbatten as Supreme Commander. American sailors said SEAC stood for the "**S**upreme **E**xample of **A**llied **C**onfusion."

OHIO
Over the **H**ill **I**n **O**ctober

In late 1940, when Roosevelt suspected America would soon be at war, he called up the National Guard for one year of active duty. In camps throughout the nation, these divisions showed up and waited and waited. OHIO was a slogan written on barracks walls and on vehicles, warning that the bored and restless men, many of whom could see no reason to be separated from their families only to cool their heels in army camps, would be heading back home as soon as their year of mobilization was over in October of 1941, even if the president didn't see fit to release them. However, when October came around, the men did accept a six-month extension. And on December 7, Japan attacked Pearl Harbor.

the Steagles
Steelers + Eagles

During the war, so many of the players from the Pittsburgh Steelers and the Philadelphia Eagles football teams were away at war that there weren't enough pros to fill the rosters. So the two teams were merged for the duration of the war.

The postwar era of the 1950s was a seemingly innocent, bland, conforming, and eagerly consuming time in the United States. With the Depression and the war behind them, all Americans wanted to do was snuggle into suburbia and give their children everything the parents had missed. However, the acronyms of the time reveal that there was plenty of conflict and tension under the Ozzie-and-Harriet smiles.

COMINFORM
COMmunist **INFORM**ation Bureau
and
COMECON
COuncil for **M**utual **ECON**omic Assistance

After Germany was defeated, the Soviet Union annexed 390,000 square miles of additional territory in Eastern Europe, including Poland, Romania, Bulgaria, Czechoslovakia, Albania, and East Germany. Eighty-seven million people were suddenly being ruled by Communist governments that took their ideological cues from the USSR through an organization called Cominform. Two years later, Comecon was set up to cover the economic aspects of turning formerly independent countries into satellites of the Soviet Union.

This Communist bloc deadlocked with the NATO countries in the newly formed United Nations and destroyed the dream the Allies had shared at Yalta in 1945 of a postwar world of international cooperation enforced by U.N. peacekeeping forces.

TASS
Telegrafnoie **A**gentstvo **S**ovietskavo **S**oyuza ("Telegraphic Agency of the Soviet Union")

The only news agency in the USSR, TASS has been called the "gatekeeper" of the Soviet Union. It controlled and censored all the news the Russian people read and also controlled all information that left the Soviet Union and was read by the rest of the world. Its worldwide organization of news correspondents doubled as a spy network. TASS was managed by the Propaganda Department of the Communist party and had a good deal to do with the frightening "Iron Curtain" that Winston Churchill saw falling between Eastern and Western Europe after the war ended.

DEW line
Distant **E**arly **W**arning

The most frightening part of the Cold War was, of course, the weaponry that would be used should the war heat up.

Some Americans built bomb shelters next to their suburban barbecue pits. Kids were trained to scuttle under their desks at school and shield their necks with their clasped hands whenever the word "Drop!" was shouted. And in the far North, from Alaska to Greenland along the 70th parallel, the United States and Canada cooperatively built a line of igloo-shaped radar stations designed to provide several hours of warning should Soviet bombers armed with atomics invade North American airspace. Any gaps in the DEW line, where there was sea instead of land, were filled in by picket ships and aircraft carrying radar.

CONELRAD
CONtrol of **EL**ectromagnetic **RAD**iation

Should the United States come under nuclear attack, all commercial radio stations were directed to broadcast the same information on the same frequency—640 KC and 1240 KC. Instructions to civilians would be sent over this emergency broadcast system.

SANE
is not an acronym, contrary to popular belief.

Called the Committee for a Sane Nuclear Policy, this ban-the-bomb group was formed in 1957. Founding members included a number of atomic scientists aghast at where their research had led the world. They often quoted the greatest physicist of them all, Albert Einstein: "I do not know how World War III will be fought. But I do know how World War IV will be fought—with sticks and stones."

KATUSA
Koreans **A**ttached **T**o the **U.S. A**rmy

In early 1950, Communist North Korea invaded non-Communist South Korea, and the U.N. sent American troops to stop the advance. The first U.S. units were seriously undermanned and the North Koreans overpowered them. In desperation, the United States drafted thousands of Korean civilians who spoke no English and had no military experience. Many of these Katusa inductees were sick, half-starved refugees. For the most part, they were used for work details, freeing up U.S. soldiers for direct combat.

Later in the war, Korean soldiers assigned to actually fight in American units were called ROKs (**R**epublic **O**f **K**orea) and the army of South Korea was also called ROK.

MIG
MIkoyan and **G**urevich

A Soviet jet fighter named for its two designers. The state-of-the-art planes were first used in Korea in 1950. MiG Alley was a series of North Korean valleys where Communist fighter planes began attacking when U.N. bombers flew missions over North Korea.

CORE
Congress **O**f **R**acial **E**quality

Though it was founded in 1942 by James Farmer and a small interracial group of Gandhian pacifists, this nonviolent yet confrontational civil rights group became widely known in the '50s. CORE militants staged sit-ins, demonstrations, boycotts, and picket lines throughout the South, demanding the right of black people to use the same lunch counters, bathrooms, and other public facilities as whites.

STOP
Stop **T**his **O**utrageous **P**urge

In 1954, the Supreme Court ruled that segregated schools were unconstitutional. Many southern school districts, which had been completely segregated until this time, attempted to "comply" with the new law by allowing a handful of black students into formerly all-white schools. The seriously ne-glected all-black schools received no attention.

Even this token integration led to a certain amount of racial tension, and in Little Rock, Arkansas, Governor Orval Faubus deliberately provoked racial fears and hatreds to fur-ther his own political career.

He'd served the two terms as state governor that were customary in his state and it was time to step down. But Faubus wanted a third term. So in September 1957, when Central High School was about to be tokenly integrated by adding nine black students to a population of 1,800 white ones, Faubus called in the Arkansas National Guard to surround the school and prevent the "integration." This action attracted vociferous white segregationists who turned into an angry mob when the nine black children attempted to enter Central High on the first day of school.

President Eisenhower sent in the 101st Airborne Division to enforce the law of the land and the entire country watched on television as federal troops beat back state troops and inflamed mobs of segregationists. Looking like a hero protecting the southern way of life against the "Yankee" invaders, Faubus was swept into office on a wave of prejudice.

After he'd closed the Little Rock secondary schools for all of the 1958–1959 school year, to "calm" the tensions his highly publicized refusal to integrate had created, the three segregationist members of the Little Rock school board proposed purging all teachers and administrators in the school system who espoused integration. A group of highly influential community leaders formed STOP in protest. The segregationists countered with CROSS—Committee to Retain Our Segregated Schools—and enlisted Faubus in fighting the "left wing country club."

When the CROSS members demanded recall elections, they themselves were unseated from the board by an electorate tired of the consequences of racial hatreds. Astute politician that he was, Faubus backed away from the issue of segregation. He served six terms as governor before retiring undefeated in 1966.

Whatever else can be said about the sixties, they certainly weren't bland and conformist. As the decade progressed, much of people's early idealistic searching for creative solutions became eroded by the constant escalation of the Vietnam War. Most of the decade's acronyms come from that war and those idealistic battlers.

WHAM
Winning Hearts And Minds

WHAM was a U.S. campaign in South Vietnam to control the native population. Though some of the methods were brutal, official sources described it as a humanitarian effort. This contradiction is reflected in the contrast between the acronym and the phrase it stands for.

ARVN ("Arvin")
Army of the **R**epublic of **V**iet**N**am
A term used by American military men to refer to South Vietnamese soldiers. Also called "Marvin Arvin," or "Viet," the South Vietnamese soldier was not generally held in high esteem by his American counterpart. An "Arvin attitude" was one that revealed a cowardly personality.

ROK RATs
Republic **O**f **K**orea **RAT**ions
The C-rations of the Korean army. The phrase was also used to refer to the marines from Korea who fought alongside U.S. and ARVN troops in Vietnam. Rok Rats had a reputation for being very tough and the Vietcong was intimidated by them.

HUeY
Helicopter, **U**tility
A nickname for a series of helicopters with the military designation UH-1. Like the amtrac swamp buggy of World War II, the huey was the transportation workhorse of the military, this time in Vietnam. It took the place of supply trucks, ambulances (called medevacs from medical + evacuation), troop shuttles, and weapons of war (when armed). The nickname is probably also a nod to Donald Duck's nephew.

NAPALM
NAphthene **PALM**itate
An incendiary jellylike chemical shot from flamethrowers or contained in bombs that was widely used by U.S. forces in battling enemy troops and destroying Communist-held hamlets. Its particularly horrible effects (flames that cling to the body) led antiwar protesters to focus their efforts on getting it banned. (They were unsuccessful.)

SAMs
Surface-to-**A**ir **M**issile
In the '50s, these weapons were called by their initialism (S.A.M.) but in Vietnam, the initialism became an acronym.

It was widely used when Russian-built SAMs defended Hanoi against American B-52 bombers in 1972.

From Vietnam, we move to the home front, a very different place from what it was in the '40s.

SNCC ("Snick")
Student **N**onviolent **C**oordinating **C**ommittee
Founded on college campuses in 1960, SNCC's evolution mirrored the gradual change of most civil rights groups during the decade from nonviolent protest to Black Power. In the early '60s, SNCC operated Freedom Schools in Mississippi to teach voter-registration skills and black history. Their work peaked in 1964 with the Freedom Summer, when hundreds of student volunteers from northern campuses rode buses into Mississippi in a vast effort to register black voters. This led to much violence culminating with the tragic murders of Mickey Schwerner, James Chaney, and Andrew Goodman.
In late '65, SNCC threw off many of the white staffers (Tom Hayden and Abbie Hoffman among them), whose philosophic, antihierarchy focus on grass-roots efforts contrasted sharply with the mostly black hard-liners who felt the civil rights movement needed to become more practical about power politics. There was less examining of personal motives and more focus on manipulating the media and changing the laws. By 1968, when H. Rap Brown became SNCC's new leader, the former advocates of nonviolent change had come to espouse the separatist beliefs of such groups as the Black Panthers. It was a long way to travel in eight years—an evolution that many activists shared during the decade of the '60s, whether demonstrating for student rights, peace, or the legalization of marijuana.

PIG
Pride, **I**ntegrity, and **G**uts
"Pig" was a favored insult that demonstrators hurled at the police who were sent to stop or control various protests. By the late '60s, radicals were shouting "Off the pigs," meaning "Kill the police." Finally, some uniformed wit fought back by turning "pig" into an acronym of respect.

YIPpie
Youth **I**nternational **P**arty
   The term gets its "pie" ending from the 1957 word "hippie" and also is partly derived from the 1930 interjection "yippee." The Yippies were a mock-political party started by Abbie Hoffman and Jerry Rubin at the end of 1967. The self-proclaimed jesters of the New Left, the Yippies staged funny, deliberately outrageous acts of challenge to the System like dropping a huge pile of dollar bills on the floor of the New York Stock Exchange. Yippies plastered the army recruiting booth in Times Square with travel posters saying "See Canada Now." In Chicago, just outside the 1968 Democratic Convention, the Yippies nominated a pig for president and announced they would put LSD in the city's water supply. (Mayor Daley stationed round-the-clock guards at the reservoirs.) The idea was to keep the System off balance, get lots of free publicity for the alternative political system the Left espoused, and have a rollicking good time doing it.

   In the '70s, there was less expectation and thus less fear of change as people turned inward and away from politics. Watergate made cynics of many former political idealists and a faltering economy led those who had ridden high on the spending boom of the '50s and '60s to reevaluate. Perhaps the world, even the world of wealthy America, was not a bottomless cornucopia we could always draw from. The sexual revolution and a burgeoning Women's Liberation movement were signs that the war in the streets had come home to the home itself.

CRP ("Creep")
Committee to **R**eelect the **P**resident
   Five months before the sweeping reelection of Richard Nixon in November of 1972, five men with electronic eavesdropping equipment were arrested in the Democratic party headquarters situated in a well-known Washington, D.C., hotel. Unfortunately, the wheels of justice ground so slowly that Nixon won the election before the scandalous practices of his reelection campaign came to light. (Instrumental in uncovering the story was a team dubbed "Woodstein" by the press—

Carl Bernstein + Bob Woodward of *The Washington Post*.) As the American public watched the tainted story of Watergate unfold on television, CRP came to be called "Creep."

In 1978, when the pardoned but none the less ex-president Nixon proposed visiting Oxford University, a group who opposed his visit called themselves **C**ommittee to **R**esist the **E**fforts of the **E**x-**P**resident—CREEP redux.

WITCH
Women's **I**nternational **T**errorist **C**onspiracy from **H**ell

A group of actress/writers in the early '70s who called themselves "a guerrilla-theater squad." They aligned themselves with the Weatherwomen and other radical feminists in challenging male supremacy in leftist politics as well as in the more traditional arenas.

OPEC
Organization of **P**etroleum **E**xporting **C**ountries

Though founded in 1960, this group became widely known, and feared, in the 1970s. It was created in Baghdad, Iraq, by frustrated countries who had leased oil concessions to various international petroleum companies. The companies had the unfortunate habit of lowering crude-oil prices without consulting the leaders of the countries who owned the oil. OPEC was a sort of "Let's take back our streets" response, and the member nations insisted on negotiating with the petroleum companies to determine the price of oil. The original members were Iran, Kuwait, Saudi Arabia, and Venezuela. (There's also NOPEC—**N**on-**OPEC**—another group of oil-producers including Angola, China, Egypt, Malaysia, Mexico, and Oman.)

In 1973, with the outbreak of the Arab-Israeli War, OPEC became much less conciliatory. By this time, the organization had grown to include Algeria, Ecuador, Gabon, Indonesia, Libya, Nigeria, Qatar, and United Arab Emirates and controlled four fifths of the oil reserves of the non-Communist world. OPEC began raising the price of crude oil without any input from the companies pumping it. And raising it. And raising it some more. The result was serious economic dislocation in most First World countries.

If OPEC had managed to maintain its unified posture, it's

interesting to speculate who might be running the world to-day. However, internal conflicts between members (revolu-tionary Iran versus the conservative kingdom of Saudi Arabia; Iran versus Iraq; Iraq versus Kuwait, etc.) have limited its effectiveness. OPEC survives, but no longer holds the world for oil ransom.

Petrodollar
petroleum + dollar
　　In 1973, when OPEC began some serious muscle flexing and quadrupled the price of crude oil, American dollars began flowing at an alarming rate out of American pockets into Arab hands. Countries like Saudi Arabia had such a large dollar surplus that they used these petrodollars for loans and other investments in America.

Stagflation
stagnation + inflation
　　When OPEC quadrupled the price of oil, it meant that everything dependent on oil was going to become more expen-sive. Because practically everything is ultimately dependent on energy, and oil provides that, worldwide inflation began in the mid-seventies. Unfortunately, high prices meant that businesses had to cut back on expenses, which meant letting employees go. So economic growth stagnated.
　　The government was caught in a bind. If it tightened the money supply to control inflation (which was as high as 1.5 percent a month), that meant businesses could borrow less money so they'd have to tighten their belts even more, letting more workers go. On the other hand, if the government low-ered interest rates so people could borrow more money, infla-tion would intensify.
　　Stagflation was also called Slumpflation (slump + infla-tion) and Inflump (inflation + slump). Later, in 1978, Hesifla-tion (hesitation + inflation) set in. This was a condition where economic growth was intermittent and inflation continued to be high.

WIN
Whip Inflation Now
　　During the Ford administration (1974–1976), as the gov-ernment struggled with the slumpflation bind, federal officials

had major newspapers print an enlistment form for "inflation fighters." Readers were asked to cut out a form reading "Dear President Ford, I enlist as an Inflation Fighter and Energy Saver for the duration. I will do the very best I can for America."

The first one hundred thousand people who filled in their names and addresses and mailed in the form received a red button with the word WIN in white letters.

One group opposing the slumpflation-fighting package Ford finally presented to Congress called itself LOSE—Let Others Share Equally.

big MAC
Municipal **A**ssistance **C**orporation

In June of 1975, New York City ran out of money. After bitter negotiations among bankers, city officials, and state legislators, a new state agency, named playfully after a hamburger (those financiers are such devils with words), was created to alleviate the financial crisis. Big MAC offered long-term municipal bonds backed by specially earmarked city sales taxes. Response by investors was tepid, unfortunately, but in the end the Big Apple pulled through.

MEOW
Moral **E**quivalent **O**f **W**ar

Three months into President Carter's administration, in 1977, he sent his first major piece of legislation to Congress—an extremely complex package aimed at reducing our dependence on oil and therefore controlling inflation. Carter told the nation that solving America's energy problem was the moral equivalent of war. (That is to say, instead of fighting the Arabs for the oil, the moral solution is to lessen our dependence on oil.) The response on Capitol Hill was unbelievably negative. By proposing to raise gas taxes yearly, penalize gas guzzlers, put a cap on automobile sticker prices, and control the cost of natural gas, the bill managed to offend an enormous array of powerful interests. And because Carter hadn't wooed the key members of Congress who might have smoothed the way, they didn't fight for him.

The fight lasted eighteen bitter and divisive months and the bill came out much lessened in power. Carter's mishandling of Congress was derisively called MEOW—a pussy-cat approach to a situation calling for a lion.

Blaxploitation
black + exploitation
What do the movies *Shaft*, *Superfly*, and *Cleopatra Jones* have in common? They all had action galore, blood by the bucketful, tough-talking, tall-black-and-handsome heroes, smoldering women, and a soundtrack full of soul music. Community leaders from the NAACP and CORE might have complained that the gangsters, pimps, and pushers with their tireless muscles and lack of brainpower were terrible role models for young black men, but Hollywood kept putting out blaxploitation movies because black audiences flocked to them. There was even a *Blacula* (black + Dracula) movie at the height of the fad. The trend lasted from 1970 to 1974.

PUSH
People **U**nited to **S**erve **H**umanity
The Reverend Jesse Jackson founded this self-help black organization in 1972. PUSH promotes economic independence among minorities. It also sponsors an anti-drug program for inner-city students.

ROAR
Restore **O**ur **A**lienated **R**ights
In September 1974, when Boston city schools opened for the fall semester, the scene was reminiscent of Little Rock, Arkansas, in the bad old '50s. Mobs of white parents, protesting busing, joined their boycotting children in throwing rocks at incoming buses of black students. The protesters marched on City Hall, carrying an Irish flag with ROAR emblazoned on it and when Senator Edward Kennedy tried to reason with them, he was shoved away and harassed from the street. One parent even shouted, "Why don't you let them shoot you like they shot your two brothers?"

Palimony
pal + alimony
Living together became quite a common arrangement in the '70s and some of those relationships were quite long-lived.

When actor Lee Marvin broke up with Michelle Triola, his live-in girlfriend of six years, she took him to court and sued for alimony (half of the $3.6 million he'd earned during the years they were together). With the help of famous Hollywood divorce lawyer Marvin Mitchelson, the dispute reached the California State Supreme Court, which agreed to hear the case, citing the "radically changed social mores" of the times.

The dispute stimulated over a thousand similar palimony lawsuits, including ones against Peter Frampton and Flip Wilson. Courts mostly awarded the plaintiffs large sums for rehabilitation purposes but not full alimony. And prenuptual agreements, toasted at times with Champale (champagne + ale), became common between would-be cohabitors where one member of the couple was wealthy. The poorer lover had to agree not to demand a portion of the richer lover's earnings and/or estate should the couple part. There was often a sizable "severance" reward offered in exchange.

Ah, the '80s: glitter and corporate greed and conspicuous consumption, and scandals galore. It was a good time to be rich. And if you weren't, at least you could gloat when the monied and the powerful went to jail.

Contragate
Contra + Watergate
What a tangled web President Reagan's top advisers wove, and without even involving the CIA. Since Congress had passed legislation forbidding any material aid to be sent to the Nicaraguan Contras, sending money to these right-wing guerrilla fighters was against the law. But what if no one knew? In 1985 the president's personal covert-operations gang secretly diverted their earnings from undercover arms sales to Iran and sent the money on to their favorite counterrevolutionaries in Nicaragua. "Iranscam" or "Iranamok," as journalists also called it, made the president look either derelict in his duties as overseer of his staff or actively involved in the scandal. The remaining two years of his second term in office lacked much of the high moral conviction Reagan had conveyed to his admirers during his first six years.

Abscam
Arab + scam
   The FBI dressed up several of its operatives as rich Arabs looking to buy favors from members of Congress and netted seven congressmen and a senator in its two-year sting operation. The 1982 trial, which included videotapes of public officials accepting $25,000 and $50,000 bribes, caused Harrison A. Williams, Jr., from New Jersey, to resign his Senate seat.

Televangelist
television + evangelist
   The Jim and Tammy Show became a whole new kind of show in the '80s and the swagger in Jimmy Swaggart took on new meaning. And what about Oral Roberts announcing that if he didn't get $8 million immediately, he would die? What they all had in common was enormous religious charisma, very wide TV coverage, and too much access to money. Jim Bakker, after having an extramarital affair with church secretary Jessica Hahn, paid her a large sum of church money to keep quiet. Mr. Swaggart indulged his libido with Debra Jo Murphree, who later posed for *Penthouse* and told all. There was lots of vicious infighting and sobbing confessions among televangelists in the second half of the decade, much of it right on television.

PATCO
Professional **A**ir **T**raffic **C**ontrollers **O**rganization
   On August 3, 1981, more than 13,000 air traffic controllers walked off the job in a dispute over wages, working hours, and retirement benefits. President Reagan broke the strike, jailing five of its leaders, slapping the union with a $1 million a day fine for every day it struck, and firing any employee who didn't immediately return to work. More than eleven thousand people permanently lost their jobs. The president justified his actions by calling PATCO's walkout illegal since the controllers were federal workers bound by a no-strike oath.

the Chunnel
channel + tunnel
   A few hardy souls have swum the English Channel, but in 1986, France and Great Britain announced plans for digging

a two-way railway tunnel all the way under it to connect the two countries. This is the largest European construction project ever. It is scheduled to open in 1993 and it is estimated that the trip along the thirty-mile route will take half an hour. Not for the very claustrophobic, perhaps, but certainly for the hurried.

POSSLQ ("Possel-cue")
Person of **O**pposite **S**ex **S**haring **L**iving **Q**uarters

By the '80s, living together was something many people did before they married. But the language hadn't kept up with social change. There really wasn't a good word to use when referring to the person you romantically lived with. People tried "Significant Other," "Roommate," "Domestic Partner," "Boy/Girlfriend," "Lover," "Live-In," and lots more, but none of them was quite right. In 1980, the U.S. Census Bureau took its shot with a sociological code word for an unmarried person with whom you live.

USA for Africa
United **S**upport of **A**rtists for Africa

On January 28, 1985, many of America's top recording artists gathered in Los Angeles to record an album called *We Are the World*. The $50 million that the album earned was donated to charitable organizations focused on helping the needy of Africa. The contributing artists included Lionel Ritchie, Michael Jackson, Tina Turner, Bruce Springsteen, Ray Charles, Diana Ross, Bob Dylan, Billy Joel, Paul Simon, and Stevie Wonder.

The success of the effort sparked more charitable concerts, videos, and albums. Live-Aid raised $40 million for African famine relief. Farm-Aid, headlined by Willie Nelson and other pop country singers, contributed $10 million to the cause of the American farmer. In a decade characterized more by greed than generosity, these group accomplishments were a heartwarming contrast.

CHAPTER 5

The Groups We Belong To—Part I

IF YOU JOIN a group in its start-up phase, you will almost certainly have a meeting where you throw around possible names for your fledgling organization. And sure as water is wet, someone will suggest an acronym as you munch your way through that slowly hardening mound of sweet rolls and sip your weak coffee.

Judging from our findings, the acronym pushers win the day in an amazing number of cases. Why? Perhaps because a single word functions almost like a photograph—the right word is worth a thousand wrong ones. It suggests the tone, the direction, the energy, the meaning, all at the same time. And it's clever besides.

The groups here are organized by the passion they promote or reject. Incidentally, should you find your own passions stirred by any of these causes and wish to join a group, we include the addresses of many of the following organizations in an Appendix at the back of the book.

Cigarette smoking in public has become a very emotional issue since science has shown that even smoke we inhale from someone else's cigarette can endanger our health.

ASH

Action on **S**moking and **H**ealth

The granddaddy of the anti-smoking groups, ASH was founded by John Banzhaf, a young man fresh out of law school who had just begun work for a large New York legal firm in 1967. Only two years earlier, the Surgeon General had announced that cigarette smoking was unhealthy and cigarette ads remained the number-one kind of TV commercial.

Banzhaf's story reads like a modern-day version of David and Goliath. With only his legal wits and against strong recommendations from his employers (whose major client was Philip Morris), Banzhaf challenged the FCC to provide equal time for pro-smoking and anti-smoking viewpoints on television and radio. When the FCC agreed, the lords of the powerful tobacco industry rose up against him. They appealed the FCC decision and worked to have the trial moved to a court deep in tobacco country, where Banzhaf wouldn't have stood a chance.

Banzhaf managed to hold his own even though such expected allies as the American Cancer Society and the American Heart Association refused to back him. Apparently they were far more comfortable doing research and public education than taking an activist stand. Finally he attracted the support of people on the staff of Harvard Medical School, who in turn brought in other heavyweight supporters. With prestigious names on the ASH letterhead, Banzhaf was able to raise funds to publicize his organization and build a reputation.

Banzhaf lost his position with his law firm but instead became the unsalaried head of ASH, named for the end of a cigarette. And in the twenty-five years since its founding, ASH has helped abolish cigarette ads on television, end smoking on airplanes, and limit smoking in many public places. It takes legal action to protect the rights of the nonsmoking majority.

GASP

Group **A**gainst **S**mokers' **P**ollution

Founded in 1971 by Clara Gouin, GASP works to educate the public about the dangers of secondhand smoke. There are fifty local chapters. In the '70s, the group bestowed several Ventilator Awards for clearing the public air of tobacco smoke. Jesse Steinfeld, the U.S. Surgeon General who sponsored the first government study of the effects of secondhand smoke, was an early winner.

Other anti-smoking groups include FANS (**F**resh **A**ir for **N**on-**S**mokers) and SHAME (**S**ociety to **H**umiliate, **A**ggravate, **M**ortify, and **E**mbarrass Smokers).

A couple of pro-smoking groups: CIGARS (**C**ommittee **I**nsuring and **G**uaranteeing **A**nyone's **R**ight to **S**moke) and COUGH (**C**ongregation **O**rganized by **U**nited **G**enial **H**ackers).

Another emotion-laden issue is drugs: alcohol, marijuana, and the harder substances. Powerful, attractive, dangerous, drugs are the focus of many groups.

MADD
Mothers **A**gainst **D**runk **D**riving

An organization one million strong that was founded in 1980 to act as the voice of victims of drunk-driving crashes. MADD encourages more stringent laws against drunk driving and works with teachers of driver's education. The organization also holds an annual candlelight vigil for people who have died as a result of the lethal mix of alcohol and automobiles.

SADD (**S**tudents **A**gainst **D**runk **D**riving), founded in Maryland in 1981, has fifty state groups. SADD works to raise public awareness of the dangers of alcohol, drugs, and driving.

DAMM
Drinkers **A**gainst **M**ad **M**others

A Detroit group with one hundred members, founded in 1984, that lobbies to protect the rights of social drinkers. DAMM opposes breathalizer tests, mandatory seat-belt laws, and other such legalized acts that the organization believes infringe on drinkers' constitutional rights. The group advocates personal discipline in place of legal restraints and objects to special-interest groups such as MADD using legislation to express their views.

DARE
Drug **A**buse **R**esistance Education

A widespread educational program for children in elementary and secondary schools that uses local police officers as teachers. The program, begun in Los Angeles in 1983, focuses on preteens in grades 5 and 6, teaching them how and why to refuse drugs in social situations. Much time is spent on assertiveness training and on building self-esteem. Literature is sent home to parents to help them help their kids. The motto of the now nationwide organization is "Dare to Keep Kids off Drugs."

Parents Against DARE, a group from Colorado, fears that having police officers discuss drugs with children could well lead to civil-liberties violations. There have been several instances where children have confessed that their parents are users and those parents have been arrested.

DARE classes are typically offered as an option in elementary schools rather than a requirement.

DAWN
Drug **A**buse **W**arning **N**etwork

One way the government can gauge how well its anti–drug-abuse programs are working is by polling hospital emergency rooms. More than five hundred hospitals report the incidence of drug-related emergencies to DAWN, which compiles the information and passes it on to the National Institute of Drug Abuse. Former President Bush often referred to DAWN reports when discussing his administration's progress in fighting drug abuse.

CAMP
Campaign **A**gainst **M**arijuana **P**lanting

Summertime is when the marijuana crops ripen in the far northern counties of California. So summer is when commando-type strike teams composed of people from federal, state, and local law agencies attack the illegal fields with helicopters, long-handled brush cutters, and fire. In the mid-eighties, residents of Trinity and Shasta counties came to expect the spotting helicopters as soon as the weather began to warm. The five-year program was reportedly quite successful in wiping out what was California's largest cash crop.

NORML ("Normal")
National Organization for the Reform of Marijuana Laws

A public-education organization working to decriminalize the use, possession, and cultivation of marijuana. NORML was started in 1970 and has 80,000 members.

STASH
STudent Association for the Study of Hallucinogens

In 1967, law-enforcement officials often distorted the truth about hallucinogenic drugs in an effort to frighten potential users and justify the drugs' illegal status. Kids and their parents were routinely informed that marijuana use, for example, inevitably leads to heroin addiction.

A student named Leif Zerkin believed that a more rational look at drugs would foster a healthier attitude toward these substances whose use was as old as civilization itself. For fourteen years his organization published books, pamphlets, and a scholarly journal in an effort to disseminate more accurate information about hallucinogens. Law officials' initial response was extremely negative, but in the end, even officers in the armed forces were distributing these well-researched materials, convinced that truth was a more potent tool than fiction in halting drug abuse.

BACH
Business Alliance for Commerce in Hemp

A Los Angeles–based organization working to legalize marijuana and to resume the commercial use of hemp for paper, building materials, and pulp. (Such use is currently illegal.) BACH proposes regulating marijuana in the same way as alcohol. Growing it for private consumption and using it for medical reasons would become legal. The group points out that for every acre of hemp planted, we could preserve 4.1 acres of forest.

Another organization for marijuana legalization is BLOSSOM (Basic Liberation Of Smokers and Sympathizers Of Marijuana).

A couple of odd patterns turn up in acronymic organizations about sexuality. Prostitution groups almost all have animal names and groups advocating no sex education in schools almost all start with "P."

JACGUAR
Johns **A**nd **C**all **G**irls **U**nited **A**gainst **R**epression

A small group from New York founded in 1978 that works to legally safeguard the civil rights of prostitutes and their customers. JACGUAR also wants to decriminalize prostitution. Their monthly magazine is called *Oldest Profession Times*.

COYOTE
Call **O**ff **Y**our **O**ld **T**ired **E**thics

A prostitutes' activist group from San Francisco.

There's also PONY (**P**rostitutes **O**f **N**ew **Y**ork) and ASP (**A**ssociation of **S**eattle **P**rostitutes). Plus there's the slogan of a prostitutes' group in Honolulu: DOLPHIN (**D**ump **O**bsolete **L**aws—**P**rove **H**ypocrisy **I**sn't **N**ecessary).

HUMP
Hookers **U**nited **M**ostly for **P**rofit

The official prostitutes' union of the United States.

CLAP
Citizens **L**obbying **A**gainst **P**rostitution

Folks ranged on the other side.

SIECUS ("Seek-us")
Sex **I**nformation and **E**ducation **C**ouncil of the **U.S.**

Formed in 1964 to assure that all people, including adolescents, the disabled, sexual minorities, and the elderly, have access to clear and objective answers to their questions about sexual issues. The organization's library in New York City has the largest collection of material on sexuality and sexuality education in the world. SIECUS staff members work with school boards and many other governmental agencies as well as distribute the many publications of the organization. Its membership includes many doctors, educators, and religious leaders.

POPE
Parents for **O**rthodoxy in **P**arochial **E**ducation
A group against sex education in school. Other similar groups: POSE (**P**arents **O**pposed to **S**ex **E**ducation), PAUSE (**P**eople **A**gainst **U**nconstitutional **S**ex **E**ducation), POPS (**P**eople **O**pposed to **P**ornography in **S**chool), and POSSE (**P**arents **O**pposed to **S**ex and **S**ensitivity **E**ducation).

ROMP
Recovery **O**f **M**ale **P**otency
A self-help group that was founded in 1983 for impotent men and their partners. ROMP also holds training conferences for doctors and psychologists who work in the field.

People often join a group in order to gain power through numbers. Some groups apply this power directly to the political process.

NOW
National **O**rganization for **W**omen
Founded in 1966 to achieve full equality for women, this nationwide group has grown to 280,000 members. (More than 10,000 new members joined up in the four months after Clarence Thomas was confirmed to the Supreme Court.) NOW uses litigation, lobbying, a PAC dedicated to bringing women into national office, and demonstrations. (Three quarters of a million people marched on Washington in March of 1991 for reproductive freedom.)
LATER (**L**adies' **A**fter**T**houghts on **E**qual **R**ights) appeared in the '70s as a group opposed to some of NOW's goals. Another opposing group was THEN (**T**hose **H**ags **E**ncourage **N**euterism).

ACORN
Association of **C**ommunity **O**rganizations for **R**eform **N**ow
A group started in 1970 that is dedicated to helping local neighborhoods gain power in the institutions that dominate their lives. A national organization with eight hundred local groups, ACORN focuses on poor and moderate-income fami-

lies and helps them fight such things as utility rate increases, high prices for prescription drugs, and inadequate housing.

LASER
League for the **A**dvancement of **S**tates **R**ights

A group founded in Utah in 1977 that promotes the "Sagebrush Rebellion," an organized political attempt by conservatives in western states to gain control of millions of acres of federally owned land.

TINCUP
Time **I**s **N**ow, **C**lean **U**p **P**olitics

In the late '70s, Orange County in Southern California suffered a spate of political fund-raising scandals. TINCUP was the campaign reform movement that led to strict controls on how much money a county supervisor could accept from a donor and still vote on that donor's project.

TAJ
Taxpayers **A**gainst "**J**"

"J" was a ballot measure asking for money to build a new jail. This opposing group's slogan was "We need jails, not a Taj Mahal."

GAP
Government **A**ccountability **P**roject

Let's say you work for a government agency that is taking bribes to change zoning laws so that high-rise apartments can tower over single-family homes. If you as an individual blow the whistle on your employer, chances are you will lose your job, even if you succeed in calling attention to the illegal activity.

GAP was organized in 1975 to give legal and strategic advice to people who are in a position to expose waste, threats to public health and safety, illegality, or repression. The group's name calls attention to the gap between the law and reality in these difficult situations.

HALT
Help **A**bolish **L**egal **T**yranny

Ever fume at the excessive tangles of the legal system and how much money it takes to get out of its coils? Say you're involved in a fender-bender and everyone walks away in perfect health. Even the cars are fine. Next thing you know you're being sued for major medical injuries, workmen's compensation, psychological trauma, and—who knows?—maybe the greenhouse effect. By the time your lawyer and their lawyer get through sending foot-thick depositions back and forth, setting court dates, wheeling and dealing on the settlement, etc., etc., the mess has cost you extraordinary amounts of time, money, and molar-grinding frustration. There's got to be a better way.

HALT was established in 1977 to simplify legal language and procedures, to establish simple and affordable litigation, and to reform our laws on attorney regulation. This Washington, D.C., group is 150,000 members strong.

TRIM
Tax Reform IMmediately

Formed in 1977, TRIM is a project of the John Birch Society that proposes to cut taxes so as to reverse the growth of government control. It publishes the congressional voting record on big money bills and offers a speakers' bureau and library.

CAUTION
Citizens Against Unnecessary Tax Increases and Other Nonsense

A group formed in St. Louis in the early '70s that opposed a large bond issue.

On the international scene, there are several acronymically named organizations that extend aid to the needy.

CARE
Cooperative for American Remittances to Europe
and
Cooperative for American Relief Everywhere

When World War II was over, Europe was devastated by famine. Twenty-four American charitable agencies banded together to help, calling their umbrella organization "Cooperative for American Remittances to Europe." Americans paid fifteen dollars to send a CARE package of food to a starving family. CARE directed the American relief effort until 1948, when the broader-based Marshall Plan took over.

Today CARE has changed its name (Cooperative for American Relief Everywhere), the field of its endeavors, and the manner in which it offers help. With almost seven thousand people on staff and a yearly budget of $321 million, it operates in thirty-nine Third World countries, teaching self-help, training health-care workers, giving disaster aid, and still providing food to the hungry.

AID
Agency for **I**nternational **D**evelopment

Established in 1961 as part of the State Department, AID works to solve severe economic problems in developing countries in which the United States has a special interest.

UNICEF
United **N**ations **C**hildren's **E**mergency **F**und

UNICEF began just after World War II as an American charitable organization which sent food, clothing, blankets, and medical supplies to suffering children in war-blasted Europe. After Europe recovered, the organization came under the auspices of the United Nations and in 1963 won the Nobel Peace Prize for its work in healing, feeding, and educating the children of the world.

UNESCO
United **N**ations **E**ducational, **S**cience, and **C**ultural **O**rganization

After World War I, the leaders of the Allied nations created the League of Nations with the avowed purpose of preventing any more war. One of the philosophic tenets of the League was that war begins in the minds of men so that if prejudice and ignorance could be erased, then people wouldn't fight. The International Institute of Intelligent Cooperation was formed to promote worldwide learning.

UNESCO is based on this organization. One of its first tasks after World War II was to rebuild the educational systems of countries conquered by the Nazis. The group worked to discredit Nazi master-race ideas and to encourage the spread of democratic beliefs.

Today UNESCO works to train teachers, to combat illiteracy, and to promote appreciation of different national cultures. Though almost all the countries in the U.N. belong, both the United States and Britain withdrew in the mid-eighties, charging that the organization allows restrictions on freedom of the press and suffers from wasteful management methods.

WHO
World **H**ealth **O**rganization

This is the major health agency of the United Nations. WHO is a huge organization that broadcasts a daily epidemic report, establishes international quarantine regulations, and assists members in many health-related activities such as eradicating major diseases and training health professionals.

Three American governmental groups aiding Americans:

VISTA
Volunteers **I**n **S**ervice **T**o **A**merica

A War on Poverty program envisioned and initiated by John F. Kennedy as part of his effort "to get the country moving again." After six short weeks of training, volunteers are assigned to a year of service in urban ghettos, Alaskan Eskimo villages, migrant worker camps, and other such impoverished sites. Living at poverty level themselves, volunteers reside among the poor and share their skills and time. Since the program has yet to evolve concrete, specific goals, perhaps the most obvious result of VISTA is to expose the middle-class volunteers to the reality of how their poor fellow citizens live their lives.

HUD
(United States Department of) **H**ousing and **U**rban **D**evelopment

Lyndon Johnson proposed HUD, along with Medicare and several other federal organizations, as part of his ambitious plan to create "The Great Society" in America. (The escalating war in Vietnam overshadowed these efforts to make the country a more equitable society.) HUD still exists and its many local offices help the old and those with low income afford housing.

OSHA
Occupational **S**afety and **H**ealth **A**dministration

How much radiation should you be exposed to if you work in a nuclear power plant? What is an acceptable noise level in a factory? Until OSHA appeared in 1971, the answers depended on what state and even what city you worked in. OSHA has established nationwide standards in the workplace. These are the people who inspect the places where we work, and if they find we aren't safe, propose penalties and issue deadlines to our employers.

Helping organizations and acronyms go together like a horse and carriage.

LIFE
Love **I**s **F**eeding **E**veryone

A Los Angeles food collection and distribution program started in 1984 by Hollywood stars Dennis Weaver and Valerie Harper. By 1992, LIFE was salvaging four million pounds of food per week to feed one hundred thousand homeless people. The group issued a star-studded album called *Raise the World* and arranged with Mobil Oil Company to train former gang members for work in major corporations as part of the Rebuild L.A. effort after the 1992 riots.

ACTION
American **C**ouncil **T**o **I**mprove **O**ur **N**eighborhoods

Founded in 1967, ACTION seeks to improve the quality of life for the disadvantaged in urban areas. The group encourages women and minorities to study in the sciences, offers AIDS education, and serves as an advocate for the urban poor.

Project ANGEL
Assist **N**eighbors by **G**iving **E**nergy for **L**iving

Every two months, when Angelenos get their water and power bills, they are encouraged to add a little extra money to their checks. The money ($1.3 million in 1983, for example) is used to help poor people in L.A. who are behind on paying for the water and electricity they use.

DEAF Inc.
Developmental **E**valuation **A**djustment **F**acility

A New England agency that helps the hard of hearing learn independent living skills such as responding to visual signals for a ringing doorbell or telephone. DEAF Inc. also sponsors the telephone relay service for the state of Massachusetts in which hearing partners work as translators of phone messages for hard of hearing customers.

GLAD
Greater **L**os **A**ngeles Council on **D**eafness

The umbrella organization for more than forty-five California agencies and groups serving the hard of hearing. GLAD offers social clubs, maintains a pool of available sign-language interpreters, and sponsors religious, health, education, and many other sorts of groups.

SHHH
Self **H**elp for **H**ard of **H**earing People, Inc.

A volunteer organization in Maryland that works as an advocate in many areas of concern for deaf people. The group's journal *Shhh*, with a readership of 200,000, is the only magazine designed specifically for the hard of hearing.

BOLD
Blind **O**utdoor **L**eisure **D**evelopment

A Colorado organization established in 1969 that designs downhill-ski opportunities for the blind. The group also helps local clubs make it possible for blind people to skate, bike, horseback ride, and participate in many other such outdoor sports.

PRIDE Foundation
Promote **R**eal **I**ndependence for the **D**isabled and the **E**lderly

An organization in Connecticut that designs all sorts of implements and garments to make it easier for people with physical limitations to dress and groom themselves independently and to manage their own cooking and other housework. The group also provides workshops where the products are demonstrated.

WISE
Westside **I**ndependent **S**ervices to the **E**lderly

A Los Angeles organization that helps approximately 35,000 seniors annually with transportation, day care, and other needs.

CHUMS
Cancer **H**opefuls **U**nited for **M**utual **S**upport

CHUMS sponsored self-help groups of cancer "victors" (as opposed to "victims") around the country for several years. The groups were led for the most part by psychiatrists or counselors who themselves had had a history of cancer. Members met to exchange information regarding treatments and to explore the emotional side effects of their disease. The group functioned through most of the 1980s but has recently closed down.

CHAPTER 6

The Groups We Belong To—Part II

THE FIRST GROUP most of us belong to is the family we are born into. Many organizations have arisen to fill in the gaps that can sometimes be found in families.

VOICES
Victims Of Incest Can Emerge Survivors
Founded in 1980 in Chicago, VOICES is a support network for people who have experienced incest and are scarred by it. The group helps victims find effective psychological help, trains health professionals, and works to educate the public about the prevalence and consequences of incest and the methods of prevention.

STOP-IT
Survivors of Trauma for the Overall Prevention of Incest and Trauma
A Los Angeles–based think tank staffed by volunteers who work to prevent child rape and abuse.

VOCAL
Victims Of Child Abuse Laws
A group that supports the legal prosecution of those people who falsely accuse others of abusing children. VOCAL seeks to reform the current child-abuse laws.

WEAVE
Women Escaping A Violent Environment

A Sacramento-based support group for battered women. A complementary group for men, based in San Francisco, is MOVE (Men Overcoming ViolencE).

CUB
Concerned United Birthparents

An organization founded in 1976 that focuses on improving the processes of adoption. CUB advocates open birth records and support groups to prevent mothers from giving children up for adoption if a better choice can be found.

A group with similar goals is the ALMA Society (Adoptees' Liberty Movement Association), which is made up of adults who were adopted, foster children, siblings separated by adoption, and natural parents who gave children up for adoption. The society helps adoptees find their natural parents.

NOCIRC
National Organization of Circumcision Information
Resource Centers

A group that hopes to end routine infant circumcision. NOCIRC is an umbrella organization created in 1981 for the many circumcision information centers nationwide. The organization publishes a newsletter questioning the medical necessity for circumcizing newborns. This information is sent to 16,000 hospitals and individual medical offices.

NICE
Neighborhood Involvement in Children's Education

A program in which senior citizens volunteer to become foster grandparents to children with special needs.

EXXCEL
Educational EXcellence for Children with Environmental
Limitations

A pilot program co-sponsored by the University of Southern California, a pair of apartment-complex developers, and several local public schools in the heart of Los Angeles. EXXCEL has built a low-rent housing complex and offered some of the units to students from the university in exchange for their tutoring the children of the other tenants in the complex. The tutors, doctoral students in education or psychology, also work with teachers from the public schools that the children attend. The complex includes a study room with computers and reference books designed for the children and their tutors. The program even gives children who get high grades free trips to Disneyland.

PURE
People **U**nited for **R**ural **E**ducation

A grass-roots organization in Indiana founded in 1977 that opposes reorganizing rural school districts into centralized, bureaucracy-heavy ones. PURE believes that small autonomous districts produce the most individualized and enriched education.

Organizations concerning Native Americans have some evocative names.

AIM
American **I**ndian **M**ovement

An activist Native American group that works to regain a "warrior spirit" among its people. It was formed in 1968, mostly by urban American Indians, to encourage self-determination among their people and to establish international recognition of their treaty rights. In 1972, armed AIM activists wearing their characteristic red headbands staged a demonstration at Wounded Knee, South Dakota, that gained national attention.

Five years later, AIM members were involved in a mysterious shootout with the FBI on the Pine Ridge Indian Reservation in South Dakota in which two federal agents and one Indian were killed. Three major AIM activists were accused of murdering the FBI agents, and one man, Leonard Peltier, was convicted. He is currently serving two concurrent life sentences.

Peltier's trial was highly controversial. His lawyer, the famous William Kunstler, claims that much of the evidence offered by the FBI was clearly tampered with and that Peltier was made to be the fall guy because someone had to pay for the "resmurs" (reservation + murders) of FBI agents. Apparently many people agree with this assessment. Two movies have been made in recent years about the incident, one a documentary narrated by Robert Redford, called *Incident at Oglala*, and the other a drama closely based on the actual happenings, called *Thunderheart*. Both movies support Kunstler's claims.

Pine Ridge was experiencing a veritable reign of terror by armed vigilantes called GOONS (**G**uardians **O**f the **O**glala **N**ation) in the months before the incident. The reservation was run by nontraditional Indians who sided with the various federal agencies (Bureau of Indian Affairs, FBI, etc.) in wanting to assimilate with white culture.

Traditional Indians resented these "Uncle Tomahawks," especially since they controlled almost all the jobs on the desperately poor reservation. Traditionalist protests were met with violence, which escalated to stunning proportions. Houses were attacked with fusillades of bullets, and many women, children, and elders were killed. AIM was called in for protection.

When the two FBI agents, armed strangers, drove up to an AIM camp, some of the Indians overreacted out of fear. But who did the actual killing is not clear. The FBI dispatcher who was recording the last messages of the two agents changed his story later as to time and the type of car leaving the scene (to fit with the FBI's scenario). Supposed eyewitnesses to Peltier's presence at the scene turned out to have been badly intimidated by the FBI and later denied seeing him there. A mysterious Mr. X has claimed that he is the actual murderer. But Leonard Peltier remains in prison.

WARN
Women of **A**ll **R**ed **N**ations

A South Dakota grass-roots organization of Native American women that works to solve many of the issues facing Indians today. One major focus is the exploitation of mineral resources on Indian land by multinational corporations. Other areas of concern include political imprisonment, miscarriages of justice, and sterilization abuses.

* * *

Environmental organizations are rife with acronyms. And it seems as if every other one is called GASP.

MUSE
Musicians **U**nited for **S**afe **E**nergy

Remember the "No Nukes" concert in September of '79? Three hundred thousand people attended the rally and listened to the music of such rock stars as Jackson Browne, James Taylor, and Crosby, Stills and Nash as a protest against the proliferation of nuclear power plants. The money earned at the concert was used to fight the growth of nuclear-energy use. And the nonprofit organization that administered this money was called MUSE.

SUFFER
Save **U**s **F**rom **F**ormaldehyde **E**nvironmental **R**epercussions

A Minnesota-based organization founded in 1980 that lobbies against poisonous fumes.

GASP
Group for **A**lternatives to **S**preading **P**oisons

This organization works to teach people how to avoid using toxic household and garden chemicals like weed killers or oven cleaners. (Some other GASPs: **G**roup **A**gainst **S**mokers' **P**ollution, **G**als **A**gainst **S**moke and **P**ollution, **G**reater **W**ashington **A**lliance to **S**top **P**ollution.)

SLOBB
Stop **L**ittering **O**ur **B**eaches and **B**ays

Members of SLOBB collect cans and plastic bags from local beaches in Orange County, California, and hold demonstrations to raise the public's awareness of the littering problem.

ENCORE!
ENvironmental **CO**ntainer **RE**use

A California group that buys up used wine bottles, sterilizes them, and sells them back to the wine industry to be used again.

EPIC

Environmental **P**rotection **I**nformation **C**enter, Inc.

This is a group that seeks to protect the endangered spotted owl in northern California. Since the owl's habitat is old-growth forests, saving the owl will also limit the activity of the logging industry, a goal of this organization. EPIC was founded in 1977 and functions as a resource center for volunteer activists in northern California.

Kids F.A.C.E.

Kids **F**or **A** **C**lean **E**nvironment

In 1989, a bright, concerned nine-year-old girl named Melissa Poe wrote a letter to then President Bush asking that he put up billboards urging Americans to stop polluting their environment. Many weeks later, she received his answer—a form letter thanking her for not using drugs.

Her initial frustration ended up galvanizing her to make her own efforts, with startlingly visible results—250 billboards were put up across the country after she and her parents enlisted the help of a local billboard company and suggested some environmental billboards as public-service announcements.

Melissa Poe went on to organize an environmental club, the first Kids F.A.C.E., among her Nashville, Tennessee, schoolmates and continued her antipollution efforts. Today there are more than six hundred such clubs across the country and the Kids F.A.C.E. newsletter goes out to 30,000 members, including many teachers. The organization is sponsored by the enormous Wal-Mart retail chain. (By the way, Bush later sent an apologetic follow-up letter to the young activist.)

YES

Youth for **E**nvironmental **S**anity

A nonprofit organization started in Santa Cruz, California, that is run entirely by people aged fifteen to twenty-one. They put on shows with theater acts, slides, and speeches, all designed to inspire teenagers to come to the aid of their environment. YES runs summer training camps to teach fundraising, publicizing, and other such organizational skills. Sponsors include many well-known actresses and actors as well as Jesse Jackson, Frances Moore Lappé, and David Brower (former head of the Sierra Club).

Animal rights activists are some of the most colorful people in the groups striving for a Green Revolution. And their organizations give us some lively acronyms too.

TRAFFIC
Trade **R**ecords **A**nalyses of **F**lora and **F**auna **I**n **C**ommerce
The information-gathering arm of the World Wildlife Fund. More than thirty years old, this international organization has 800,000 members. Armed with the latest TRAFFIC statistics about the illegal flow of ivory into the Far East or the death rate of parrots captured by poachers in Brazilian rain forests, World Wildlife Fund officials fight to protect endangered species around the globe.

CITES
Convention on **I**nternational **T**rade in **E**ndangered **S**pecies (of Wild Fauna and Flora)
A United Nations affiliate that monitors and coordinates information on international trade. One hundred countries have signed the 1973 CITES treaty, agreeing not to import or export endangered species or their products. More than twelve hundred animals are protected by this agreement. However, smugglers sometimes circumvent the law by stealing an endangered animal from a country that's signed the treaty and selling the animal in a neighboring country that hasn't signed.

SAFE
Save **A**nimals **F**rom **E**xtinction
An early name for the Wildlife Preservation Trust, Intl., which is the American support group for the famous zoo of the prolific British author Gerald Durrell. Durrell, a passionate lover of everything that flies, swims, or crawls, started out as an adventurous animal collector for zoos. Shocked at the number of depleted species he kept encountering during his work, he opened his own zoo. Unlike most zoos, the Jersey Wildlife Preservation Trust is designed for the express purpose

of breeding endangered animals and releasing them back into their wild environments in healthier numbers.

WHOA!
Wild **H**orse **O**rganized **A**ssistance

A Nevada foundation begun in 1971 that's committed to the welfare and freedom of wild horses and burros in the West. WHOA! maintains a national research center with a library and museum as well as several visitor's centers located on wild-horse ranges. Members conduct field studies on numbers, health, and behavior patterns of the animals, hoping to help the wild horses recover their former numbers. (Wild horse populations have shrunk from two million at the turn of the century to fewer than 70,000 today.)

GOAT
Give **O**ur **A**nimals **T**ime

An organization devoted to saving the endangered goats of California's offshore islands.

The last group of groups is characterized by having no particular characterization. Some are deadly serious. Many are firmly tongue-in-cheek. And a few ended up in this grab bag simply because there's nothing else like them.

BANG
Be **A**merican—**N**othing's **G**reater

A club from the city of Buena Park, California—home to the super-patriotic theme park Knott's Berry Farm. BANG is a patriotic organization that works for safe fourth of July celebrations. The group, which includes several important civic leaders, offers free fireworks and all the attendant fairground excitement to everyone who attends its Independence Day gathering.

WAR
White **A**ryan **R**esistance

A group formed in 1980 that's run out of the Southern California home of its leader, Tom Metzger. WAR promulgates the belief that white-skinned, non-Semitic people are superior to all others. It broadcasts a cable television show and has a 1,000-volume library on race and politics. Two dozen hot lines play messages that refer to non-Aryans as "mud people" and "assorted scum." Its newsletter, with a circulation of five thousand, is aimed at the "militant white worker." WAR also holds periodic Aryan festivals with lectures and seminars.

In the late '80s, WAR was taken to court by Alabama civil rights lawyer Morris Dees. He sued them for liability in the beating and murder of an Ethiopian immigrant. The murder was committed by a band of WAR members after they attended a lecture about Aryan superiority. Dee's aim was to bankrupt WAR as he and his fellow lawyers of the Southern Poverty Law Center had successfully done to an arm of the Ku Klux Klan in 1987. In late 1990, the court ordered Metzger to pay $5 million in damages for his part in the murder.

SHARPs
Skin **H**eads **A**gainst **R**acial **P**rejudice
A self-described pacifist, nonbiased gang that stages fights with neo-Nazi gangs in Southern California.

CANDLES
Children of **A**uschwitz—**N**azis' **D**eadly **L**ab **E**xperiment **S**urvivors
Dr. Josef Mengele was one of the most heinous of the Nazi war criminals. He conducted genetic experiments at Auschwitz on prisoners who were twins. CANDLES is a 200-member organization that works to locate surviving victims of Mengele's experiments to gather eyewitness accounts of the atrocities. CANDLES also honors those who died at his hands.

CORPUS
Corps **O**f **R**eserve **P**riests **U**nited for **S**ervice
Founded in 1974, this Chicago-based organization of 6,500 members seeks to support and encourage former priests who have married but who still feel a strong commitment to the Church and to helping people. CORPUS works to make possible meetings between "married and celibate priests" to discuss religious, ethical, and social issues.

SCROOGE
Society to **C**urtail **R**idiculous, **O**utrageous, and **O**stentatious
Gift **E**xchange

A Charlottesville, Virginia, group that seeks in a light-hearted way to de-commercialize Christmas. The 1,000-member organization, started in 1979, encourages members to give gifts that are inexpensive but require thought and creativity. They also recommend giving adults the gift of a contribution to a favorite charity. When choosing a present for someone sick or elderly, SCROOGE suggests an extra visit as a gift.

LAW
Ladies **A**gainst **W**omen

The 12,000 members of this Berkeley, California, group do their best to poke good-humored fun at feminist, right-wing, and generally decorous organizations. Support groups include the Moral Sorority and Another Mother for World Domination. LAW reportedly conducts stress-reducing seminars for uppity women to help them lower their collective consciousness. A committee is called Save the Stoles. LAW advocates banning books, not bombs, and operates a speakers' bureau which addresses such topics as the repeal of the women's vote and the creation of a national dress code.

Their publications include the *National Embroiderer* and *Ladyfesto*. The international arm of the organization is FLAW—**F**oreign **L**adies **A**gainst **W**omen.

CROC
Committee for the **R**ecognition of **O**bnoxious **C**ommercials

Advertising agencies would prefer to avoid winning a CROC award. It's in the shape of a toilet bowl and signifies exactly what you'd expect.

WATSUP
The **W**essex **A**ssociation for **T**he **S**tudy of **U**nexplained **P**henomena

An organization in England that keeps watch for Unidentified Flying Objects.

BLOOP
Benevolent and **L**oyal **O**rder **O**f **P**essimists

A humorous group founded as a counterpart to the Optimist clubs. BLOOP also raises money for charity and gives a Pessimist of the Year award. The annual meeting takes place on whatever Saturday falls the closest to that grimmest of days, April 15.

NOT SAFE
National **O**rganization **T**aunting **S**afety **A**nd **F**airness **E**verywhere

A satiric organization, 1,400 strong, which includes members of Congress, corporate executives, journalists, and scientists who lambaste "overkill and stupidity" in government. NOT SAFE bestows an annual "Stir the Pot" award to a person who has demonstrated great courage in the face of bureaucratic intimidation.

Its yearly publication is called *Quagmire*.

SPERMFLOW
Society for the **P**reservation and **E**nhancement of the **R**ecognition of **M**illard **F**illmore, **L**ast **O**f the **W**higs

Quick. Name something important accomplished by President Fillmore. Name anything accomplished by President Fillmore.

That's the point of SPERMFLOW, a 400-member humorous organization reportedly dedicated to the celebration of mediocrity, as epitomized by our thirteenth president. The group gives an annual Medal of Mediocrity at the president's "Dearthday Party" and collects and disseminates information on mediocre public figures.

CHAPTER 7

The Art of the Possible

POWER'S HEADY STUFF. And open political power, where you make stirring speeches and all those people out there applaud, is particularly ego-tingling. But behind the scenes, the language is less high-flown and considerably more cynical, or perhaps simply more honest.

APE
Above **P**olitical **E**xpediency
Most people in public office obediently vote the party line. From time to time, a politician departs radically from what everyone expects him or her to do, causing consternation among friends and even foes. Imagine a liberal Democrat, for example, who commonly votes for entitlement programs, suddenly speaking out against a major welfare package. This wayward elected official may have gone APE, however, for shrewd political reasons. Let's say he's received several opinion polls from his home state showing that his constituents are fed up with high taxes. Let's also say that he's up for reelection in six months. And his major challenger is making low taxes sound like a personal crusade.

Going APE may be seen as his best move to ensure his political future. Only seldom does a politico go out on a personal limb due to sincerely held beliefs.

DRAB
Don't **R**ock **A**ny **B**oats

The elected official who wouldn't dream of going APE—who lies low, makes no waves, and hopes to play the game without any challenging consequences—he or she can be awarded the DRAB accolade.

BAP
BAy of **P**igs

Since JFK was tragically killed, he has become the beau ideal of modern presidents. But had he gone on to finish out his term, we might not idealize him at all. One major reason is his serious mishandling of the Bay of Pigs invasion of Cuba, where Cuban refugees, with his administration's encouragement, staged an attempted coup against Castro's regime. Kennedy balked at sending any air support and so the refugee forces were cut to ribbons.

Today a BAP is any serious political misjudgment that leads to terrible consequences. Example: Gary Hart's BAP, where he dared the press to prove he was guilty of sexual misconduct, is a textbook case of how to lose one's constituency.

Spinnish
spin + English (also influenced by "Spanish")

Spinnish has been called the international language of politics. In the game of pool, when a player puts spin on the ball, the ball moves in a carefully planned direction. In politics, so-called "spin doctors" use carefully doctored language to manipulate the public's view of a candidate or a situation. We may come to conclusions very different from those derived from a straightforward examination of the facts.

Ronald Reagan's so-called Teflon coating had a good deal to do with the former actor's marvelous ability to deliver Spinnish. How else could he have convinced the majority of the American people that we could vastly increase defense spending while we lowered taxes and the economy would experience no negative consequences because money from the rich would "trickle down" to the rest of us?

Tripewriter
tripe + typewriter
Some people claim that political speeches are created not on typewriters but on tripewriters instead. This can lead to a serious Crap (credibility + gap), where something the size of the Grand Canyon yaws between what the public hears and what the politico actually means. (It's sometimes hard to know whether that chasm was put there deliberately by political speech crafters or whether it's the result of poor writing.)

BOMFOG
Brotherhood **O**f **M**an Under the **F**atherhood **O**f **G**od
In the mid-sixties, a journalist who'd once too often heard Nelson Rockefeller say this grandiloquent mouthful devoid of content shortened it to BOMFOG. (The governor had the unfortunate habit of dragging out the phrase at practically every whistlestop.) Today a BOMFOG is any speech long on fluff of the solemn sort and short on content.

FAT
Flush **A**nd **T**rue
If you declare your candidacy for public office, be sure you have a few FAT people in your corner. That is to say, backers who believe in you implicitly and who can supply you with large amounts of money. As your staff takes you on the road, they'll work to arrange Photops (photograph + opportunities), where you can count on getting your picture taken. If you come to a speaking engagement and there's no real issue to discuss, they'll provide you with a Tissue or two (trivial + issue). You'll sound impressive as you suggest rational solutions to unimportant problems or perhaps carefully disguised stupid solutions to real problems. As hectic day passes hectic day, you'll be grateful for your RONs (**R**est **O**ver**N**ight or **R**est-**O**f-**N**ight), where you catch as much sleep as your busy campaign schedule permits.

EMILY's list
Early **M**oney **I**s **L**ike **Y**east
A Democratic PAC (**P**olitical **A**ction **C**ommittee—see Chapter 1 for more detail) that was established in 1985,

EMILY's list raised money to elect to Congress women who were pro-choice. The phrase "Early money is like yeast" is followed by "It makes the dough rise."

EMILY's list certainly did that. In 1990 alone, the group raised $1.5 million. And certainly the PAC's efforts helped change the number of Democratic women in the House from twelve to twenty in four years.

In 1991, an analogous group was formed for electing pro-choice Republican women to the halls of Congress. The PAC calls itself WISH list (**W**omen **I**n the **S**enate and **H**ouse), and its campaign-financing efforts have aided the election of one senator and six representatives.

The fact that 1992 was labeled "The Year of the Woman" politically is undoubtedly due in part to the efforts of these PACs.

Billary Clinton
Bill + Hillary Clinton

Journalists coined this phrase when President Clinton was governor of Arkansas, referring to speculation that Ms. Clinton was so actively involved in her husband's political decision making that the couple worked together at the governership. Because Ms. Clinton was a high-powered lawyer in her own right and dedicated to social action, the claim seemed plausible.

RIP
Revelation, **I**nvestigation, and **P**ersecution

A term invented by Benjamin Ginsberg and Martin Shefter in their book *Politics by Other Means: The Declining Importance of Electors in America*. The RIP is a current method politicians use to undermine opponents. According to the authors, the Watergate scandal was used as a RIP to stop Richard Nixon's attempt to gain control over the national media. By undermining his credibility, the scandal made it impossible for the media to take his political claims seriously. More recently, according to the authors, Republicans frustrated by House Speaker Jim Wright's power grabs RIPped him by accusing him of accepting money illegally. He was censured by the House and his power much diminished.

Povertician (1977)
poverty + politician

A derogatory job title for a person who's appointed to administer a government program aimed at helping the poor. It's particularly apt if the administrator is pocketing some of the money for him- or herself.

Psytocracy
psychological + autocracy

In the 1971 book *Requiem for Democracy*, authors Lewis M. Andrews and Marvin Karlins worry that our country is headed toward an absolutist government that controls the populace with psychological behavior-modification techniques. In this psytocracy, citizens would be passive and conform willingly.

Meritocracy
merit + aristocracy

On the other hand, Michael Young, author of the 1958 book *The Rise of the Meritocracy*, imagines a twenty-first-century Britain run only by those bright enough to score at the top of universal examinations. Wealth and/or class would no longer lead to power.

Dawk
dove + hawk

Coined by *Time* magazine in 1966, the term originally referred to Republicans in the mid-sixties who opposed LBJ's war in Vietnam but who still supported using our fighting men in other situations, like sending American "advisers" to the Dominican Republic to bolster the right-wing government there. It has come to describe any person who disapproves of a war but doesn't take an antiwar stand.

Dixiecrat
Dixie + Democrat

This term originated as the nickname of a third party called the States' Rights Democrats that was formed in 1948, nominating J. Strom Thurmond for president. They returned to the fold of the Democratic party in 1952, a vocal and well-organized wing. Today a Dixiecrat is a southern Democrat whose first loyalty is to the South rather than to the party.

Narcokleptocracy
narcotic + kleptomania (+ the suffix "cracy")
    Why is it well-nigh impossible to stop the enormous flow of cocaine and other dangerous drugs from Latin America to this country? This term postulates a cabal of politicians, military leaders, and drug dealers who acquire enormous wealth by trafficking in drugs in such countries as Bolivia and Peru.

TINA
There **Is No A**lternative
    The name Margaret has many diminutives—Peggy, Marge, Greta, Rita, and the one Ms. Thatcher prefers: Maggie. However, the loyal opposition in the British Parliament called her Tina because she so often justified her harsh economic policies with the phrase "There is no alternative."

the GERBIL
Government's **E**ducational **R**eform **BIL**l
    British teachers' nickname for Margaret Thatcher's 1988 law. This was not a term of approval. Apparently the teachers were not thinking of a cuddly classroom pet, but of the gerbil's insatiable appetite and ratlike demeanor.

ACNE
Association of **C**ountries with **N**o **E**conomy
    What did American high government officials call the former USSR after it dissolved? When Secretary of State James Baker visited there in late 1991, he avoided any name at all, referring to the country in which he was making his speeches as "Here." Accompanying reporters boldly stepped into the gap, coining ACNE and also XSSR—**EX-S**oviet **S**ocialist **Re**publics.

Priviligentsia
privilege + intelligentsia
    When the head pig in George Orwell's political allegory *Animal Farm* explained why he and his fellows lived in the lap

of luxury while the rest of the supposedly egalitarian community was poor, he said that, although all animals were equal, some were more equal than others. The Party bureaucrats and intellectuals in the Soviet Union (one major group that Orwell's pigs symbolized) were dubbed the "priviligentsia" by the American academic community in the 1950s. The term became popularized by the media in the '80s and was used to refer to those Soviet citizens who, for example, never stood in three-block-long lines to buy a loaf of bread because they had access to special food shops. Gorbachev's perestroika reforms were partly aimed at eradicating this group's special status and accompanying privileges.

Guestage
guest + hostage
    In August of 1990, when Iraq invaded Kuwait, Saddam Hussein dubbed the foreign nationals he forceably detained "guests." A few weeks later, the detainees themselves invented "guestage," a more appropriate term for their status.

GOD
Government **O**bserving **D**evice
    Someone's got to.

    A few acronyms have even been used for large geopolitical entities: countries, districts, and regional policies and organizations.

PAKISTAN
Punjab, **A**fghan border states, **K**ashmir, **S**ind, and
Baluchis**TAN**
    An independent nation created by the British after World War II when their former colony of India was partitioned into predominantly Hindu India and mostly Muslim Pakistan. Partition was first proposed in 1930. The name itself was created in 1933 by Chaudhrie Rahmat Ali, a young philosophy student at Cambridge University. Ali's name for the country-to-be is particularly elegant because "Pak" also is a Persian root meaning "pure" or "holy," and "stan" is a common Urdu suffix for "land" or "place."

SOWETO
SOuth **WE**stern **TO**wnships

Until very recently, black people have not been allowed to live in Johannesburg, the capital city of the Union of South Africa. Instead, the government placed them far outside the city limits in an impoverished area called Soweto. This ghetto-suburb became internationally infamous in June of 1976. The government ruled that Afrikaans, the language of white South Africans, would be henceforth the compulsory language of instruction in all Soweto schools. When black students mounted an enormous peaceful protest, government troops met them with violent repression. In the three weeks of fighting that followed, many students were killed, teargased, or arrested and there was massive destruction of property. Soweto has become a rallying cry of black activists in South Africa.

NIBMAR
No **I**ndependence **B**efore **M**ajority **A**frican **R**ule

At the end of the nineteenth century, a British adventurer named Cecil Rhodes carved out his own economic empire in the area to the north of what would become South Africa. Rhodesia developed in many ways into a South Africa clone. In order to exploit the region's great mineral wealth, a repressive white minority ruled a country with a predominantly black majority. However, the southern part of Rhodesia remained a British colony. In the 1960s, Southern Rhodesia asked for independence. Britain refused to grant it until Rhodesian efforts to give black citizens a real voice were convincing. The negotiations for independence fell through because of this NIBMAR issue and Rhodesian leader Ian Smith illegally declared his country independent of Britain in 1965.

Years of economic sanctions followed and not a single nation recognized Smith's government. Within the country, the black majority began seriously agitating for political power. ZAPU (**Z**imbabwe **A**frican **P**eople's **U**nion) and ZANU (**Z**imbabwe **A**frican **N**ational **U**nion) were the two major organizations for change and Smith responded to their demands by banning their leaders. The groups fled to neighboring countries and mounted armed attacks on the Southern Rhodesian power structure. This civil war continued until 1980, when the government finally surrendered to pressures within and without. In Southern Rhodesia's first free election, ZANU candidate Robert Mugabe won by a landslide and the country was soon renamed Zimbabwe.

SWAPO
South **W**est **A**frican **P**eople's **O**rganization

South West Africa, rich in diamonds and uranium, had been administered by South Africa since 1920. In 1966, SWAPO, the militant black independence movement of that country, began a protracted civil war to win the country's freedom. After twenty-three years, the country of Namibia was born, with SWAPO's leader, Sam Nujoma, as its first president.

BENELUX
BElgium, **NE**therlands and **LUX**emburg

Western European countries have been working on various versions of economic union for many years. Benelux dates from September 1944, when the three neighboring countries agreed to drop customs duties among themselves. Later there was Fritalux, a similar combination uniting **Fr**ance, **Ita**ly, and Bene**lux**. In 1952, most of Western Europe joined together in the European Coal and Steel Community, and in 1958, the ties became wider with the European Economic Community, or Common Market. Members seriously diminished the major economic barriers between them, like tariffs, customs duties, and quotas. Between 1958 and 1968, trade quadrupled among the Common Market nations.

Today Benelux itself is essentially a single economic entity, with free movement of people, goods, and capital over the common borders. And the whole of Western Europe is ironing out the details of a sweeping economic coming together called the European Community, which will even have a single currency, the ECU or **E**uropean **C**urrency **U**nit. (Ecu is also the name of a European silver coin in the Middle Ages.) The new universal currency should be in place by the year 2000 and perhaps even earlier.

Wherever there's power, bureaucracy is sure to follow. And follow. And follow.

GWIBIT
Guild of **W**ashington **I**ncompetent **B**ureaucratic **I**dea **T**hroatcutters

A term invented by Republican Representative Karl E. Mundt in 1943. The gwibit is not to be confused with the kibitzer, who is content to sit on the sidelines and watch. The more actively destructive gwibit deliberately undermines progress by finding fault with any new idea. Wives and mothers working in steel-processing factories? Terrible idea—they'll foul up production. Victory gardens? We'll poison ourselves. Etc. Etc.

BE TOPS
Budget **E**mergency: **T**ime **O**ff for **P**ublic **S**ervices

The name of a budget-cutting program in San Diego, where various managers of county programs have been advised to ask, cajole, and/or pressure their employees to take unpaid vacations. The harassed employees say BETOPS really stands for **B**oard **E**njoys **T**orturing **O**utstanding **P**ublic **S**ervants.

WASTE
Wisdom, **A**cclaim, and **S**tatus **T**hrough **E**xpenditures

A fictional governmental agency from the book *Alice in Blunderland*. The book was written in 1983 by longtime columnist Jack Anderson as a satire deriding the excesses of our national bureaucracy. The agency collects, files, and forgets untold numbers of applications. It generates red tape with creative glee. Toward the end of the book, Alice gets to meet the actual waste makers. They are many and have no faces.

Corpocracy
corporate + bureaucracy

Top-heavy and entrenched ruling and regulating structures that are found in some large companies. Such companies are often inefficient and thus find it difficult to compete with competitors having leaner staffs. However, it can be difficult to force corpocrats to give up company cars, executive dining rooms, memberships in country clubs, and other jealously protected privileges.

WAWA
West **A**frica **W**ins **A**gain

Apparently wending one's way through the raging rivers of red tape is quite an art form in certain West African countries. People new to the scene, like tourists, often find themselves harassed and overcharged by highly creative bureaucrats. When they relate their tales of woe to an old Africa hand, all they're liable to receive is a regretful shrug of the shoulders and a murmured "WAWA."

FONSI
Findings **O**f **N**o **S**ignificant **I**mpact

This is the report every federal agency with a big development program wants to achieve. It presents all the reasons why the building or dam or ten-lane highway that they want to construct will have no appreciable effect on the human environment. Thus the agency can avoid preparing an environmental impact statement which might force them to reveal that their project could pose a threat to some endangered species, for example, or use an unwarranted amount of some scarce resource.

HAZOP
HAZard and **OP**erability Study

Paperwork we hope all nuclear power plants have completed. Experts examine a plant from stem to stern and then they imagine all plausible disasters that might occur—explosions, fire, dangerous chemicals escaping. For each detailed scenario, the plant must make a plan to avoid the disaster and then take all the necessary steps to do so.

GRAS
Generally **R**ecognized **A**s **S**afe

In 1958, the FDA passed a blanket approval for more than six hundred additives that were currently being used in foods, drugs, and cosmetics. In typical tangled bureaucratic fashion, the law stated that no additive could be removed from the GRAS list until it had been proved to be harmful. In the early '70s, Ralph Nader went to battle against GRAS, focusing particularly on saccharin, which had carried the GRAS label for over a decade.

Echosultants
echo + consultants

A government agency wants to spend half a billion dollars researching a controversial weapon system. The agency touts the glowing predictions that a consulting firm has made about this system. The agency is all set to spend when a nongovernmental watchdog group blows the whistle and, skeptical of the consultant's report, insists on a second opinion. Does the agency, in all good faith, go out and find a disinterested second consultant firm? Nah. They call for their trusty echosultants, a firm that the agency knows will manage to come to the same conclusions that the first firm presented.

LOSS
Look-**O**ut **S**ituation

If a bureaucrat receives a report with LOSS stamped on it, he or she had better handle the potentially damaging situation unusually well or it could mean a seriously diminished or even lost career.

CRONT
Career (how hungry for)
Reasons (wants the career)
Obedience (to the rules)
Need (to conform)
Team (belief in team play)

The people who hire fledgling bureaucrats look for these five essential characteristics in their applicants. Note the absence of traits like creativity, leadership, or a sense of humor.

CHAPTER 8

Money Makes the World Go 'Round

THAT MOST PROTEAN of substances, cash, can turn deserts into hypermodern cities (witness Saudi Arabia) and patriots into turncoats. (CIA—and, no doubt, KGB—files bulge with such cases.) Money also seems to bring out the whimsical in otherwise hardheaded financial wheelers and dealers, who recklessly invent acronyms for all sorts of ways of separating you from your greenbacks.

Let's begin with some clever wordplay from the advertising world, which shouldn't surprise us. It's their meat and drink, after all.

Anticipointment
anticipation + disappointment
Remember the blazing blitz campaign for "The New Coke" a few years back? TV commercials got us all panting for this dazzling new taste that was going to be even better than the Coca-Cola we knew and loved. And then we tasted this new phenomenon and . . . Big Ech. Our rejection was as intense as our excitement had been. That's anticipointment. Broadcast advertisers coined the term in 1988 as a warning against building the public's hopes too high. (The Coca-Cola company had to bring back the old flavor, calling it "Coke

Classic." It sold so much better than the new wunderkind that today it's hard to find a can of "New Coke" in the United States. However, it is a big seller internationally.)

Concrete
consumer + cretin

It's not pretty to think that some ad writers see us like this. In fact, they even have subdivisions for our particular styles of gullibility:

    elite concrete   —the rich
    neat concrete   —the middle class
    sweet concrete —women between seven and thirty-five
                    (the group that spends the most money)
    beat concrete   —people who are too mobile to be found
                    by creditors (the largest group)

DIBS
Discretionary **I**ncome **B**udgets

The money that's left over from our monthly paychecks that we tell ourselves we should save. The advertising world works on convincing us to use it for impulse buying.

Commerciogenic (1974)
commercial + photogenic

Food is often produced and packaged this way, with an eye to attracting the buyer to its glamorous looks. Whether the stuff actually tastes good or is good for us is another kettle of fish. Those tomatoes we've been passing up recently sure look gorgeous, but they've got about as much taste as a Baggie stuffed with sawdust.

Slophop
Smog, **L**itter, **O**verpopulation, and **P**ollution + hop

The "hop" comes from the '50s term for a post-game dance, and the whole term refers to an ad campaign that is created to improve the image of a company the public perceives as greedy and/or detrimental to the environment. Oil and car companies are common recipients of a slophop makeover.

PIGgy spots
Pain **I**s **G**ood

You've manufactured yet another aspirin-clone, given it a catchy name like Painfree or Antithrobin, and your packaging would make Picasso weep. What image will you bombard the public with on TV? Conventional advertising wisdom suggests your commercial begin with a person in serious pain. Only after potential buyers have dwelt on the grimaces and the wincing for long enough to remember their own last pounding headache do you show what your product can do.

HAG
Hidden **A**ppeal to **G**ays

The gay community is sizable and has a particular consumer profile, just like housewives or teenagers or yuppies do. So where are the marketing campaigns aimed at homosexual buyers? They actually do exist, but in deference to straight consumers' sensibilities, publicists use code words and particular images that are recognized in the gay world but that pass by the rest of the buying public.

Advertorial
advertise + editorial

This is an advertising ploy that's the opposite of the usual glossy splash ads. First used in the '60s, it's typically a full page written in small close-spaced print that appears to be an objective report about a new product. Actually, of course, it's advertising copy, as slanted and exaggerated as any glamorous photograph. The only clue to its identity is the word ADVERTISEMENT printed in very small letters at the top of the page.

SUG
Sell **U**nder the **G**uise

You get a call or a visit from someone who says they're conducting a survey. After you've answered half a dozen questions, the tenor of the conversation changes. Turns out the researcher has a product he or she thinks would be perfect for you. For a "nominal" sum, it can be mailed to your door. Guess what? You've been sugged. It's a common technique in Britain.

NORM
Naturally **O**ccurring **R**adioactive **M**aterial
Sounds like pretty benign stuff. But actually it's a public-relations term for radioactive industrial wastes—dangerous substances that are created all the time and are hard to dispose of. So firms looking for dump sites scout out sparsely populated communities that are poor, like Bracketville, Texas, located in a barren area bordering Mexico. Since such towns are fairly powerless politically, it's relatively easy to foist NORM on them. (The citizens of Bracketville got wise in time and declined the offer. Other Texas communities haven't been so lucky.)

NIMBY
Not **I**n **M**y **B**ack**Y**ard
This attitude has been called "a modern national syndrome" by the man who coined the phrase in the late '70s, Walton Rodger. A dedicated member of the American Nuclear Society, Rodger claims we automatically and vociferously reject any large project slated to be built in our immediate vicinity, be it a NORM dump, a sewage treatment plant, a freeway, a halfway house, or a nuclear power plant.

We move now to terms from the business world in general.

Administralia
administration + Australia
There's a mountaintop where CEOs and others of their ilk live, far from the madding crowd of managers, white and blue collars, and tiny take-home paychecks. Though this is a country of the mind, it is such a different space from where the rest of us live that it can be referred to as a separate continent. It is from Administralia, supposedly, that all of the business world is controlled.

Hipo
high + potential
The Wall Street Journal says a hipo (pronounced "HIGH-poe") is an employee who is bound for success on the express route.

ICE
Incidental **C**ompany **E**xpenses

A company that is audited by the IRS can expect anything its accountant filed in this category to be scrutinized first. That's because businesses commonly use ICE to cover up their padded expense accounts and other extras that favored employees are allowed to use.

ACE
Authoritarian **C**onscience **E**mployee

Personnel departments are often on the lookout for this type of person. What could be more useful to the average company than an employee who'll never complain about salaries or benefits, who'll do whatever he or she is told to do, and who never fights back? Why is the ACE such a wimp? He or she is haunted inside by the image of a thundering and judgmental authority figure.

ACE
Active **C**orps of **E**xecutives
   and
SCORE
Service **C**orps **O**f **R**etired **E**xecutives

Two volunteer organizations sponsored by the Small Business Administration that provide free consulting services to people planning to open a small business or already in business. One can get help with marketing, manufacturing, sales, etc., from people in the know.

Glocal
global + local

A major marketing concept in the early '90s that was a reaction to the previous decade's think-global expansionist style. Businessmen competing for world markets in the '80s were impressed with the Japanese ability to simultaneously create a worldwide product and adjust it for differing local needs. The Japanese called this "dochakuka" meaning global localization. The current buzzword *glocal* already has a verb form: to glocalize.

MONY
Mutual **O**f **N**ew **Y**ork

Like the green stuff it's named for, this insurance company has been around a long time. Chartered in 1842, MONY has been selling life insurance ever since. Today you can also make use of its pension and investment management services. MONY is one of the oldest and largest life insurance companies in the world.

COLA
Cost **O**f **L**iving **A**djustment

A typical union demand written into employee contracts so that inflation doesn't diminish a worker's salary.

OWL
Older **W**omen's **L**eague

Founded in 1980, this Washington, D.C., group lobbies for the rights of middle-aged to old women. OWL was instrumental in getting COBRA (**C**onsolidated **O**mnibus **B**udget **R**econciliation **A**ct) passed into federal law. COBRA allows workers who lose or leave their jobs to continue their group health insurance for up to three years. OWL also works to protect wives covered under their husbands' pension plans. Let's say a husband retires at age sixty-five and decides to draw out a good 10 percent of his pension each year after. Should he die in his mid-70s, his widow will be left with practically nothing. Husbands can no longer opt for large payments during their lifetimes if that practice will leave their widows with no income.

ERISA
Employee **R**etirement **I**ncome **S**ecurity **A**ct

A law passed in 1974 that requires any employer who offers a pension plan to provide workers with a clear written description of that plan.

ESOP
Employee **S**tock **O**wnership **P**lan

You've worked for a company for twenty-five years and one day your boss announces that your workplace is in real danger of being shut down. Funds are seriously depleted. It's curtains unless the staff can bail the company out. In return for the staff investing in the business, your boss offers stock in the company. It's a tempting offer. You keep your job and you invest in something you yourself can work to improve. Many companies have survived this way and even thrived. ESOP participation can lead to increased productivity, improved labor-management relations, and thus greater profits because the workers are in a sense working for themselves.

RIF
Reduction **In** **F**orce

First used in 1950 by federal government employees who received RIF letters. It quickly became a verb, as in "Tony's been riffed," meaning fired. Government workers often get riffed when budgets are trimmed or when administrations change. In the military, someone who's riffed has been demoted.

FSBO ("Fizzbo")
For **S**ale **B**y **O**wner

Realtors hate these. Hence the pejorative name (which first appeared in 1986). If you sell your own house, that means no commission for some hungry real estate broker.

LULU
Locally **U**nwanted **L**and **U**se

Another Realtor's term, again displaying a negative attitude.

NASDAQ (1968)
National **A**ssociation of **S**ecurities **D**ealers **A**utomatic **Q**uotation

Major brokerage houses belong to the National Association of Securities Dealers, which was founded in 1939. Today it is 6,200 strong with a staff of 1,700 and a yearly budget of $150 million. The NASDAQ Index is its computerized information system, which gives current price quotations for securities that are traded over the counter.

FT-SE ("Footsie")
Financial **T**imes-**S**tock **E**xchange
    This is the British version of our Dow-Jones Industrial Average. It is an index based on Britain's one hundred largest public companies traded on the London Stock Exchange. As with Dow-Jones, the number at any given time gives a general indication of how the stock market is faring.

GATT
General **A**greement on **T**ariffs and **T**rade
    A set of agreements on reducing tariffs, quotas, and other restrictions on trade around the world. It was signed in 1947 by 23 countries, and today is the principal organization for international trade with 105 participating countries. If the United States, to use a recent example, wants France to lower French subsidies on oilseed, and France, on behalf of its indignant soybean farmers, refuses, GATT will mediate and try to come up with a compromise that furthers open trading.

NAFTA
North **A**merican **F**ree **T**rade **A**greement
    A controversial and far-reaching economic treaty between Canada, the United States, and Mexico that was first negotiated by George Bush and then pummeled into law by his successor, Bill Clinton. NAFTA lowers tariffs and other trade barriers between the three countries, encouraging Mexican consumers to buy American and Canadian goods, while inviting American manufacturers to open factories in Mexico, where both wages and environmental restrictions are lower.
    Not surprisingly, the major opponents to NAFTA were U.S. labor unions, which were fearful that American jobs would be lost to Mexico. Democrat Clinton put his administration on the line, using everything from blatant deal making to a vice-presidential debate with naysayer H. Ross Perot on the Larry King talk show to a lineup of all five living former presidents (Nixon, Ford, Carter, Reagan, and Bush), who argued for the proposed agreement.
    NAFTA is a dramatic example of the dictum that politics makes strange bedfellows. It has got to be the only issue that Pat Buchanan, Jesse Jackson, Ralph Nader, and H. Ross Perot could agree on. They all just said no.

GAAP
Generally **A**ccepted **A**ccounting **P**rincipals

GAAP includes the conventions, rules, and procedures underlying accounting. For example, if an accountant is keeping the books for a corporation that is undergoing litigation, he or she is required to evaluate the current offers to the company, the plans the company is making for expansion, etc. The accountant then offers his or her formal estimation of these various existing conditions that may yield either future profits or losses using one of four terms: probable, reasonable, possible, or remote.

FIFO
First **I**n, **F**irst **O**ut
and
LIFO
Last **I**n, **F**irst **O**ut

A pair of terms used in everything from data processing to accounting. Imagine you have one of those In/Out file baskets on your desk. Whenever someone needs you to do something, they drop a new memo onto your In section. If you work from the bottom of the In pile through to the top, you are doing your jobs FIFO. If you start from the latest and work down, it's LIFO. If you do neither, you are either unusually talented at discriminating between necessary and unnecessary tasks or you are the boss's pampered kid.

Though there are those who become wealthy by earning higher and higher salaries, the more typical path to riches (unless you're born sucking on that silver spoon) is through investment. Now this seems like very serious business, risking one's hard-earned bucks, yet brokerage houses and banks have cavorted about with language for many years now, naming loans and funds and bonds after animals, girls, rhymes, and moonshine-swilling duffers. Doesn't mean you can't lose your shirt, of course. But it does make the whole process a little more human.

Let's begin with the bond market, which has a surprising number of acronyms. A bond is a way you can lend your government money and be paid back with interest. One kind, the U.S. Treasury bond, commonly comes in $1,000 increments. It has two parts. One you hold on to for the life of the bond, typically twenty years, and then cash in. This is the $1,000 principal you lent the government in the first place. The second part is a series of maybe 40 coupons. Over the twenty-year life of the bond, you go to the bank typically twice each year and cash in one of these slips for, say, $50. The money from the 40 coupons is your interest.

This is a pretty cumbersome process. And not very attractive to people seeking a long-term investment. In 1982, a investment company called Merrill Lynch had a brainstorm. What if they bought up millions of dollars worth of treasury bonds and separated the principal section from the interest coupons. They could cash in the coupons themselves and offer just the principal part of the bond. Of course, no one would buy a twenty-year bond if they were only going to get the same amount of money at the end that they paid originally. So Merrill Lynch offered deep discounts—50 percent or more. And they refigured the bonds so that an investor could buy in much smaller increments than $1,000. Today you can buy one of these bonds for, let's say, $50 and figure that you'll get $100 in twenty years.

These resulting zero-coupon bonds, called TIGRs (**Trea**sury **I**nvestment **G**rowth **R**eceipt), have been enormously popular with investors, so much so that many other brokerage houses and banks have gotten into the act. Lehman Brothers offered LIONs (**L**ehman **I**nvestment **O**pportunity **N**otes), Salomon Brothers created CATS (**C**ertificate of **A**ccrual on **T**reasury **S**ecurities), A. G. Becker Paribas, stretching, came up with COUGARs (**C**ertificates **O**n **G**overnment **R**eceipts), and Merrill Lynch doubled its fun with LYONs (**L**iquid **Y**ield **O**ption **N**otes).

Though clearly not as enamored of feline money monikers as Americans, the British came up with a zero-coupon bond called STAGS (**S**terling **T**ransferable **A**ccruing **G**overnment **S**ecurities) and the Aussies created the DINGO (**D**iscounted **I**nvestment in **N**egotiated **G**overnment **O**bligations).

This idea of buying up bonds and reselling them in different forms has continued to be applied to all sorts of investment situations. Paine Webber offers FIGS (**F**uture **I**ncome **G**rowth **S**ecurities) and GAINS (**G**rowth **A**nd **IN**come **S**ecurities) based on municipal bonds. Goldman Sachs has created STAIRS (**S**tepped **T**ax-Exempt **A**ppreciation and **I**ncome **Re**alization **S**ecurities), which gives the investor the added advantage of not having to pay any taxes on earnings. Salomon Brothers' LIMOS (**L**imited **I**nterest **M**unicipal **O**bligation**S**) does the same.

And even our own federal government has gotten into the act with STRIPS (**S**eparate **T**rading of **R**egistered **I**nterest and **P**rincipal of **S**ecurities), offered by the Treasury Department only to particular financial institutions. However, one of these, Shearson Lehman Brothers, has refigured its STRIPS and offered the resulting bonds to the public as TINTs (**T**reasury **INT**erest).

While zero coupon brokers sit around inventing clever acronyms (wouldn't it be great to be a fly on the wall of one of those august boardrooms during one of these creative sessions?), their fellow investment mavens have also been busy.

DRIP
Dividend **ReI**nvestment **P**lan

Instead of sending stockholders their dividends every few months, stock companies would greatly prefer to automatically reinvest the money in the company. In return, the stockholders get more shares of the stock. If you don't need the money to live on and can afford to pay taxes on money you've not been sent, it's a good way to build up your investment. Drip by drip.

HITS
High-**I**ncome **T**rust **S**ecurities

Does a company called Drexel Burnham Lambert sound familiar? It was a member of the '80s junk-bond royal family. If an investor, reasonably enough, hesitated to put his or her money into low-quality bonds even if they had very high yields, these folks offered units of a junk-bond investment trust. The trust had many different high-risk bonds in it. The theory was that by spreading your investment over many different risks, you'd be protected if a few of them went belly-up. HITS is a very '80s high-roller name, is it not?

CARS

Certificate for **A**utomobile **R**eceivable**S**

An appropriate name for a bondlike investment where your money provides debt security for two- to three-year car loans.

PIGs

Passive **I**ncome **G**enerators

and

PALs

Passive **A**ctivity **L**osses

These are investments used as tax shelters. You invest in the PIG (typically a piece of real estate or a business) and then when you get income that would normally be taxed, the debt and depreciation (the PAL) from the property or business is used to cancel out the gain. The investor suffers the loss only on paper. This was a nice setup until the 1986 tax reform. The law now states that unless the investor is actively involved in a business, he or she cannot claim any debt or depreciation the business may accrue.

PUDs

Public **U**tilities **D**istricts

You can lend practically any governmental organization money. If you purchase a PUD bond from, let's say, for example, the Department of Water and Power, the IRS is willing to exempt the interest from your federal income tax.

WHOOPS

Was**H**ingt**O**n **P**ublic Power **S**ystem

However, municipal bonds can be tricky. This one was very highly rated, but in 1983, it defaulted on $2.25 billion in bonds. That's a record in city bonds. Not much consolation to all those investors who lost their shirts.

Real estate loans and investments are rife with acronyms.

ARM

Adjustable **R**ate **M**ortgage

Suppose you want to buy a house and your folks have kicked in with a good chunk toward the down payment, so you sneak a peek at what your monthly payments would be at current interest rates and you turn a ghastly shade of pale. Just before you despairingly blow your savings on a trip to all the Hawaiian Islands, that ultrasmooth loan officer murmurs she can get you a loan rate three points below the current rate. Startled, mystified, but basically thrilled, you agree to the ARM. Were you wise?

If your income keeps rising for the next several years, it'll probably be OK. Your interest rate will certainly be moving up steadily, once or twice each year. Typically it will stop rising when it's half a point above what you'd have paid if you'd gone for the higher rate initially. And from there, the interest rate will fluctuate along with the market for the entire life of your loan.

GEM
Growing Equity Mortgage

You're doing well and have every expectation of doing better as time goes by. So you buy a house, and though the interest rate remains the same, your payments keep swelling. Why? The extra part of your payment is paying off part of the principal so that you actually own more and more of the house. Even though you start with payments based on a twenty-five-year loan, you'll actually own the house free and clear in fifteen years.

SAM
Shared Appreciation Mortgage

This one's a fixed-rate loan. And as the years go by (twenty-five or thirty) and you slowly pay the bank back, your house will almost certainly appreciate in value. Here comes the twist. The bank has an equity interest, so if you sell the house before the twenty-five or thirty years are up, the bank gets a portion of the house's higher price.

RAM
Reverse Annuity Mortgage

You've paid off that twenty-five- to thirty-year loan and the house is yours. You retire. Gosh, Social Security, investments, that pension fund just don't go as far as you imagined they would. You don't want to sell the family manse and squeeze yourself into one of those narrow condos. Well, the bank will let you retain the ownership of your house and live there and pay you a monthly stipend. Of course, that means that each month you will owe the bank more money. When do you pay the piper? These loans are usually given to elderly people, sometimes with a shortened life expectancy. If you don't pay back the loan, your estate will. So your house will eventually be sold, but you won't lose it.

GNMA ("Ginnie Mae")
Government **N**ational **M**ortgage **A**ssociation

If you send your house payments to the bank that lent you the money, you might reasonably assume that your loan is owned by that bank. Turns out that banks typically sell their mortgages to other companies. (The bank makes its money from the up-front fees it charges—what it calls "points.")

The three biggest buyers of home loans are linked to the federal government. Ginnie Mae, begun in 1975, is the largest, buying up FHA (Federal Housing Administration) loans. Freddie Mac (Federal Home Loan Mortgage Corporation), started in 1974, is the second largest. Its stock is owned by the Federal Reserve Banks. And the third, begun in 1953, is Fannie Mae (Federal National Mortgage Association), which is government sponsored though the stock is privately owned.

Here's how it works: One of these secondary mortgage companies buys up thousands of home loans. They repackage them and offer the individual investor shares. You buy a share of Ginnie Mae, let's say. This means you are lending many homeowners a small part of their home loan. So every month you get sent parts of house payments. This sum fluctuates unpredictably because a home often gets sold off before the whole home loan is paid or the owner will renegotiate the loan if interest rates go down. If this happens, you get your chunk of whatever the paid-off loan comes to. It's not as simple as just buying a T-bill, but the yield is considerably higher.

This way of repackaging loans is lucrative and makes more money available for loans so lots of other companies have jumped on the bandwagon. Hence we have Sallie Mae (Student Loan Marketing Association), which increases the money available to students, Maggie Mae (Mortgage Guaranty Insurance Corporation), Carrie Mac (California Association of Realtors Mortgage Assistance Corporation), Sunny Mac (Solar and Energy Conservation Mortgage Corporation), Nellie Mae (New England Educational Loan Marketing Corporation), Sonnie Mae (State of New York Mortgage Agency), and Sammie Bee (Small Business Administration), which guarantees loans to small businesses.

OPPOSMS
OPtions to **P**urchase **O**r Sell **S**pecified **M**ortgage **S**ecurities

OK—here's the next wrinkle. Merrill Lynch Mortgage Capital Corporation buys lots of shares in Ginnie Mae, Fannie Mae, etc. Then they create a customized investment: You can get various expiration dates, prices, coupons, size of issues, whatever. So you're buying a piece of a chunk of pieces of home loans. As long as you get the folding stuff, right?

CHAPTER 9

You're in the Army Now

THE MILITARY WORLD is a strikingly hierarchical place, full of divisions and their exacting definitions. And every twig of every branch seems to have its own abbreviation. Acronyms abound. We'll start with the granddaddy of them all.

SNAFU
Situation **N**ormal, **A**ll **F**ouled **U**p

(The more profane-mouthed military men use another word for "fouled," of course. You're welcome to substitute it for "fouled" in the list that follows if you prefer your language raw.)

Snafu was coined in 1940 in England by soldiers fighting both the Germans and the often impossible maze of their own army's rules and regulations. American GIs picked up the word and spread it throughout the world. It's easy to imagine a bunch of soldiers pinned down by enemy fire huddling in their foxholes, cursing the official mistake that probably got them into the mess, and inventing a new variation of *snafu* to cheer themselves up. Your tireless acronym researchers have unearthed twenty-two members of the Clan of Snafu, and all of them are slight variations on a single theme: If there's any way to tangle things up so that a situation becomes completely unworkable, the military will unerringly find that way.

SNEFU
Situation **N**ormal, **E**verything **F**ouled **U**p

SUSFU
Situation **U**nchanged; **S**till **F**ouled **U**p

SNRAFU
Situation **N**ormal, **R**eally **A**ll **F**ouled **U**p

TOFU
Things **O**rdinary: **F**ouled **U**p

TARFU
Things **A**re **R**eally **F**ouled **U**p

TASFUIRA
Things **A**re **S**o **F**ouled **U**p **I**t's **R**eally **A**mazing

FUBAR
Fouled **U**p **B**eyond **A**ll **R**ecognition

TAFUBAR
Things **A**re **F**ouled **U**p **B**eyond **A**ll **R**ecognition

FUBB
Fouled **U**p **B**eyond **B**elief

FUMTU
Fouled **U**p **M**ore **T**han **U**sual

SAPFU
Surpassing **A**ll **P**revious **F**oul-Ups

SAMFU
Self-**A**djusting **M**ilitary **F**oul-Up
     That is, even if the emergency in the field that caused the powers-that-be to create a snafu were to change, the snafu would adjust itself to make the new situation just as unworkable as the original one.

SABU
Self-**A**djusting **B**alls-**U**p
"Balls-up" is British for "Foul-up."

NABU
Non-**A**djusting **B**alls-**U**p

TABU
Typical **A**rmy **B**alls-**U**p

IMFU
Imperial **M**ilitary **F**oul-**U**p

JAAFU
Joint **A**nglo-**A**merican **F**oul-**U**p

JANFU
Joint **A**rmy-**N**avy **F**oul-**U**p

JACFU
Joint **A**merican-**C**hinese **F**oul-**U**p

TUIFU
The **U**ltimate **I**n **F**oul-**U**ps

COMMFU
Complete **M**onumental **M**ilitary **F**oul-**U**p

Most military acronyms are considerably less cynical.

NEACP ("Kneecap")
National **E**mergency **A**irborne **C**ommand **P**ost
In Washington, D.C., there is a state-of-the-art jet plane that is always ready to take off at a moment's notice. Let's hope it never will. If it ever does take flight, it will be carrying the president of the United States to safety as the nation's capital endures a nuclear attack.

CINCUS ("Sink-Us")
Commander IN Chief of the **U**nited **S**tates Navy
This title was used before World War II. After Pearl Harbor, when the navy reorganized, one change very deliberately made was the Commander's formal title. From 1941 on, he was known as COMINCH—**COM**mander **IN CH**ief (U.S. Fleet).

NATO
North **A**tlantic **T**reaty **O**rganization
After World War II, when it became clear that the USSR was attempting to take over as much of Europe as possible, the United States, Canada, and most of the nations of Western Europe (Italy, France, Portugal, Luxembourg, Belgium, Denmark, the Netherlands, Great Britain, Norway, and Iceland) joined together to prevent the further spread of communism. Set up in 1949, NATO's military array contains both conventional forces and defensively deployed nuclear weapons. Today, with the Cold War at an end and Germany reunified, will the West need armed forces in Europe aimed at communism?

SEATO
South **E**ast **A**sia **T**reaty **O**rganization
A regional defense alliance created in 1954 and disbanded in 1977 after the war in Vietnam demonstrated its ineffectiveness. Original members were the United States, Great Britain, France, Australia, New Zealand, Thailand, the Philippines, and Pakistan. South Vietnam, Cambodia, and Laos joined later, and during the war in Vietnam, there were SEATO soldiers from Australia and Thailand fighting with the South Vietnamese.

EGADS
Electronic **G**round **A**utomatic **D**estruct **S**ystem
At Cape Canaveral, when a missile that's already in flight must be destroyed, this is the name of the signal that's used.

DEFCON
DEFensive Readiness **CON**ditions
When a military unit is operating under normal peacetime conditions, DEFCON 5 is the code word used to describe its level of readiness for an actual operation. As war becomes

more likely, units move into greater states of readiness. DEF-CON 2, or "double take," means close to being ready to move out, and if a unit is DEFCON 1, or on full alert, it is at maximum readiness and war may be imminent.

MOPP
Mission **O**rientation **P**rotective **P**osture

An army term from the '70s that refers to both the likelihood of chemical attack and the level of protection offered by special clothing against nerve gases. MOPP 1 means the enemy force has chemical weapons but is unlikely to use them. Soldiers wear only the heavy charcoal-lined overalls but keep rubber boots, gas masks, protective hoods, and rubber gloves handy. MOPP 2 means chemical weapons use is somewhat more likely, so boots are also worn. With MOPP 3, chemical weapon use is likely and soldiers wear all but their gloves. Their hoods may be open or closed. MOPP 4, the level under which American soldiers in the Gulf War of 1991 were operating much of the time, requires that soldiers use the full protection because chemical-weapon attack is expected.

SAC
Strategic **A**ir **C**ommand

One of the sixteen major air commands that make up the U.S. Air Force. This is the one in charge of the long-range nuclear strike force. TAC (**T**actical **A**ir **C**ommand) is another, in charge of fighter aircraft. SAC was created in 1946 and was the prime U.S. instrument of nuclear deterrence throughout the '50s. TAC had a major combat role in Korea, Vietnam, and the Persian Gulf.

KISS
Keep **I**t **S**imple, **S**tupid

This is a directive used in the army to remind strategists and tacticians that the more complex their planning becomes, the more likely it is that the operation will not work.

DINFO
Defense **INFO**rmation

The public-relations office of the Pentagon.

BOGSATT
Bunch **O**f **G**uys **S**itting **A**round **T**he **T**able
A Pentagon term for a major style of making decisions.

COTS
Common **O**ff **T**he **S**helf
What the army calls a standard piece of equipment.

GOGO
Government **O**wned, **G**overnment **O**perated
Pentagon slang for a facility that doesn't belong to the private sector and that presumably can get the requisite work done right away.

BASH
Bird **A**ircraft **S**trike **H**azards
A navy term for the problem of planes striking birds.

SLIG
Sucker, **L**owbrow, **I**diot, **G**oodwill-buster
A 1944 term for a cultural faux pas committed by an Allied soldier in a neutral country during World War II. The Algiers news correspondent who reported the word warned that a slig feeds the Axis propaganda machine. That is, if an American GI drunkenly tells a Turkish bartender that the women of his country smell like goats, both the bartender and his native customers may find their sympathies moving closer to the Nazis.

FAIRS
Fair **A**nd **I**mpartial **R**andom **S**election System
The military draft.

TAD
Temporary **A**dditional **D**uty
A term that the officer who gets assigned the TAD may react to with a certain amount of skepticism.

RETREAD
REtiree **TR**aining for **E**xtended **A**ctive **D**uty
Old soldiers never die, as General MacArthur once said. Like certain batteries, one might add, they keep going and going and going . . .

EXPOSE
EX-**P**artners **O**f **S**ervicemen for **E**quality

An organization founded in 1980 whose 5,000 members are divorced spouses of military personnel. The group works to change the laws concerning how military benefits, particularly retirement pay, will be divided after the couple separates. EXPOSE has achieved legislation for direct payment of child support and alimony to former spouses by the military.

CLAM
Chemical **L**ow-**A**ltitude **M**issile

An air force weapon infamous for its lame name. Harry Reasoner of CBS News once said, "You can tell a girl you spent World War II on the crew of a 155-millimeter howitzer and sound like a devil of a fellow, even if you never got past Fort Riley, Kansas. But how will it sound if you spent World War III, all seventeen minutes of it, manning a CLAM?"

TOW missile
Tube-launched **O**ptically tracked, **W**ire-guided missile

After 1968, whenever the infantry went on attack, a jeep or an armored car could shoot this anti-tank missile. The missile was guided by signals picked up by the wire attached to its body.

HARM
High-Speed **A**nti-**R**adiation **M**issile

A weapon used by the air force to knock out Libyan radar sites (1986) and also in 1991 against the Iraqi air defenses. It's fired from an aircraft in the general vicinity of radiation-emitting sources. Then it "listens" for radar signals, locks on, and attacks the source of the signals.

SLAM
Stand-off **L**and **A**ttack **M**issile

Another weapon used in the Gulf War. SLAM is also the acronym for an earlier missile used in Vietnam—the **S**uper-sonic **L**ow-**A**ltitude **M**issile. There was also an operation in Nam called SLAM—**S**eeking, **L**ocating, **A**nnihilating, and **M**onitoring—which worked to coordinate reconnaisance information and firepower.

SEALs

SEa-**A**ir-**L**and units (or soldiers)

During the war in Vietnam, American and South Vietnamese navy commandos joined to create a special force that ran secret intelligence operations both on land and in the water. Today SEALs are the navy's elite and special operations teams. Their work typically runs to underwater demolition and reconnaissance missions.

SEALORDS

South**E**ast **A**sia **L**ake, **O**cean, **R**iver and **D**elta **S**trategy

A joint operation of U.S. and South Vietnamese forces whose purpose was to cut enemy supply lines from Cambodia through the various waterways. In 1971, the Vietnamese navy took over the whole operation.

INFANT

Iroquois **N**ight **F**ighter **A**nd **N**ight **T**racker

A U.S. helicopter in the Vietnamese war that flew at night and attacked enemy positions with Gatling guns and rocket launchers.

The war in Vietnam generated a good deal of acronymic slang, mostly coined by the enlisted men.

DEROS ("deer-rose")

Date of **E**xpected **R**eturn from **O**ver**S**eas

Young men drafted and sent to Vietnam knew exactly how long they were assigned to stay there. Typically it was a year stretch except for marines, who got thirteen months. A common form of depression suffered by American soldiers in Nam was called the "deros blues syndrome," where men overwhelmed by long-term tension and stress became obsessed with the desire to escape.

This counting-the-hours-till-I'm-home attitude is certainly not limited to the draftees in Nam, though seasoned military officers have reported that it was more intense and more pervasive there than in earlier wars. From the Korean War, we have the term FIGMO—**F**-ck it, **I**'ve **G**ot **M**y **O**rders. Officers talked about the "figmo attitude," where a soldier who had received his separation papers didn't care what happened to his unit or in the war anymore. A more recent version is FUJIGMO—**F**-ck **Y**ou, **J**ack, **I G**ot **M**y **O**rders. Like DILLIGAF (**D**o **I L**ook **L**ike **I G**ive **A F**-ck), it's an expression of indifference and mild defiance.

STRAC (or STRACK)
Soldier **T**rained and **R**eady **A**round the **C**lock

Enlisted men called one of their number a "Strack" if they considered him a good soldier who stuck exactly to the rules and regulations. An officer using the term meant the guy was sharp, prepared, on the ball. The acronym originally came from **STR**ategic **A**rmy **C**orps, a group of units in a high state of combat readiness. It's also been said to stand for "**Sh**-t, **T**he **R**ussians **A**re **C**oming."

WETSU
We **E**at **T**his **Sh**-t **U**p

When a soldier was assigned to a unit he considered dangerously gung-ho, he'd belittle them by calling them Wetsus.

BUFF
Big **U**gly **F**at **F**ellow

An air force nickname for the eight-engine B-52 bomber, also known as the "Stratofortress." This long-range heavy bomber has been the mainstay of the U.S. **S**trategic **A**ir **C**ommand (SAC) since the late '40s. (It was a B-52 that dropped the bomb on Hiroshima.) Originally designed to carry nuclear weapons, it was used in Vietnam to deliver conventional bombs. BUFF was originally a term of affection by SAC pilots but it was used in Nam disparagingly. SAC then forbade flight crews to use the acronym. There was also the SLUF or **S**hort **L**ittle **U**gly **F**ellow, nickname for the A-7 Corsair attack aircraft.

LRRP ("lurp")
Long **R**ange **R**econnaissance **P**atrol

Elite five to seven man army teams that went deep into the jungle to spy out enemy positions and activities. They often went more than ten kilometers beyond the front line, where they could receive no support from the artillery. It was a dangerous job calling for highly skilled personnel. The men got their special training at a military in-country school called Recondo (reconnaissance + commando).

One perk provided by the army for these patrols was pre-cooked, freeze-dried lightweight meals called LRPRs ("lurps")—**L**ong **R**ange **P**atrol **R**ation. They were much less bulky and much tastier than C-rations, the food most of the regular troops were given.

The name of the patrol was changed twice. After LRRP, it was called LRP or **L**ong-**R**ange **P**atrol, and after 1969, the men were simply called "Rangers."

FUBIS
F-ck **Y**ou, **B**uddy, **I**'m **S**hipping Out

Used when a soldier disliked an officer's order.

FIAP
F-ck **I**t **A**nd **P**ress

That is, don't worry—just press on with whatever you're supposed to be doing.

FIDO
F-ck **I**t, **D**rive **O**n

You're a soldier driving a jeep along a recently cleared path through the jungle and there's an ominous column of smoke up ahead. You give your buddy sitting next to you an alarmed look. "Fido, man," he says, waving you on.

The area of the military that most haunts the general American public, and the rest of the world as well, is the nuclear arsenal and the war that could be fought with these doomsday weapons. Some of the acronyms are blackly humorous.

MAD
Mutual **A**ssured **D**estruction

Coined by Donald Brennan, an American military strategist, at the Hudson Institute in the early '70s. It's shorthand for the reason the United States and the former USSR have been trying to agree on nuclear disarmament since the 1950s. Here's the MAD scenario: Both sides have stronger offensive nuclear weapons than defensive ones, so when the first country sends over its bombs, though much of the second country's arsenal will be wiped out, enough weapons will survive to retaliate. Thus both sides will be destroyed.

OOPS
Occasionless **O**rdered **P**reemptive **S**trike
World War III begun by accident.

NO FUN
NO **F**irst **U**se of **N**uclear Weapons

NUTS
Nuclear **U**tilization of **T**arget **S**trategy
A nuclear war where the bombs will be sent to destroy military targets and will avoid civilian centers.

NORAD
NORth **A**merican Air **D**efense Command
A joint U.S.-Canada command in charge of defending against armed enemy aircraft, and ballistic or Cruise missiles launched against North America. The main operating headquarters is inside Cheyenne Mountain in Colorado Springs, Colorado. The system includes radar and communication networks, various early warning systems, and fighter-interceptor squadrons. The electronic supersystem that integrates the information from all these sources is SAGE (**S**emi-**A**utomatic **G**round **E**nvironment).

ASAT
Anti-**SAT**ellite weapons
Satellites are vital to both the United States and the former USSR's defense against nuclear weapons since they provide early warning, surveillance, and communication linkages. In the early '60s, the United States began experimenting with weapons systems designed to destroy enemy satellites in space and the USSR followed. ASATs, if used, could be particularly destabilizing to the nuclear balance between the superpowers

because they would destroy nuclear warning systems. The ASAT, therefore, is extremely dangerous and thus an important bargaining chip in superpower negotiations.

FOBS
Fractional Orbital Bombardment System

The 1966 Outer Space Treaty states that neither superpower will place nuclear weapons in orbit. FOBS gets around it by placing them in a low earth orbit and having them reenter the atmosphere over the target before completing a full revolution of Earth. Being in outer space for much of the journey, FOBS avoids most radar detection.

MIRV (1970)
Multiple Independently Targetable Reentry Vehicle

A missile with several nuclear warheads, each of which can be sent to a different target. The MIRV greatly increases the destructive capabilities of an individual missile. The 1972 MARV (**MA**neuverable **R**eentry **V**ehicle) added to the MIRV the ability to change the speed of the missile in order to avoid interception.

AWACS
Airborne Warning And Control System

In 1970, U.S. Air Force planes carrying specialized radar equipment began patrolling European skies. This new system of enemy bomber detection would give European countries five minutes' warning instead of three in the event of a Soviet air strike.

SALT
Strategic Arms Limitation Talks

On November 17, 1969, the United States and the Soviet Union began a round of negotiations to reduce the production of strategic nuclear weapons. In one form or another, we've been working on it ever since. Even Ronald Reagan, the man who refused to ratify the sweeping limits of SALT II, opened his own new round of talks, called START (**ST**rategic **A**rms **R**eduction **T**reaty) in 1982. Today, with the former USSR dissolved and the Cold War over, the nuclear arsenals of the superpowers are being dismantled much faster than SALT negotiators ever dreamed possible. It looks to be the end of a worldwide nightmare begun more than forty years ago—the dawn of a new day.

CHAPTER 10

Overt and Covert Operations

SQUAD CARS, PATROLLING police officers, those traffic cops who scan your driver's license with a judgmental frown—these are law enforcement made visible. Perhaps it's their very overtness that explains the light use of acronyms, which can be cloaking, in the field of police work.

Interpol
INTERnational Criminal **POL**ice Organization
　　Police from 143 different countries pool their computer data to track down terrorists, drug traffickers, smugglers, counterfeiters of foreign currency, and other such international criminals. The voluminous records are kept in the Interpol headquarters located in Lyons, France. Once a criminal is located, member countries extradite him or her to the country where the criminal will be tried.
　　The organization was originally founded in 1923 but during World War II, the Nazis ransacked the records and Interpol had to start up again from scratch in 1946.

TASER
Tele-**A**ctive **S**hock **E**lectronic **R**epulsion
　　This stun gun used by police to temporarily immobilize a person gets its name from Tom Swift and his Electric Rifle.

The device was patented in 1974 and its name is trademarked. (Taser is also influenced by the word "laser.") The Taser looks something like a flashlight and can fire two darts carrying 50,000 volts into a person from fifteen feet away. There are no permanent effects to the body. The Taser became infamous in mid-1992 when its use on Rodney King of Los Angeles was videotaped for the world to see and judge.

A spin-off of Taser is the Dazer (dog + taser), a trademarked name for an ultrasonic whistle that mail carriers can use to ward off threatening dogs.

RICO
Racketeer-**I**nfluenced and **C**orrupt **O**rganizations

The nickname of a federal law created in 1970 to catch the leaders of organized crime. (Rico is the name of that classic gangster played by Edward G. Robinson in *Little Caesar*.) The Constitution forbids the arrest of a person for simply belonging to any organization (even if that organization is the Mafia), so RICO instead makes it a crime to "racketeer" and defines that term very widely. If a person commits two illegal acts within ten years that are seen as part of a pattern involving a criminal enterprise, he or she can be indicted as a racketeer. RICO has been used against the Cosa Nostra, the Teamsters, Michael Milken, and César Chavez. Though the Justice Department has issued guidelines, many people feel that RICO is still too broad in its powers. Because simply being indicted means that all of one's assets are frozen, it can be used as a threat by large corporations to stop smaller, poorer groups from demanding their rights. For example, a small union threatened with a RICO suit by the large business they are striking against might well drop the strike. The union would have no way to pay its members enough money to keep striking and still feed their families. Congress is working to limit RICO's use without weakening its original purpose—to stop mobsters.

FALCON
Focused **A**ttack **L**inking **C**ommunity **O**rganizations and **N**eighborhoods

In an attempt to bring ruined neighborhoods decimated by crack wars back to life, the Los Angeles Police Department and federal law enforcement teams have targeted 135 L.A. "hot spots" to clean up. Since they watch those houses like hawks, the acronym is apt. Another LAPD effort is the CRASH detail—**C**ommunity **R**esources **A**gainst **S**treet **H**oodlums. This is a division of ten detectives that specializes in gangs.

GHOST
Graffiti **H**abitual **O**ffenders **S**uppression **T**eam

A somewhat less hard-nosed LAPD effort that places undercover transit police on city buses to bust youthful spray-paint artists who get an urge to express themselves on the way to school.

FIST
Federal **I**nvestigative **S**trike **T**eam

Long-term fugitives are searched out and captured due to the pooled resources of law enforcement at the federal, state, and local levels.

IRIS
Infra**R**ed **I**ntruder **S**ystem

Used first in 1972, the IRIS is an alarm system that sends a steady beam of infrared light across doorways. If someone steps through the doorway and interrupts the beam, that sets off the alarm.

Burgrep
burglary + report

Considering all the reports policemen have to write, it's surprising there aren't more acronymic bits of shorthand. There's BOLO (**B**e **O**n the **L**ook**O**ut for), ROB (**R**elieve **O**f **B**ooty) and a set of terms from Philadelphia: REAP (**R**ecklessly **E**ndangering **A**nother **P**erson), PICK (**P**ossession of an **I**nstrument of a **C**rime) and POW (**P**rohibited **O**ffensive **W**eapon).

On the other hand, the various Secret Services abound in shortened words—probably all part of the impulse to disguise that's basic to covert activities.

BOSS
Bureau **O**f **S**tate **S**ecurity

The acronym was invented in 1969 but the secret service of the Union of South Africa was organized in 1962 to bring all of the different security systems of the country under one department. It was a paramilitary organization that was given great latitude in its methods of suppressing perceived subversive activity. Amnesty International and other human-rights organizations have much documented evidence of torture and killing that have taken place under BOSS auspices. In 1978, a scandal brought down the Vorster government in South Africa, and with it Vorster's close friend General Hendrik van der Berg, the sinister director of BOSS. Under the new Prime Minister Botha, BOSS was reorganized, renamed DONS (**De**partment **O**f **N**ational **S**ecurity), and ordered to clean up its image.

SAVAK
SAzman-i Ittila'at **VA** Amniyat-i **K**ishvar (National Security and Intelligence Organization)

The Iranian secret service under Mohammed Reza Shah Pahlavi, shah of Iran, that was formed with the guidance of U.S. and Israeli intelligence officers in 1957. By the '70s, it employed 15,000 full-time officials and thousands of informants who worked to suppress any opposition to the Pahlavi regime. Censorship was intense and pervasive. SAVAK came to have virtually unlimited powers, detaining, torturing, and murdering thousands of political prisoners. Hit men were even sent into foreign countries after Iranian students who spoke against the shah. SAVAK was officially dissolved in 1979 by Khomeini after the revolution.

GULAG
Glavnoye **U**pravleniye **LAG**erei (Russian for Chief Administration of Corrective Labor Camps)

A collection of forced labor camps established by Stalin for political prisoners and criminals. They are administered by the Russian secret service. The term became well known in 1974 when Aleksandr Solzhenitsyn's book *The Gulag Archipelago* was published.

COINTELPRO
COunter**INTEL**ligence **PRO**gram

An FBI program of domestic spying established in the '60s and early '70s that attempted to disrupt those activities by individuals or groups that the agency defined as threatening to domestic security. For example, leftist student groups were harassed, faked letters were sent to sow discord between various liberal organizations, and disinformation was leaked to the press. After Richard Nixon was elected in 1968, COINTEL-PRO "dirty tricks" were stepped up considerably.

REPULSE
Russian **E**fforts to **P**ublish **U**nsavory **L**ove **S**ecrets of **E**dgar

In the mid-sixties, J. Edgar Hoover was the target of a KGB plot worthy of James Bond's nemesis SPECTRE. A man in LBJ's administration was arrested on a morals charge and the Russians tried to link Hoover to the same questionable activities. The FBI mounted a counteroperation with the code name REPULSE.

PICKLE
President's **I**ntelligence **C**hec**KL**ist

Every day our Chief Executive has a PICKLE dropped on his desk by the CIA—that is, a report of CIA activities.

NSSM ("Nissim")
National **S**ecurity **S**tudy **M**emorandum

During the Nixon and Ford administrations, knotty national security problems were thrashed out during secret meetings and any decisions or clarifications were written up in NSSMs. When Jimmy Carter took over, his staff proposed changing the name to Presidential Study Memorandum. This new title lasted less than twenty-four hours. Someone tried the new acronym and realized they'd be sending around "Piss-ems."

Crants
cover + grants

Let's say you have a company that does various kinds of chemical research. A representative of the CIA approaches you, wanting you to do a study of nerve gases. How are they going to get you a government grant to fund your work? They can't publicly solicit funds for a secret project. So instead, you win a grant to examine, let's say, the effects of ozone on egg laying or some such fallacious topic. You get your crant money and they get their secrecy.

Comint (1969)
communications + intelligence
One of the divisions of the U.S. spy network, Comint intercepts enemy communications. Humint (human + intelligence—1977) is the actual spy division. Elint (electronics + intelligence) listens in on ship and aircraft electronic messages. Sigint (signal + intelligence—1972) is a combination of Elint and Comint.

Psyop
psychological + operations
The various forms of psychological warfare, including brainwashing, propaganda, programming, and torture.

Harsubs
harassment + substances
Spies use these nonlethal materials to give their fellows in enemy spy agencies nausea, diarrhea, and other discomforts. A stink bomb is also considered a harsub.

COP
COver **P**rotection
This is the "mild-mannered reporter" cover identity that a spy hides behind while he or she is busy with secret activities.

JIB
Jack **I**n the **B**ox
Let's say the CIA knows that a car containing several of their operatives is under surveillance by unfriendly observers. The operation requires that one of the CIA operatives exit the car without the enemy knowing it has happened. So a dummy, the JIB, is used to fool the observers into thinking that the car

still has the same number of occupants after one agent has sneaked out.

DAME
Defense **A**gainst **M**ethods of **E**ntry

During the 1950s, the Army Intelligence School in Maryland offered prospective agents a three-week course in this subject. Two weeks and six and one-half days were spent teaching how to pick locks and break into safes. The last afternoon covered stopping others from doing so. At graduation, agents received a state-of-the-art set of lock picks.

DASE (**D**efense **A**gainst **S**ound **E**quipment) similarly taught how to bug rooms and tap phones.

Legat
legal + attaché

Just prior to World War II, J. Edgar Hoover began planting spies in American embassies abroad and calling them Legats. The practice spread until it was worldwide. Today a Legat functions as a liaison in a foreign country between the local police and the American law enforcement officers.

MICE
Money, **I**deology, **C**ompromise, and **E**go

The CIA uses this acronym to sum up the four most common reasons a KGB officer might defect to the West. (Do the Russians have an analogous acronym for the CIA?)

CHAPTER 11

Take Two and Call Me in the Morning

THERE'S A SECRET LANGUAGE doctors speak to each other in the hospital. And it's not meant for patients to overhear. It's not especially complex or scientific, but it can be insulting and it is almost always funny or at least irreverent. Why? Imagine twelve or eighteen or even twenty-four straight hours of rushing from mangled body to frightened suffering face to unheard-of complication and all with Death grinning at your shoulder. Every patient and every patient's family needs you to be a tower of strength. Some tension might build up, no?

So you tell a nurse that her comatose patient is CTD—hospitalese for Circling The Drain—i.e., about to die. It's black humor and somehow you both feel better. Laughter, especially in the face of death, is good medicine.

GOMER
Get **O**ut of **M**y **E**mergency **R**oom

Typically an old and decrepit patient, often brought to the hospital from a nursing home, who has lots of problems. Whatever the doctor does isn't going to improve a gomer's quality of life very much and the patient will soon return. Also used to refer to a patient who's always whining and asking for some kind of treatment and doesn't necessarily need it. First used in 1966. It's possible that the term originally came from the TV hillbilly character Gomer Pyle or even from the Scottish word *gomerel*, meaning "simpleton."

There are several variations. A gomere (go-MARE) is a female gomer. Sometimes a gomer of either gender is called a "gome" for short. In Vietnam a gomer was a soldier who was always kvetching. And when interns in a hospital send out for food instead of eating that bland in-house stuff, they often use what are called gomer bowls. These are the kidney-shaped, plastic, individually wrapped tubs meant to be used by patients for vomit or phlegm.

GOK or GORK
God **O**nly **K**nows or **G**od **O**nly **R**eally **K**nows

What you've got when all the doctors working you up can't figure out what's wrong. A phrase often heard between hospital staff members: "that gorked-out old gomer."

SHPOS ("Shpahss")
Sub**H**uman **P**iece **O**f **S**h-t

Unaffectionate term for a patient, commonly found in emergency rooms, who's either deranged and/or addicted to drugs, and who's often neglected him or herself to the point of no return.

MOPES
Medical **O**ut**P**atient **S**ervice

Surgeons are renowned in the field of medicine for the attitude "when in doubt, take it out." They tend to look down on other types of doctors who don't do "real" (cutting) medicine. They are particularly derisive about the doctors responsible for patients whose problems are so "minor" that the patient doesn't even need to stay in the hospital. Hence the cutting nickname, which can refer to any nonsurgeon.

OOPS!
Out **O**f **P**elvis

On the obstetrics floor, the nurses keep a big board which they frequently update regarding the status of their laboring patients. When it turns out that a woman has come in early and her baby's head isn't engaged yet, so that labor hasn't really begun in earnest, the nurse writes "Oops!" by the patient's name.

Hematomato
hematoma + tomato
An accumulation of blood outside the blood vessels, where it doesn't belong. A slang word for hematoma, which can be as minor as a bruise, or as serious as life-threatening subdural hematoma, where the blood vessels of the brain are leaking blood into the space between two of the brain linings.

SICU ("Sick-you")
Surgical **I**ntensive **C**are **U**nit
Jocular slang for the place where the most seriously ill patients are cared for. Other Intensive Care Units have their own nicknames:

MICU ("Mick-you") for **M**edical **I**ntensive **C**are **U**nit
NICU ("Nick-you") for **N**eurological **I**ntensive **C**are **U**nit
CICU ("Kick-you") for **C**ardiac **I**ntensive **C**are **U**nit
PICU ("Pick-you") for **P**ulmonary **I**ntensive **C**are **U**nit

Neomort
neo + mortal
Coined by Willard Gaylin, an American psychiatrist, in 1974 to describe a patient whose brain is dead but whose body is being kept alive by machinery because the person has willed his or her body to science. Organs will be taken when another person needs them. Other words for this anomalous body: biomort, respirated cadaver.

PUP rounds
Pick **U**p the **P**ieces
What the doctor or nurse just arriving for a shift on the ward does first—checks out the status of his or her patients by talking to the staff whose shift is about to end.

BIBA
Brought **I**n **B**y **A**mbulance
Something commonly heard on PUP rounds: each new patient's name, age, race, sex, problem, and how the patient entered the hospital.

LOPS
Length **O**f **P**atient **S**tay
 The acronym suggests the attitude of the hospital toward long-staying patients.

AMPLE history
Allergies, **M**edications, **P**revious major illnesses, **L**ast meal, **E**vents leading to injury
 A mnemonic acronym used to help interns in the emergency room remember what to ask incoming patients. The meaning of the acronym also reminds these new doctors to keep it short.

ROMI
Rule **O**ut **M**yocardial **I**nfarction
 The first thing to do when diagnosing a patient who comes in with chest pains—check for heart attack.

CABG ("Cabbage")
Coronary **A**rtery **B**ypass **G**raft
 One of the most common kinds of surgery done in modern hospitals—fixing broken hearts.

C.O.L.D.
Chronic **O**bstructive **L**ung **D**isease
 This is pronounced as an initialism but still thought of as an ironic acronym. That's because the condition is usually eventually fatal as opposed to the mildest of mild problems— the common cold.

MOPP
Nitrogen **M**ustard, **O**ncovin, **P**rocarbazine, and **P**rednisone
 A chemical brew used in chemotherapy to kill cancerous cells. Other mixtures are called CHOPP, COPP, and BLAM. (We'll spare you the chemical compounds they stand for.) The medicines are injected using large syringes filled with various clear lollipop-colored fluids like bright purple or orange.

PERRLA
Pupils **E**qual, **R**ound, **R**eactive to **L**ight and **A**ccommodation
 How a patient's eyes should look if there's no serious head injury. When concussion is suspected, the eyes are checked

periodically for any changes from this norm. (By the way, accommodation is the method your eyes use to adjust to seeing at different distances.)

DOC
Died of **O**ther **C**auses

Not disease and not accident. A similar term from Britain: DOMP—**D**iseases **O**f **M**edical **P**ractice.

Outside the pressure cooker of the hospital, the acronyms are lighter.

BRAT diet
Bananas, **R**ice, **A**pple sauce, **T**oast

The diet your pediatrician will probably recommend when your baby has diarrhea.

RICE
Rest, **I**ce, **C**ompression, **E**levation

What to do for a sprain: Get off the injured body part, use ice and elastic bandaging to control the swelling, and get that leg or arm above the level of your heart to help the excess fluid from the swelling drain off.

ECHO virus
Enteric **C**ytopathogenic **H**uman **O**rphan virus

A mysterious type of virus that seems to turn up in people who have various kinds of meningitis (swellings of the covering of the brain and spinal cord), intestinal distress, and respiratory illnesses. However, it isn't known to cause any of these diseases. Hence the name "orphan."

Medicide
medicine + suicide

Dr. Jack Kevorkian's term for his highly controversial practice of setting up machinery that will allow patients who request death to kill themselves. The people he typically assists are suffering from painful degenerative diseases like advanced multiple sclerosis or terminal lung cancer. Many medical professionals are aghast at this practice and "Doctor Death," as he is sometimes called, is in danger of prosecution.

Laetrile

LAEvo-mandeloni**TRILE**-beta-glucuronic acid

Whew—you can see why they shortened it. A chemical compound derived from apricot pits that has been used in treating cancer but has not yet been proven an effective agent.

ELISA

Enzyme-**L**inked **I**mmuno**S**orbent **A**ssay

A test used first in 1985 to make sure that blood supplies weren't contaminated by the AIDS virus.

GRID

Gay **R**elated **I**mmunodeficiency **D**isease

An early name for AIDS.

NIROscope

Near **I**nfra**R**ed **O**xygen Sufficiency + scope

Three short minutes is the maximum length of time the human brain can survive without oxygen. Longer deprivation means irreversible damage. Thus, when you're having surgery and the anesthesiologist puts you under, he or she must constantly monitor your brain's oxygen level. The NIROscope is an instrument that manages to shine infrared light through both the skin and the bony skull to the brain. By measuring the amount of light that comes back, the anesthesiologist can instantaneously evaluate the brain's oxygen level. This superb noninvasive technique was developed in 1982 by Dr. Frans Jobsis, professor of physiology at Duke University.

GIFT

Gamete **I**ntra-**F**allopian **T**ransfer

There is no greater gift to an infertile couple than the ability to give birth to a child of their own. Medical science keeps making advances in this area, and the aptly named GIFT technique was developed in the mid-1980s as a step along the way. An egg and sperm are collected from the couple and inserted into one of the woman's fallopian tubes. At that point, the egg should be fertilized naturally and pregnancy proceeds in the usual way from there.

TENS
Transcutaneous Electrical Nerve Stimulators

A portable mechanical painkiller effective for many people, even though no one really knows why. Here's how it works. You clip to your belt or clothing a battery-operated generator about the size of a pack of cigarettes. Two or more electrodes connected to it are placed on your skin where you are having pain. Whenever your arthritis or childbirth or postoperation site starts to trouble you, you press a button and a mild current of electricity flows through the area. More often than not, you'll get good to very good relief.

Why's it work? Maybe the electricity manages to garble the pain message your nerves are sending to your brain. Or perhaps the current stimulates your body to release its own natural opiate—endorphins. Someday the doctors will know for certain, but for now, the pain relief will do.

Endorphin
endogenous + morphine

A protein produced in the brain that, like morphine, relieves bodily pain. It may improve our immune systems and elevate our moods as well. The research to date suggests that regular aerobic exercise, meditation, prayer, and certain kinds of relaxation training lead to increased levels of endorphins in the body. Phenomena as diverse as "runner's high" and pain relief after acupuncture can be explained by this morphinelike chemical. A suggestive finding is that alcoholics, drug addicts, and people with clinical depression have all been found to have unusually low levels of endorphin.

SQUID
Superconducting QUantum Interference Device

The newest relative of the CAT scan and the PETT. You trust your head to this device that looks like an old-fashioned beauty-parlor hair dryer. No X rays and nothing injected, yet what comes out is a three-dimensional picture of your brain at work. The SQUID measures the extraordinarily faint magnetic fields that are produced when nerve cells in the brain fire. Mechanical mind reading may not be far away.

BEAM

Brain **E**lectrical **A**ctivity **M**apping

Doctors measure our brain waves with the electroenceph-alogram or EEG. The data appears on reams of paper strips which can be hard to read. The BEAM takes this information about the brain's electrical wave patterns and displays it as a colored topographical map that changes through time. Doctors have used the resultant "movies" to diagnose everything from dyslexia to epilepsy to schizophrenia, as well as to pinpoint brain tumors.

POSSUM

Patient **O**perated **S**elector **M**echanisms (In Latin, *possum* means "I am able.")

A nickname for an electronic device used in Britain that enables a paralyzed person to use a typewriter, a telephone, and several other machines.

MEDLARS

MEDical **L**iterature **A**nalysis and **R**etrieval **S**ystem

A 1964 computerized reference file for doctors looking for the latest medical information. It indexed 2,300 periodicals but took more than a week to gather and send relevant information.

Medline (Medlars + telephone or communications Line) superseded Medlars in 1972. Instead of a week or more, doctors can now receive requested information in minutes.

PLASMA

Parents' **L**eague of **A**merican **S**tudents of **M**edicine **A**broad

Financially strapped, missing their kids, these parents need each other's support like a bleeding patient needs a transfusion of life-giving plasma. Other medically relevant organizations: GREEN (**G**uild to **R**evive **E**xhausted **N**urses) and MEND (**M**edical **E**ducation for **N**ational **D**efense).

Psychologists and medical doctors often speak disparagingly of each other's assumptions, approaches, and successes. Yet the more we learn about brain chemistry, the more it seems that a heart attack and a hallucination are members of the same family. In the years ahead, even tumors may be treated as much by insight as by surgery. And schizophrenia may yield to the surgeon's scalpel. But for now, the science of the mind is separate from that of the body.

YAVIS
Young, **A**ttractive, **V**erbal, **I**ntelligent, **S**uccessful

A term coined in 1976 describing the sort of client who seems to benefit the most from our current forms of psycho-analysis. A pretty sad state of affairs, since people in emotional pain are often none or only a few of the above.

Affluenza
affluence + influenza

A psychiatric disorder described in the mid-eighties by California psychiatrist John Levy following his study of the children of wealthy people. He found that many people who expected to inherit riches felt guilty, lacked motivation, acted emotionally immature, and often found life boring. Perhaps having everything is more delightful as a daydream than as reality. Perhaps.

DIMS
Disorders of **I**nitiating and **M**aintaining **S**leep

A category used by specialists in sleep disorders. A person with this condition may have difficulty getting to sleep, may wake frequently, may wake excessively early in the morning, and/or may find his or her sleep nonrestful. The treatment of DIMS depends on the cause, which may be anxiety, depression, a stressful event, or other such difficulties.

HALT
Hungry? **A**ngry? **L**onely? **T**ired?

Members of Alcoholics Anonymous have learned to check themselves with this slogan whenever they feel tempted to take a drink. If they can pinpoint the feelings that are leading them into danger, then it's much easier to eat or confront their anger or find a friend or simply hit the sack than to succumb to self-destruction.

EST (written *est*)
Erhart **S**eminars **T**raining

A system of consciousness-raising and self-realization that was created in 1971 by Werner Erhardt. Participants (five or six hundred at a time) paid several hundred dollars to be told they were "assholes," to kowtow to Gestapo-like trainers who often denied food and even bathroom visits to their trainees, and to spend sixty hours over a pair of weekends listening to lectures and each other's confessions. Why? Apparently to get "it," "it" being a sort of existential awakening. Erhardt taught a New Age version of the power of positive thinking: Since you create everything that happens to you, you can get whatever you want. An uncomfortable corollary: Since this is true for each of us, there is no need to offer help to anyone else—they're busy creating their own reality and can't make use of our help anyway.

est has changed over the years. It's now called The Forum and most of the rough stuff has been dropped. The focus is more on how to increase effectiveness at work. But the underlying philosophy is the same—you are the only actor in the play you continuously write.

JINS
Juveniles **I**n **N**eed of **S**upervision

A legal term for kids who are not criminals or in other ways burdens to society but whose parents find them impossible to control. These children or adolescents with behavior problems are often confined to institutions and there is some concern in the legal community that their rights are not being protected. Different states have different terms for the same kids: CINS (**C**hildren **I**n **N**eed of **S**upervision), PINS (**P**ersons **I**n **N**eed of **S**upervision), and MINS (**M**inors **I**n **N**eed of **S**upervision).

WAIS
Wechsler **A**dult **I**ntelligence **S**cale

A test that measures that illusive and fascinating entity, general intelligence. Similar to the Stanford-Binet, the granddaddy of all such measures, the WAIS was developed in 1939 and revised in 1955. The ten subtests, evaluating such skills as block design and vocabulary, must be administered individually by a trained person and scored using carefully standardized parameters. In 1949 Mr. Wechsler created the WISC (pronounced "wisk"), the **W**echsler **I**ntelligence **S**cale for **C**hildren, which is designed for children ages six to sixteen. It was revised in 1974. And in 1967 came the WPPSI (pronounced "Whip-see"), the **W**echsler **P**reschool and **P**rimary **S**cale of **I**ntelligence, which works with children between four and six and a half. Earlier than four years of age, every child is a genius. Ask any parent.

CHAPTER 12

From Lasers to Quasars

FROM A SCIENTIFIC point of view, the twentieth century is an extraordinarily exciting time to be alive. Mysteries long believed to be unsolvable, like the workings of the human brain, are yielding bit by fascinating bit to the scrutiny of scientists and the ever more powerful machines at their disposal. As knowledge expands exponentially, language must stretch to keep pace and often in a hurry. Microscopically and telescopically, there's an acronymic world out there.

ACHOO
Autosomol **D**ominant **C**ompelling **H**elio**O**phthalmic **O**utburst

By any chance, do you find yourself sneezing the moment you step outside into bright sunlight? Or when you enter a brightly lighted supermarket? If you do, it's all your parents' (and their parents') fault. There is actually a genetically inherited tendency to yield to that irresistible nose tickle when moving from relative darkness to vivid light.

RFLP ("Riflip")
Restriction **F**ragment **L**ength **P**olymorphism

How do scientists "read" our genes? For example, how can they predict a fetus will have Down syndrome from looking at a few fetal cells? Since 1985, they've used a technique called "riflip mapping." At a certain spot on a particular chromosome, if they find abnormally long bits of DNA cut with a particular chemical, they know that Down syndrome will occur. Other inherited diseases and conditions have their own characteristic abnormalities. Riflip mapping is proving invaluable in learning about genetic illness.

REM
Roentgen **E**quivalent **M**an
and
RAD
Radiation **A**bsorbed **D**ose

REM and RAD are measurements of radiation. REM, (named for Wilhelm K. Roentgen, the German physicist who discovered X rays), is the unit that measures the amount of radiation being absorbed by a living being. RAD measures the same thing absorbed by nonliving things.

The average American absorbs .36 REM every year from various sources. A single X ray gives you about .006 REM. Currently the law allows a worker in a nuclear plant to absorb 5 REMs per year, but many people believe this amount is dangerous. A lethal dose is between 500 and 1,500 REM but, of course, all kinds of damage can occur at considerably lower levels of exposure.

SCRAM
Safety **C**ontrol **R**od **A**x **M**an

This term originates with the Manhattan Project—the group of people who built the first atomic bomb during World War II. In those early days, a major safety precaution was provided by special control rods suspended by ropes over the nuclear reactor. Should anything go wrong, the SCRAM cut through the ropes with his ax, allowing the rods to fall into the reactor and stop the fission reaction.

Today's technology has moved beyond ropes and axes but nuclear technicians still use the acronym SCRAM for any sudden shutdown of a nuclear reactor that involves using the control rods.

ALARA
As **L**ow **A**s **R**easonably **A**chievable
A term from nuclear engineering having to do with radiation levels, decontamination, and other such delicate matters.

Plantimal
plant + animal
Aw, come on—another hoax like the old dog/cat hybrid? Nope. This term was invented in 1976 to name the cell formed when an animal cell is fused with a plant cell. And the resulting plantimal cell is actually alive. Fifty years from now, when you want a couple of tomatoes, maybe all you'll have to do is open the screen door and call, "Here, Red, old boy. Come get a fertilizer bone."

RAND Corporation
Research **AN**d **D**evelopment
In 1946, though World War II was over, the U.S. military community believed that the postwar world would require a strenuous and continuous application of science to weaponry and other technologies of combat. In order that this focus, honed to a fine point during the war, would not be lost, the air force contracted with Douglas Aircraft Company to create the nation's first "think tank"—project RAND. Its first assignment was to study the feasibility and military usefulness of an artifact that in 1946 only science-fiction fans had heard of— an artificial earth satellite.

Today the RAND Corporation is a private nonprofit company based in Southern California that studies everything from urban transportation to drug abuse. The same intellectually independent style exists today as it did in the '50s, when RAND thinker Herman Kahn and his group created the "scenario technique" to think about the unthinkable: the strategic use of nuclear weapons.

RADAR
RAdio **D**etecting **A**nd **R**anging
First used in 1941, this electronic device can locate an object by sending out a radio wave that intersects with that object. The wave then bounces back to the receiver. By mea-

suring how long it takes the wave to bounce back and what direction it's bouncing back from, the radar mechanism can pinpoint where the object is. The return bounces show up as "blips" or points of light on the screen of the device.

LIDAR
light + radar (or **LI**ght **D**etecting **A**nd **R**anging)

An application of the radar principle to meteorology. Light beams are used to measure cloud height and patterns, air turbulence, visibility, and other weather phenomena.

SONAR
SOund **N**avigation **A**nd **R**anging

Electromagnetic waves like radio or light can't travel very far in water, so in order to have an underwater locational device, it is better to use sound waves instead, which work wonderfully. (Consider whale song.) Sonar is used to detect, locate, and classify submerged objects. It can work passively by simply listening. Or it can actively send "pings," pulses of sound, into the ocean and analyze the echoes reflected from undersea objects.

LASER
Light **A**mplification by **S**timulated **E**mission of **R**adiation

Light, whether from the sun or a sixty-watt bulb, normally radiates out in all directions. It may heat us up or brighten a room, but in its ordinary form, it certainly isn't capable of substituting for a knife during delicate surgery on a knee or an eyeball. Or accomplishing the indelicate but certain destruction of an entire satellite. Ordinary light is what scientists call "incoherent"—it's made up of many different wavelengths and colors and it travels in all directions at once.

However, when it is compressed into a single beam of one wavelength going in one direction only, light in this coherent form can be enormously powerful and/or exact. That's what a laser beam is. The term itself was coined by scientist Gordon Gould in 1957.

There are those who claim that LASER also stands for **L**ucrative **A**pproach to **S**upport **E**xpensive **R**esearch.

MASER
Microwave Amplification by Stimulated Emission of Radiation

A microwave is another kind of energy wave, like a light wave only lower in frequency. When microwaves are made coherent, the resulting maser beams can be used like radar and might be even more effective in locating objects.

GRASER
Gamma-Ray Amplification by Stimulated Emission of Radiation

Yet another laser-type device, this time making high-frequency gamma rays coherent. Like the laser, it can be used to cut or to destroy. The word was invented in 1974.

QUASAR
QUASi-stellAR radio source

The term was created by scientist Hong Yee Chiu in 1964. It refers to some mysterious sources of powerful radio waves, the most distant known objects we humans have encountered in the universe. Scientists' best guess is that quasars are baby galaxies, evolving in deep space as much as fifteen billion light-years from Earth. No well-accepted theory accounts for why they emit such enormous amounts of energy.

PULSAR
pulse + quasar

Another mysterious source of radio waves far out from Earth, this time emitted in short intense bursts at very precise intervals. One widely accepted theory is that a pulsar is what's left after a small star has gone supernova and then collapsed into itself. The pulsing is caused by this enormously dense star rotating.

LINAR
line + star

Will we ever invent FTL (Faster Than Light) travel and find out what all these tantalizing beeps and flashes really are in the deep reaches of space? The linar (coined in 1970) sends out waves of extraordinary energy that can be measured by using the spectral lines of particular chemical compounds.

WIMP
Weakly **I**nteracting **M**assive **P**article

Pick a galaxy—any galaxy. Now measure the mass of all the stars. And then measure the mass of the whole galaxy. Should be about the same number, right? Well, it turns out that the mass of an entire galaxy is about ten times the mass of all of the stars in it. Odd. What makes up the other nine tenths of the mass? Some scientists speculate that this unseen matter is made up of enormously heavy collapsed stars like black holes or brown dwarfs. Others believe that huge amounts of subatomic particles, called WIMPs, make up the difference in mass. So WIMPs are theoretical, but the theory is taken pretty seriously in astrophysical circles.

Parsec
parallax + second

If we ever do take short hops from Betelgeuse to Alpha Centauri, how will we measure the distances we travel? Measuring space travel in miles is like measuring people in numbers of atoms. The parsec, equaling 3.26 light-years (19.2 trillion miles), might work better. (By the way, Parallax is a geometric term concerning the measurement of direction and Second is a tiny unit used to measure angles. Glad you asked.)

Rectenna
rectifying + antenna

Imagine the power at our disposal if we had space stations beaming microwaves down to Earth to be received by a rectenna and converted into electricity. The term was invented in 1975. Hopefully the device (and the station) will be invented ASAP. Electricity bills would plummet.

Pixel
picture + element

Did you ever wonder how television pictures are sent to your screen? They are actually made up of about 70,000 little dots or pixels. Each pixel's color and brightness are controlled by which electronic signals reach it and tell it what to do. (Turn green, stay off, etc.) All 70,000 working in concert over and over make Madonna wiggle or Peter Jennings tell you about the latest disaster.

AMIGO
Ants, **MI**ce, **GO**phers
A device that sends out electromagnetic waves to painfully stimulate the nervous systems of many unwanted creatures in and around the home. The animals are either killed or chased away, making the name "amigo" rather ironic from the creatures' point of view.

CANDU
CANada **D**euterium Oxide—**U**ranium
A hearty name (coined in 1963) for a particular type of nuclear reactor used in Canada.

Positron
positive + electron
Remember the "solar system" model of the atom? In the center is the nucleus, made up of the positively charged protons and the neutrally charged neutrons. Circling around the nucleus, like little orbiting planets, are the negatively charged electrons. And the whole atom is balanced because the number of positive protons equals the number of negative electrons.

It turns out that atoms aren't always balanced like this, and nuclear physicists started examining this anomaly both theoretically with mathematical models and physically with particle accelerators and atom smashers. And what they have been finding out for the last forty-five years is that the building blocks of the universe are tinier, more various, and more delightfully balanced than anyone had suspected.

For one thing, it looks like anti-matter really exists. In an anti-matter atom, the positron (an electron with a positive charge) circles a nucleus with anti-protons (which have a negative charge).

Many of these sub-subatomic particles have portmanteau names because the particles themselves seem to be either combinations of other particles or mirrors of other particles. The tauon (tau + meson), for example, is like an electron but is enormously heavy (relatively speaking). It lasts only one trillionth of a second before breaking down into a muon (mu + meson) and an electron. Then there's the pion (pi + meson). Both the pion and the muon were predicted to exist by Japanese physicist Hideki Yukawa before the particles were actually discovered. He won a Nobel Prize for his extraordinary mathematics.

Finally there's the IMP (**I**ndeterminate **M**ass **P**article), a hypothetical particle that has no mass when it's not moving. Rather impish activity—dropping in and out of existence.

GUT
Grand (or **G**eneral) **U**nified **T**heory

Albert Einstein once said that God does not play dice with the universe. He believed that when we humans finally figure out how everything fits together, the big picture will be breathtakingly beautiful in its simplicity and perfection. He came to believe that the four known forces of nature would turn out to be intimately related—in fact, would be four expressions of one grand idea. (The four forces, by the way, are gravity, electromagnetism, the strong nuclear force that holds protons together, and the weak nuclear force that has to do with radioactive decay.) He spent the last thirty years of his life searching for the connection between all four forces. He never found it.

Some scientists believe that if Einstein couldn't find it, it must not exist. But the search goes on. Currently a relationship has been found between the last three forces, but gravity still has to be brought into the equation. Some believe that the GUT will finally be achieved when anti-matter partners are found for all existing subatomic particles. This idea is called SUSY—**SU**per **SY**mmetry.

On October 4, 1957, the Soviet Union launched the world's first artificial satellite, Sputnik I. And the image of our country as America the Invincible took a beating around the world—particularly when our first highly publicized rocket, Vanguard TV3, blew up on the launch pad two months later. The British press dubbed our effort "Kaputnik." We followed in February of 1958 with a rocket that broke up in flight, nicknamed by the press "Flopnik." Another failure was aptly named "Stayputnik." Explorer I did finally make it in 1958 and discovered the Van Allen radiation belts that circle the Earth. And the space race has continued ever since (at least until the USSR dropped out), full of three-letter initialisms and charming acronyms.

NASA
National **A**eronautics and **S**pace **A**dministration
One of the first things the United States did after Sputnik started beeping at us was create this independent government agency in 1958 to oversee research and development of vehicles and activities for space exploration. Today NASA is an enormous enterprise, responsible for both technological and astrophysical research; rockets, shuttles, and other transportation in space; tracking and monitoring of signals from space; developing a space station.

NASA has developed and overseen such world-renowned programs as the Apollo flights that landed humans on the moon and the unmanned flights like Viking, Mariner, Voyager, and Galileo that explored the other planets of our solar system.

EROS
Earth **R**esources **O**bservation **S**atellites
Interior Secretary Udall pulled a fast one on NASA in the '60s. He wanted a satellite launched that would observe Earth from space and NASA was dragging its collective feet. So Udall puckishly announced that his department (the Interior Department?) was launching a research satellite of its own named for the Greek god of erotic love. (NASA is renowned for its need to name space vehicles with great dignity.) The hoax worked. In 1970 NASA did launch ERTS (**E**arth **R**esources **T**echnology **S**atellite) to survey land forms. Even for NASA this name was dull. It was changed to Landsat in 1972.

Contrary to popular belief, however, NASA does occasionally evince a sense of humor. Note the term PLACID, standing for **P**ay**L**oad **A**board, **C**aution **I**n **D**escent. And LOB for **L**aunch **O**perations **B**ranch. And PLOP for **P**lantary **L**anding **O**bservation **P**ackage. Not knee-slappers maybe, but not bad.

MECO
Main Engine Cut Off

A 1981 term for the moment during a space flight when the ship's primary engine is shut down.

BURP
Back Up Rate of Pitch

When the computer on board a spacecraft changes the ship's position, there is a light jerking motion as if the spaceship had expelled some gas.

Capcom
capsule + communicator

When manned spacecraft are sent out from Earth, communications are maintained with the astronauts through a whole roomful of officials called unofficially Mission Control. (The official name is the acronym MOCR, pronounced "Moecur," which stands for **Mission Operations Control Room**.) The officer who does most of the actual talking with the astronauts is the Capcom, a person who has trained along with the space crew.

Near the Capcom sits the Guido (guidance + officer) who is the chief navigation officer, the engineer in charge of the flight. Next to him or her is the Fido (flight + dynamics + officer), the engineer responsible for the trajectory, velocity, changes in direction, elevation, and other flight dynamics.

One of the major complaints of the daring test pilots who became the first U.S. astronauts was that there was little if any actual piloting to be done in space since everything was controlled from the ground. Sounds like a reasonable complaint.

Lox
liquid + oxygen

An early (1959) word for rocket fuel. There's also Gox— gaseous + oxygen.

FLATs
First Lady Astronaut Trainees

In 1959, a group of thirteen women began medical testing in New Mexico to become astronauts. They were the first U.S.

women candidates for the job and they called themselves FLATs. The project ran secretly for three years and then the whole idea was dropped. Why? NASA issued one of their typical Catch-22 explanations: The women weren't military test pilots. (But the military wasn't accepting female test pilots.) Some astronauts have a different explanation. Unlike its Soviet counterpart, apparently NASA feared that the American public would have been offended if male and female astronauts slept together in the same space capsule. (The women candidates scored generally higher than the men in many of the physical parameters measured by NASA doctors: withstanding pain, heat, noise, G-force, etc.)

Castronaut
Castro + astronaut

The American nickname for the first Cuban in space.

MASTIF
Multiple **A**xis **S**pace **T**est **I**nertia **F**acility

NASA's theory of how to train an astronaut for space travel was to subject the candidate to every physical challenge the scientific team could imagine might occur on a flight. Candidates practiced accomplishing the various maneuvers while rolling from side to side, tumbling head over heels, being jerked in different directions, etc. The MASTIF was considered by many candidates to be the wildest ride of all, since they had to accomplish tasks while being moved in several ways at once.

PLSS ("Plis")
Portable **L**ife-**S**upport **S**ystem

This is a big square backpack, named in 1968, that astronauts on the moon carried when exploring the surface. The PLSS holds four hours' worth of oxygen and regulates the temperature inside the space suit. The final two used by the first humans on the moon were left there along with other used-up equipment, as well as some scientific instruments and symbolic objects like an American flag. Why? Every ounce a space vehicle must carry costs the moon in expensive rocket fuel.

DACT

Disposable **A**bsorbent **C**ollection **T**runks

Did you ever wonder what an astronaut does when he or she is inside one of those very complex space suits for hours at a stretch and nature calls? You can't just unzip and let fly. Early astronauts were connected up with a plastic bag that stayed inside their suits. (Buzz Aldrin, the second man on the moon, actually had his bag break and the contents land on his left foot. He took very sloshy steps on the lunar surface.)

Today, when astronauts on the shuttle flights need to urinate, the men use hoses directly attached to them and the women use a kind of space diaper—the DACT. Thank goodness the apparatus is used only when people are inside pressure suits and pressure suits are not needed very often.

SARAH

Search **A**nd **R**escue **A**nd **H**oming Beacon

Spaceflights in the early days all ended with the rocket jettisoned and the people aboard returning to Earth in a small capsule that "splashed down" into the ocean. If everything went according to plan, the capsule would land right on target, where a boat and its accompanying helicopter were waiting. But sometimes splashdown was miles away, and then the SARAH would direct the search planes to the waiting astronauts.

LEM

Lunar **E**xcursion **M**odule

This term emerged in the mid '60s when NASA was gearing up for landing the first humans on the moon. The plan called for the actual spaceship to stay in orbit around the moon while two of the three astronauts took a much smaller vehicle, the LEM, down to the moon's surface. The first LEM that actually set its stilted and saucer-footed legs on the lunar surface was called the Eagle. On Sunday, July 20, 1969, at 4:17 in the afternoon Eastern Standard Time, Neil Armstrong sent the famous message from the moon: "The Eagle has landed."

Armalcolite
Arm (for Neil Armstrong) + Al (for Edwin "Buzz" Aldrin)
+ Col (for Michael Collins) + "ite"

One of the most common minerals found on the moon, an oxide composed of iron, titanium, and magnesium, that turned up in the first sample of moon rocks brought back by the three above-mentioned astronauts after humanity's first visit to the moon.

Mascon
mass + concentration

A 1968 term for a geological phenomenon first noted on the moon and later on planets and their own moons throughout the solar system. Approximately thirty miles below the surface lie massive concentrations of dense matter.

KREEP
K (the chemical symbol for potassium) **REE** (rare earth elements) **P** (phosphate)

A mineral found on the moon in the early '70s that looks like yellow-brown glass.

MOUSE
Minimum **O**rbital **U**nmanned **S**atellite of **E**arth

In 1953, a scientist named S. Fred Singer came up with a great concept—a weather satellite. He even invented a cute name for it, but his MOUSE was launched in name only. It wasn't until 1960 that the first actual weather satellite began surveying Earth, and its name was far less charming: TIROS (**T**elevision and **I**nfra**R**ed **O**bservation **S**atellite). Since 1960, more than forty TIROSes have gone into orbit, with the result that 100 percent of Earth's surface is now monitored. (Before the TIROS program began, only 20 percent was regularly surveyed.) Thousands of lives have been saved as a result of the satellite net's earlier hurricane warnings. And all this surveillance has been a boon to the science of meteorology. So how come the nightly weather report is still just a guesstimate? Though predictions have gotten more accurate, we'll probably never be able to achieve 100 percent. There're just too many variables that affect weather.

Intelsat
international + telecommunications + satellite

The majority of satellite names are portmanteaus, with the last syllable being "sat" for satellite. Intelsat, for example, is owned by a consortium of more than seventy nations. The consortium was formed to promote and direct global communications and has sent up several satellites. Other satellite names: Marisat (maritime + satellite) for ship communication, Amsat (amateur + satellite), Domsat (domestic + satellite) for a type restricted to a specific country, and Comsat (communications + satellite) for a type used to transmit information from one specific point to another. A great satellite project name that leaves out the "sat": BIRDDOG (**B**asic **I**nvestigation of **R**emotely **D**etectable **D**eposits of **O**il and **G**as).

CLASS
Chrysler **L**aser **A**tlas and **S**atellite **S**ystem

Imagine starting up your car and by punching a couple of buttons, you activate a color video map that shows you your location and your destination. Sure beats squinting at the fine print of a paper map and snarling as you try folding it up again.

Now imagine that as you drive, the video map keeps track of where you are. Sound like twenty-second-century technology? Well, the Chrysler Corporation has CLASS on the drawing boards right now. To put the system into operation would take a large net of satellites, each transmitting a unique signal to ground-station computers. The computers would interpret the different signals and get a fix on the object. This information would be sent, using laser video disc technology, to your in-car screen. So when your preschooler whined, "When are we going to be there, Daddy?" you could say, "In six-point-three minutes, darling," instead of "Soon—and quit smearing the back of my head with your frozen yogurt."

Project SETI
Search for **E**xtra **T**errestrial **I**ntelligence

There is a handful of BIG questions we Earthlings brood about and astrophysics contributes one of them: Is there really anyone else out there in the universe or are we all alone? If other space-faring races exist, where in the name of James T. Kirk are they? If we consider the billions upon billions of planets circling the stars, it seems statistically impossible that Earth is the only planet that has managed to come up with a living being capable of sustaining a technological civilization. Probability theory suggests that there are thousands of life forms capable of advanced thought scattered throughout the universe. But as far as we can tell, we've never been contacted. We've never come across a single artifact or broadcast or whatever.

It's a puzzler, all right, with respected scientists lined up on both sides. The people who started Project SETI, however, weren't satisfied with theory. Starting in 1960 and continuing up to the present day, certain scientists have been listening for artificially generated electronic signals like radio, television, and radar waves from various nearby stars. (The assumption is that advanced civilizations would have to have evolved modes of communication similar to our own.) Even though the budgets for these various projects have always been small, the listening devices have gotten bigger and more sophisticated through the years.

However, to date we haven't overheard a single whisper. Aha, say those who argue we're all alone. But actually, in all of the last thirty-plus years of scanning, we've only examined one tenth of 1 percent of the stars we need to check to have a reasonable shot at success. This number is about to be doubled in a single swoop. On Columbus Day, 1992, the California Institute of Technology began a SETI project with enormously enhanced listening powers. So the betting window's still open.

A couple of well-known SETI devotees are Carl Sagan and Steven Spielberg. Sagan, scientist and author of popular science books, has worked for many years to coax bigger budgets from NASA for this search he believes in deeply. And Spielberg featured SETI in his movie *E.T.* That government agency the kids and their knobby-knuckled friend were trying to outrun and outfly? SETI. Spielberg later funded Project META (**M**egachannel **E**xtra **T**errestrial **A**ssay) in 1985, which upgraded the scanning equipment in one of the major SETI projects so that 8.4 million radio channels could be examined.

E.T.—please, phone here!

CHAPTER 13

RAMs, BITs, and WOMBATs

ACRONYMS AND COMPUTERS were womb mates, birthed by the same strenuous World War II era. Both have flourished and multiplied, like giant fraternal twins, ever since that time. It is no surprise that the world of computers teems with acronyms.

Almost all of the earliest computers had acronymic names.

ENIAC
Electronic **N**umerical **I**ntegrator **A**nd **C**alculator (Computer)

The first general-purpose nonmechanical computer looked like something out of a Buck Rogers movie—walls of flashing vacuum tubes, panels of switches, scurrying white-coated scientists ministering to it—and it was bigger than your average house. The U.S. Army shelled out half a million dollars between 1943 and 1946 to build ENIAC. (Today's average personal computer is considerably more powerful and will set you back less than $2,000—plus it takes up a tabletop.)

BINAC
BINary **A**utomatic **C**omputer

With the ENIAC as a springboard, development of new computers flourished in the late '40s and early '50s. BINAC was another effort of J. Presper Eckert, Jr., and John Mauchly, the two scientists who created ENIAC. EDVAC (**E**lectronic **D**iscrete **V**ariable **A**utomatic **C**omputer) in 1951 was one of the first computers that could store substantial programs. And at Cambridge University, British scientists created EDSAC (**E**lectronic **D**elayed **S**torage **A**utomatic **C**omputer).

UNIVAC
UNIVersal **A**utomatic **C**omputer
Walter Cronkite can take credit for introducing the electronic computer to the American public on an evening in November of 1952. Americans had gone to the polls to decide whether war hero Dwight D. Eisenhower or bespectacled intellectual Adlai Stevenson would lead the postwar world. UNIVAC, the first commercially available computer, had predicted a landslide victory for the general who masterminded D Day. But for several hours, Cronkite had to keep this prediction a secret from the millions watching him because CBS executives didn't trust the newfangled gadget.

When his bosses finally let Cronkite tell the public that UNIVAC had accurately predicted not only Eisenhower's victory, but that he would win by a landslide, America became fascinated by the new machine. Until IBM began to dominate the computer market several years later, the name UNIVAC was synonymous with computers to the average American.

The first widely distributed computers were huge and enormously expensive. Only large corporations, universities, or government agencies could purchase them. Typically the computer itself was housed in a separate temperature-controlled building or section and kept behind wide glass windows that nonexperts could peek through and watch the arcane activity of the busy electronics experts. If you wanted something accomplished by the computer (a rocket's trajectory calculated or an atomic reaction modeled), you would typically have to fill out a work order, send it to the experts, and hope that there was time available on the machine to solve your problem. (Today's large computers, still called mainframes, are enormously more powerful, and buying a hour of mainframe time will set you back a pretty penny. They are used only for huge projects, where mind-bending amounts of memory are required.)

FUD factor
Fear, **U**ncertainty, and **D**oubt

FUD is often used to describe the way the IBM sales force did business in the '60s and '70s.

Imagine you are a buyer for a major corporation and you're told to purchase a mainframe computer system for a million-plus dollars. You look at your options. Big Blue (as IBM is often called) is the market leader, selling over 75 percent of the computer systems. Some IBM competitors offer less expensive computers. Some offer better technology. You are tempted to choose one of these competitors. But your biggest fear is doing the wrong thing. What if you go out on a limb and get fired for making a million-dollar mistake?

IBM, being the mainstream system, is "safe." Your IBM salesman intimates that the Brand X computer is unreliable, that Brand Y's company is financially unstable, etc. So you choose IBM and then you can rest easy. That's FUD at work.

Of course, IBM denies ever training its sales force in FUD tactics.

BUNCH
Burroughs, **U**nivac, **N**CR, **C**ontrol Data, **H**oneywell

With IBM bestriding the mainframe world like a colossus, its competitors were first called "the seven dwarfs." When two of them, RCA and GE, dropped out of the computer market in the '70s, the remaining five met to discuss competitive business strategies in order to survive. But the uneasy alliance of the BUNCH never really managed to make a dent in Big Blue's seemingly invincible armor.

DEC ("Deck")
Digital **E**quipment **C**orporation

In the early '60s, this small company brought out a computer system for $120,000. Since the cheapest mainframes cost more than a million dollars, this "minicomputer" was received with great enthusiasm. As the '60s and '70s went on, DEC grew to become second in sales to IBM. Though the machines weren't as powerful as mainframes, the mini still delivered enormous bang (or byte) for the buck. Plus the smaller machine offered more flexibility. Instead of having to use a mainframe to figure out your payroll each month, which is like using a two-ton boulder to swat a mosquito, a company could buy a minicomputer for such tasks.

Although everyone calls the company "deck," DEC prefers to call itself Digital.

As the mini was to the mainframe, so the microcomputer is to the mini: more flexible and amazingly less expensive. The reason? The invention and creative utilization of the semiconductor chip. One kind of chip, called the microprocessor, acts as the "brain" of the computer, and is about half the size of a playing card. And a memory chip, about the size of a long fingernail, can hold a million "bytes" or pieces of information. With its chip technology, the microcomputer, sitting on a desk, is capable of storing more information than the house-sized ENIAC. The fifty-year evolution of computer technology is truly one of the wonders of the world. As has been pointed out, if the automobile industry had developed at an analogous pace, we could now buy a Rolls-Royce for $2.75 and drive it three million miles on a single gallon of gas.

INTEL
INTegrated **EL**ectronics

A major manufacturer of the chips that serve as the microcomputer's "brain," Intel was chosen by IBM to manufacture the microprocessers for its enormously successful personal computer. Until recently, when Intel's patent rights to this chip were successfully challenged in the courts, the company had a monopoly on all microprocessor chips used in IBM and IBM-compatible computers. (That's a lot of chips!) Even minus the monopoly, Intel chips dominate the market.

PET
Personal **E**lectronic **T**ransactor

Way before the IBM PC and the Macintosh, in the late '70s, Commodore put out a microcomputer you could simply take out of the box, plug in, and compute away on. It practically followed you home from the store. This was an early attempt to create a "user-friendly" machine. But like the Pet Rock, the PET computer was popular for only a few years before it faded into oblivion.

Microsoft
microcomputer + software
The most successful software company of all time. Its founder, Bill Gates, was a student at Harvard in the mid '70s when he heard about a hobbyist computer-building kit being manufactured by a tiny company in New Mexico called MITS (**M**icro **I**nstrumentation **T**elemetry **S**ystems).

According to the myth that circulates through the industry, Gates called MITS on a lark and asked if it would be interested in having him develop a language that would work on this computer it called the Altair. When it gave him the go-ahead, he supposedly wrote the whole program in about a week. Though he'd never even seen the Altair, the program worked the first time it was tried on the machine. (That's kind of like stepping up to the plate and hitting three home runs in a row off a superstar pitcher.)

Bill left Harvard and Microsoft was born. The company has developed major software for practically every new microcomputer that has come along, including the IBM PC. Today Bill Gates is a billionaire. You may have heard of some of his company's products: Windows, Word, MS-DOS, Excel, etc. etc.

Just as the names of computers and their companies are quite acronymic, so are many of the terms used to describe how the computer actually works.

DOS ("dawss")
Disk **O**perating **S**ystem
Let's say you've typed a letter to your sweetie on your IBM PC and you want to print it out. So you hit "P" (or whatever your code is) for print. How does the machine know what to do?

When you type in "P," that tells the word-processing program (the software package you use when you write) what you want to do. The program tells the DOS, the fundamental instructions built into the machine that control the computer's various components (keyboard, printer, video screen, disk drives, etc.) and make them work together.

Then the DOS connects deep inside the computer, to its "brain" or CPU (**C**entral **P**rocessing **U**nit) and says in machine language, "Print, you fool."

"Roger Wilco," says the CPU and tells the printer (which you've hopefully turned on), "Print that sucker." And with a clatter or a grunt, depending on your model, the printer presents you with your letter.

As you might imagine, DOS is a significant program in the computer world. IBM personal computers commonly use a version called PC-DOS and IBM clones (computers that aren't manufactured by Big Blue but can use the same programs) use a sister operating system called MS-DOS. DOS has sold over fifty million copies to date, making it the best-selling software product of all time.

SCSI ("Scuzzy")
Small **C**omputer **S**ystem **I**nterface

A SCSI device is one type of connection that lets the CPU tell the printer, "Print that sucker." If the CPU is the brain, then a SCSI device is the nerves that connect to the muscles of the computer.

RISC
Reduced **I**nstruction **S**et **C**omputer

Your average CPU has instructions for many different activities. Some genius realized that, for most programs, only a small number of these instructions are actually used. So why not create a simpler CPU chip that contains only the commonly used instructions? The RISC chip was born. It's not only cheaper than the regular CPU chip but it's faster as well. Seems like a good Risc to take.

ROM
Read **O**nly **M**emory

This is where the permanent information is stored that tells the CPU of the computer how to print and other basic functions. It's called "read only" because it can't be changed.

RAM
Random **A**ccess **M**emory

When you typed in your love letter, the information was stored in your computer's RAM. That's a kind of short-term memory. The letter will disappear when you turn off the computer. If you want to save your sweet nothings, you can print an extra copy (called a "hard copy") or have the computer store them on a disk.

GUI ("Gooey")
Graphical **U**ser **I**nterface

Ten years ago, to get a computer to do anything, your only choice was to type commands in an arcane language—COPY A:\AUTOEXEC.BAT C:\DOS, for example. One small mistake and the computer spat out "Bad Command" and made you do the whole thing again.

Today the trend is to make your directions to the computer graphical. A list of choices, sometimes represented by pictures, or "icons," appears on the screen and you move a cursor (with a little gadget called a "mouse") onto the option you want. Hit the button and, *voilà*—you're in business.

Bit
binary + digit

Imagine you're explaining how your computer works to an inquisitive four-year-old, the kind of kid who asks "But why?" every time you think you've answered their question. Six or seven "why's?" into the process, you'd be talking about bits—the fundamental unit of information that the computer "thinks" with.

A bit is so small that it takes eight of them, called a byte, to stand for a single letter of the alphabet, for example. A computer bit can be in two different states. One is "on," which is made by a microscopic switch that allows the electricity to flow through it. The other is "off," made by a switch that doesn't let the electricity through. If it's on, it's a 1 and if it's off, it's a 0. The language made from these 1's and 0's is called "binary."

Long combinations of 1 and 0 become codes for numbers, letters, and other major symbols. The letter "I," for example, might be 01001001. Seems like "I love you" would take a while for the computer to produce, doesn't it? And a whole love letter? Days.

Well, it turns out that a computer can "flip" 2.5 million switches in a quarter of a second. That's because the flipping is electronic and electrons move at the speed of light. So instead of your letter being produced over several days, it seems to appear instantaneously on the computer screen as you type it.

MIPS
Million **I**nstructions **P**er **S**econd

A unit of measurement that indicates how fast your computer works. "Instruction" is computerese for "flip." The more powerful your computer, the higher its mips rating is. A typical microcomputer or PC averages one to three mips. Your typical mainframe has something in excess of fifty mips.

WYSIWYG ("Wizzy-wig")
What **Y**ou **S**ee **I**s **W**hat **Y**ou **G**et

You print out your love letter, complete with a couple of heartfelt poems, take a look at the hard copy, and it's just not right. It doesn't look as good as it looked on the screen. Maybe the lettering isn't as artistic. Maybe the poems aren't spaced just the way you wanted them.

The salesperson who sold you the word-processing program promised that it would produce **WYSIWYG** mode on your computer so that what you create on the screen is exactly what you'll see when you print your document. Well, like most people who want to make a sale, he or she exaggerated.

What you usually get might be called **WYSISWYG** ("Wizzy-swig")—**W**hat **Y**ou **S**ee **I**s **S**ort of **W**hat **Y**ou **G**et. Some people call it **WYSIWYG-MOL** ("Wizzy-wig mole")—**W**hat **Y**ou **S**ee **I**s **W**hat **Y**ou **G**et, **M**ore **O**r **L**ess.

Finally, some cynics suggest that we give up our dreams and just accept **WYGIWYG** (Wig-ee-wig)—**W**hat **Y**ou **G**et **I**s **W**hat **Y**ou **G**et.

Computers can do amazing things, everything from designing a car to writing a song to telling you what to eat for breakfast (after you've told it all about your tastes, of course). In some cases, all you need is a software program. In others, software plus hardware is required. Many of these capabilities have acronymic names.

CAD
Computer-**A**ided **D**esign

With CAD programs, architects can design buildings and engineers can design machines. The user draws a three-dimensional image on the screen and makes design modifications simply by pressing a few computer keys. Then the program can simulate mechanical stress tests to determine if there are any weaknesses in the design. All this is done before any manufacturing actually takes place. Saves time, money, and materials.

CAM
Computer-**A**ided **M**anufacturing

When a machine part is actually manufactured, it is often created by other special machines that are designed to automatically drill, cut, and assemble parts. These special machines often contain computers that can be programmed by engineers to drill, let's say, a quarter-inch hole every six inches, insert rods in each hole, etc., etc.

CAM is often used in conjunction with CAD. These CAD/CAM programs make it possible to automate the entire manufacturing process all the way from the original idea to the finished machine.

BOMP
Bill **O**f **M**aterials **P**rocessor

A database is an organized collection of related information stored on a computer. An example of a database would be a list of a company's employees, complete with everyone's date of hire, salary, sick-leave days taken, efficiency rating, etc., etc. If the boss needs to lay off someone, for example, he can ask the computer to print a report showing employee salaries in order of size and another showing efficiency ratings in order and then compare the two.

BOMP was one of the first database management programs, developed by IBM in the early '60s. A successor to BOMP was DBOMP (**D**ata**B**ase **O**rganization and **M**aintenance **P**rogram). If you ever wondered who put DBOMP in da BOMP, da BOMP, da BOMP . . . well, it was IBM.

VisiCalc
visible + calculator

VisiCalc was the original spreadsheet program. A spreadsheet stores information in tabular form. For example, let's say you're a grocery store exec and you need to know which cereals you should reorder. So you ask the spreadsheet program to print up a table showing how many boxes of each cereal have sold in each of the last twelve months. Your computer obliges with a nice little table. Each month is represented by one horizontal column and each cereal is represented by one vertical column. Makes it easy to compare the sale figures of, let's say, Frosted Chocomalt Honey Flakes to those of Hearty Bran Nuggets, though you probably know the winner without looking.

VisiCalc was designed in the late '70s to run on the Apple II personal computer and the program's success was largely responsible for the early growth of the Apple computer. This was the first program perceived by small-business owners to be truly practical and they bought it in droves. However, when the IBM-PC entered the market, a new version of VisiCalc wasn't developed for this popular machine and another company created Lotus 1-2-3 instead, which took over the spreadsheet market while VisiCalc became invisible.

OLIVER
On-**L**ine **I**nteractive **V**icarious **E**xpeditor and **R**esponder

A program designed to make daily decisions for you. First the program asks you lots of questions, including what decisions you need to make. Then it calculates away and finally tells you which side of the bed to get out of tomorrow or whether to buy that Porsche. The program was invented by Oliver Selfridge who, no doubt, asked his program what he should name it.

Modem
modulator + demodulator

A device you can add to your computer that makes it possible to send information (data) from your machine to someone else's machine by using the telephone. The modem takes your data, which is in digital form (that 1 or 0 language), and translates it into an audio form that can be sent over regular phone lines. Then the modem on the other end changes the audio message back into digital language and the second computer can read it. It's even faster than Federal Express. Every fax machine, of course, has a modem.

Sys-op ("Sis-op")
system + operator

You want to play chess with someone in Buenos Aires or Beijing? How about asking hundreds or even thousands of computer users whether they would recommend a new program? Or asking several people to take a look at a report you've written? If you subscribe to a bulletin-board system, you can do any of these things with ease.

The system typically is housed in a central location with several linked computers and several phone lines. The Sys-op is the person responsible for organizing the bulletin board, posting bulletins, troubleshooting problems, and making sure that the users get what they need.

When you want to connect, you call up through your modem using your computer, and send any messages you want. You can also check to see if anyone left you a message (a chess move?), join conferences with other users, etc. The diversity of activities to be found on a bulletin board is amazing.

One of the larger systems is GENIE—**G**eneral **E**lectric **N**etwork for **I**nformation **E**xchange.

MIDI
Musical **I**nterface **D**igital **I**nterface

Invented in the mid-eighties, the MIDI is the logical next step after the music synthesizer. The synthesizer creates electronic music and the MIDI feeds that electronic data into the computer, where a musician can edit it in innumerable ways.

Much of the music we hear in current movies and television is created with MIDI systems.

LAN
Local **A**rea **N**etwork

Suppose your business has several people working on personal computers. Pretty soon, everyone wants to share data files with one another. With a LAN, you connect cables between the computers and then everyone on the network can send information to anyone else. LANs are used when the computers are within a few hundred feet of each other. For connecting up more distant users, a WAN (**W**ide **A**rea Network) is used. The WAN is a series of LANs connected over telephone lines.

CD-ROM (Seedy Rahm)
Compact-**D**isk **R**ead-**O**nly **M**emory

A weighty set of encyclopedias may soon seem as quaint to us as windup record players. CD-ROM is a new technology that uses the same kind of disks you play in your CD player to store computer data. It's so efficient that the information from a whole encyclopedia set can be stored on a single four-and-a-half-inch disk. There's so much room on the CD that story extras like photographs or actual sound recordings (bird song, train whistles), things that require incredibly long strings of data, can be stored with ease. CD-ROM is about to revolutionize computer games. With so much more memory at their disposal, companies will be able to offer graphics and sound that will make games almost like movies.

Imagine how long it would take if a programmer had to talk with the computer in binary! Instead, computer programmers have developed languages that translate binary into far more efficient forms of communication. Hotshot programmers are always manipulating languages, devising new "dialects" as it were, that are more effective at getting the programmer where she or he wants to go. Whole new languages emerge from time to time as well, many of them acronymically titled.

BASIC
Beginner's **A**ll-Purpose **S**ymbolic **I**nstruction **C**ode

One of the earliest languages, BASIC was developed in the mid-sixties by two Dartmouth professors in order to teach students to program. Unlike many languages that are full of alien-looking symbols, BASIC has English words and pronounceable instructions. Amazingly long-lived in an environment where languages, programs, and whole technologies last as little as two or three years, BASIC is still used by more people than any other computer language.

Fortran
formula + translation

The favorite language of number crunchers, Fortran was developed in 1959 and was the first language to become widely used. It was designed to solve mathematical problems and is still commonly used for math today. So much of the mathematical programming of the past used Fortran that even though there are far more powerful languages available today, many everyday applications still use Fortran. The next time you fly the friendly skies or enjoy pictures sent back from a distant planet, think about the thousands of Fortran computer hours that made it possible.

COBOL
COmmon **B**usiness-**O**riented **L**anguage

Along with BASIC and Fortran, COBOL was the other early language (circa 1962) to enjoy widespread acceptance. It was designed to take over such business activities as inventory control, billing, and payroll. The rapid growth of IBM in the '60s and '70s is due in large part to the increased productivity of businesses that installed IBM computers to run COBOL programs. When a computer sends you the same bill (that you paid six months ago) several times in a row, that's a COBOL glitch.

Algol
algorithmic + language

An algorithm is a step-by-step procedure for solving a mathematical problem. It's like a recipe for a solution. Algol makes it easier to use algorithms on the computer. The language had its heyday in the '60s and was more popular in Europe than in the United States.

JOVIAL
Jules's **O**wn **V**ersion of the **I**nternational **A**lgebraic **L**anguage

Not satisfied with Algol and other similar languages, Jules Schwartz of SDC, a major software company, invented his own language in the early '60s. And who better to name his creation after than himself? JOVIAL was used primarily by the air force.

MUMPS
Massachusetts **U**tility **M**ulti-**P**rogramming **S**ystem

A language developed at Massachusetts General, Boston's largest hospital. The language was used to create hospital programs to manage inventory, patient, or billing files. These programs could be used by individuals at terminals spread throughout the hospital. This was quite innovative in the mid-sixties, when the language was written. It proved so practical that MUMPS spread across the country in health-care facilities. You could call it one of the few "good" epidemics.

SIMPLE
Simulation of **I**ndustrial **M**anagement **P**roblems with **L**ots of **E**quations

This language is used in computers found in factories. (Remember CAM programs?) The computers tell the factory how to use its machinery to turn out products. Changing "lots of equations" to a "simple" language is one way of creating a user-friendly environment.

PROLOG
PROgramming in **LOG**ic

When writers create future worlds, whether the twenty-fourth century of *Star Trek* episodes or the upcoming time of 2001, computers in the stories seem to think in almost human ways. Even today, there are several languages that program the computer to "think" logically, as a person would. PROLOG is one such AI (**A**rtificial **I**ntelligence) language. Another is GLIB—**G**eneral **L**anguage for **I**nstrument **B**ehavior. And a third is ALICE—**A** **L**anguage for **I**ntelligent **C**ombinatorial **E**xploration—which is used by mathematicians to represent logical constructs. Its name is a nod to that famous professor of mathematical logic, C. L. Dodgson, also known as Lewis Carroll, whose wonderland was filled with logical paradoxes.

Most of us think of computer people as fairly buttoned-down types—the IBM sales force in its pinstriped uniform, for example, or the fellow at the bank who might remove his suit jacket during business hours once or twice a year. But there's a whole other computer world, or perhaps underworld, operating at the same time—the midnight realm of the computer hacker.

Hackers are fascinated by computers in the same way that hot-rodders are obsessed with cars. The hacker "plays" passion-ately with programming. Typically, though not necessarily, the hacker is young, nerdy, a night owl, highly casual in dress, and anti-conformist. Invariably the hacker displays a high level of intelligence applied to systems analysis, a phenomenal memory for exact detail, and a love of logical puzzles.

Over the years hackers have evolved their own subculture, communicating mostly through the "Net," as they call Internet, and other widespread, sometimes worldwide webs of intercon-nected bulletin boards. The wild and creative slanguage they've invented is, predictably enough, rich with acronyms.

LISP
Lots of **I**rritating **S**uperfluous **P**arentheses

A derogatory nickname for an early computer language designed to manipulate lists. The real LISP stands for **LIS**t **P**rocessing Language and hackers find it too clumsy. These intellectuals of the keyboard have similar attitudes toward BASIC and COBOL. In fact, hackers claim that many potential hackers are lost when young people use BASIC too much and get into "bad habits" like spaghetti logic, the programming equivalent of run-on sentences. COBOL, a weak, verbose, flabby language from the hacker viewpoint, can cause a dis-ease called COBOL Fingers, where the fingers are worn down to nubs with all that excess typing.

WIMP environment

Windows, **I**cons, **M**ice, and **P**ull-down menu (or sometimes **P**ointer or **P**rogram)

These features are all methods that software developers have invented to make the computer easier to use for nonexperts. So, of course, hackers think WIMPs are for sissies and prefer to connect more directly with the computer for superior flexibility.

Netiquette

net + etiquette

Unlike most people, hackers seldom if ever meet their closest friends in the flesh. Instead they meet in the Net. Often a hacker won't even know the name of someone she or he talks to nightly for years. But they will know the input code of this friend—kind of like a trucker's CB handle.

With all this socializing going on, a set of behavioral rules has evolved, and if you break the rules, lots of people will criticize you with nasty messages written in all capital letters (bulletin boardese for screaming). One cardinal bit of netiquette is that no commercial plugs are allowed.

GNU

Gnu, **N**ot **U**nix

A major activity on bulletin boards is the sharing of programs. Many hackers believe that all programs, or software, should be free to anyone who wants to use them. GNU is a software compiler that distributes programs without charge to anyone using the Net. It is financed by an organization called the Free Software Foundation which is run by a famous older hacker named Richard Stallman. The foundation promotes something they call "copyleft" on software as opposed to "copyright."

DRECNET

drek + net

Remember DEC, that big computer manufacturer second to IBM in the '60s and '70s? Well, hackers call their DECNET software DRECNET, referring to the Yiddish word *drek* for "dirt" or "garbage." That's because DEC helped design a bulletin-board system, and then when they put out the software to allow people to get on the board, it was incompatible (computerese for didn't fit). Hackers can be quite unforgiving of error.

ICE
Intrusion **C**ountermeasure **E**lectronics

A term coined by a hacker named Tom Maddox and popularized by science-fiction writer William Gibson in such cyberpunk novels as *Neuromancer* and *Mona Lisa Overdrive*. The novels create a world where hackers connect their brains with a computer (surely the ultimate interface) and actually see and float in the universe of the Net. If they get caught breaking into private systems that are protected by ICE, the software will send lethal electricity back through the intruder's computer.

Though today's hackers can't "plug in" to the computer, they do fall into a "hack state" at times, an alternative state of consciousness where the world seems to fade away and they become the programming they're doing. It's similar to what happens to a jazz musician when his or her improvising takes on a life of its own and becomes simply wonderful.

PHALSE
Phreakers, **H**ackers, **A**nd **L**aundry **S**ervice **E**mployers

Hackers are always looking for new worlds to conquer, new puzzles to unravel, and one obvious challenge is the security systems that government agencies create to protect their computerized information. Some hackers have dedicated many hours to penetrating a military database or a secret-service file—just because it's there.

The government has come to take a dim view of this activity, as you might imagine. PHALSE is an East Coast group of computer trespassers who were raided by the FBI. The "phreaker" part of the name refers to another illegal hacker activity—creating electronic "phreak" boxes that can be used to circumvent the phone company's system of charging calls to your phone.

GIGO
Garbage **I**n, **G**ospel **O**ut

When most computer people say GIGO, they mean **G**arbage **I**n, **G**arbage **O**ut—shorthand for if you give the computer bad information, it will give you incorrect conclusions. Hackers take it a step further. Their version of GIGO is a sardonic comment on the human tendency to trust anything a computer says.

FISH
First **I**n, **S**till **H**ere

Remember those business-accounting acronyms FIFO (**F**irst **I**n, **F**irst **O**ut) and LIFO (**L**ast **I**n, **F**irst **O**ut)? Those terms are used in the computing world to talk about the order in which computers process multiple tasks. Hackers add FISH as a jokey way of pointing out that some process on the computer has stopped cold. And when any bulletin-board network is running very slowly, it's called a "FISHnet."

PLOKTA
Press **L**ots **O**f **K**eys **T**o **A**bort

Sometimes a hacker has some program cooking and just can't get it to respond to any reasonable command or query he types. Last resort is to plokta, where you press both hands flat on the keyboard in an attempt to get any reaction from the uncooperative system. This is the hacker version of kicking a recalcitrant pinball machine.

WOMBAT
Waste **O**f **M**oney, **B**rains, **A**nd **T**ime

A hacker is said to be "wrestling with a wombat" when he or she gets entangled with a programming problem that is both uninteresting to the hacker community in general and unlikely to benefit anyone even if it is solved.

YABA
Yet **A**nother **B**loody **A**cronym

The hacker's answer to the question, "What is wysiwyg?" The term was coined at Cambridge University by a computer maven who preferred a more original name for a new program instead of the traditional acronym.

CHAPTER 14

A Veritable Potpourri

THERE ARE SOME FIELDS of life where acronyms flourish without the slightest bit of tending. Look at military language or computer jargon. But even in the stoniest soils, a hardy little acronym or portmanteau will, here and there, poke out its bright frisky head. In areas as disparate and unlikely as coin collecting, candy, and ancient Jewish philosophy, the acronym has found a toehold. In slightly more welcoming regions, like letter writing, aviation, and baseball, there are whole colonies of portmanteaus and acronyms waving vividly in the breeze. Some of the most prized blossoms pop up in fields where you'd least expect them.

SHADES OF TRUTH

LIE
Limited **I**nformation **E**stimation

LIAR
Lexicon of **I**nconspicuously **A**mbiguous **R**ecommendations
    Coined by Robert T. Thorton of Lehigh University.

207

WAG
Wild-**A**ssed **G**uess

SWAG
Scientific **W**ild-**A**ssed **G**uess

ASK
Anomalous **S**tate of **K**nowledge

OOH OOH
On the **O**ne **H**and, **O**n the **O**ther **H**and

DUPE
Decidedly **U**nscientific **P**olling **E**nterprises

Writer and political commentator William F. Buckley is famous (or infamous) for his use of obscure words. One book reviewer was assigned the latest Buckley tome and spent a good deal of time with a dictionary in hand. Exasperated, he sent a list of the "Buckleyisms" he'd looked up to about twenty journalism professors, asking how many of the words these vocabulary experts actually knew. Not one professor knew them all and most knew less than half. The reviewer felt vindicated by his DUPE, though he did call the process a "non-prophet organization."

LOCALITIES

BOWASH
BOston to **WASH**ington corridor

A term used by Realtors and other businesspeople. As the outer suburbs of one metropolis creep toward the outer suburbs of the other, the two cities show signs of merging into a single economic zone, a megalopolis.

Other potential mergings: BOSNYWASH (**Bos**ton, **N**ew **Y**ork, **WASH**ington D.C.), CHIPITTS (**CHI**cago to **PITT**sburgh), and SANSAN (**SAN** Francisco to **SAN** Diego).

NoHo and SoHo
North of **Ho**uston and **So**uth of **Ho**uston

Two areas of New York City in lower Manhattan which have become avant-garde centers for the arts. The nicknames are influenced by a similar area of London called the Soho district.

PAWN
Poole, **A**berley, **W**orthington, and **N**olen

A very small town in Lane County, Oregon, which was named for four of the first settlers in the area. Each of the four men who were instrumental in getting the post office established donated the first letter of his last name. The acronymic name was suggested by Willis Nolen but the first postmaster was Monroe Poole.

TONGUES

Japlish
Japanese + English

A Japanese college student aiming toward a job in telecommunications might major in "masukomi" with a focus on "terebi." These are Japlish for "mass communications" and "television" respectively. There's lots of Japlish in baseball: after the ump yells, "Pray bollo," a player usually gets several storiku before he makes a hitto. Japlish was one of the first terms (1960) invented to describe the inroads of English into other languages. Another is Hinglish, referring to a particular style of Hindi spoken in India after the British decamped. And the amalgam Spanglish, typically spoken by Spanish-speaking immigrants learning English, second-generation Hispanic Americans when talking to those immigrants, and housewives when demonstrating the use of the microwave to their Hispanic housekeepers, is probably the most common blended language in America.

Another candidate is Yinglish. Leo Rosten has written several books on this comical and rich mix of Yiddish and English. There's even AmerEnglish (or AmeroEnglish) to describe a merging of the two dialects of our common language.

Franglais
Français + Anglais

The French are a proud people, dedicated to keeping their language pure and logical. So when Americanisms began creeping into French after World War II, there was a great hue and cry among French intellectuals. Dr. René Etiemble, professor of comparative languages at the Sorbonne, wrote a scathing book in the '60s about the subject called *Parlez-Vous Franglais?*. He even suggested true French words for such objectionable coinages as "le drugstore."

Siglish
sign + English
The sign language most often used by hearing people to communicate with their deaf friends. Siglish is actually a pidgin form of Ameslan (**AME**rican **S**ign **LAN**guage) that uses the same word order as spoken English and has other such simplifications. Most hearing people assume that there's basically one sign language for English, but actually there are several.

Ruston
Russian + Houston
In July of 1975, miles above the earth, Russian astronaut Alexei A. Leonov crawled through a tunnel created by linking an American Apollo spacecraft with a Soviet Soyuz one and knocked on the Apollo hatchway door. Tom Stafford, an American astronaut, said in Russian, "Who's there?"

This was the beginning of a two-day joint space project between the superpowers that yielded hordes of publicity photos and a new form of astronaut slang—Ruston. The Russians also claimed that Stafford's thickly accented Russian justified a name of its own—Oklahomski.

Yerkish
Yerkes + English
An artificial language using geometric symbols for words. It was successfully taught to several chimpanzees who pecked away at specially constructed computer keyboards to ask their human trainers for a banana or a hug. The term was coined in 1973 by American psychologist Duane M. Rumbaugh in honor of Robert M. Yerkes, the world's foremost authority on the great apes in the '20s and '30s.

MEMORY AIDS

ROY G BIV
Red, **O**range, **Y**ellow, **G**reen, **B**lue, **I**ndigo, **V**iolet

Many of us met up with Roy in elementary school during science class, when the teacher was talking about the colors of the rainbow. And this little memory device served us well in later science courses when we had to come up with the order of the colors in the spectrum. If we went on to college in any of the physical sciences, we probably met or invented many more such mnemonics.

SCALP
Skin, **C**onnective tissue, **A**poneurosis, **L**oose connective tissue, **P**eriosteum

A medical school mnemonic for the five layers of the scalp. Another good one is RUM (**R**adial, **U**lna, **M**edian) for the nerves entering the hand.

GEOGRAPHY
George **E**merson's **O**ld **G**randmother **R**ode **A** **P**ig **H**ome **Y**esterday

A mnemonic for learning how to spell one of those words we used to show off with in grammar school.

TRAF
Toss, **R**efer, **A**ct, **F**ile

A process for using quick decision-making to wade through a mound of paperwork. (Even quicker, though possibly less efficient in the long run, is the late Friday afternoon use of the "circular file.")

GASP
Grip, **A**im, **S**tance, **P**osture

Before you swing that golf club, here's what to think about, according to most golf instructors.

CIGAR
Controls, **I**nstrumentation, **G**as, **A**ltitude indicator, **R**adio

What a pilot needs to check before takeoff.

PEP
Projection, **E**nunciation, **P**ronunciation

A good TV anchorperson scores high in these three skills.

FACE
"**F**," "**A**," "**C**," and "**E**"

The musical notes that every piano student learns in the first few months. From the bottom of the musical staff to the top, these are the notes in the four spaces.

ST. WAPNIACL
State, **T**reasury, **W**ar, **A**ttorney General, **P**ost Office, **N**avy, **I**nterior, **A**griculture, **C**ommerce, **L**abor

An absolute godsend for pre–World War II school-children, who memorized the names of all the departments of the federal government *and* their chronological order by simply remembering the name of one saint.

BRAIN MEASUREMENT

GIFT
Group **I**nventory for **F**inding Creative **T**alent

A paper and pencil psychological test that evaluates such areas as imagination, independence, and range of different interests. Elementary school kids who score high on the GIFT are considered unusually creative and may be put in gifted classes.

SAGES
Screening **A**ssessment for **G**ifted **E**lementary **S**tudents

A more traditional group test for giftedness that checks on such areas as reasoning and school-acquired information. An individually administered section looks at a student's creativity, or at least at the part involved in fluency of ideas.

APART
Adelphi **P**arent **A**dministered **R**eadiness **T**est

One of the big questions about preschoolers is when will a child be ready to enter first grade. Many educators believe that children who start too early are at serious risk for all sorts of later problems, both academic and social. But many parents feel that their child has been slighted if a school suggests that their kid wait an extra year before entering. APART is a twenty-minute test that parents themselves can give their child to find out if Jason or Jennifer is ready for the big step up.

STUDENT LOANS

PLUS
Parent **L**oans to **U**ndergraduate **S**tudents

If you have a financially dependent son or daughter who's enrolled in a higher-education program at least half time, the federal government will lend you up to $4,000 a year at a low interest rate and give you up to ten years to pay it back. There's also ALAS—**A**uxiliary **L**oans to **A**ssist **S**tudents.

HEAL
Health **E**ducation **A**ssistance **L**oan

This federal loan goes directly to a student enrolled in a health-profession program at a school which participates in the HEAL program. The student doesn't have to begin paying back the money until nine months after she or he finishes school and can take from ten to twenty-five years to pay the money back.

LETTER WRITING

SWAK
Sealed **W**ith **A** **K**iss

After a yearning young woman wrote and sealed a long letter to her soldier or sailor fighting overseas, she would often press her bright-lipsticked lips to the seal of the envelope or write S.W.A.K. instead. Englishwomen did the same, with a slight variation—SWANK (**S**ealed **W**ith **A** **N**ice **K**iss).

HOLLAND
Home **O**ur **L**ove **L**asts **A**nd **N**ever **D**ies
   Or
Have **O**n **L**ittle **L**ace **A**nd **N**o **D**rawers

A more impassioned alternative, one way or the other, that some young women on the home front used to seal their

letters. Their boyfriends might answer with NORWICH—
KNickers **O**ff **R**eady **W**hen **I** **C**ome **H**ome.

BOLTOP
Better **O**n **L**ips **T**han **O**n **P**aper

In peacetime, several playful acronyms were substituted.
BOLTROP was one and SWALBAKWS (**S**ealed **W**ith **A** **L**ick
Because **A** **K**iss **W**ouldn't **S**tick) was another. FLAK (**F**ondest
Love **A**nd **K**isses) recalled Nazi artillery and general nagging
in peacetime.

Winging It

JATO
Jet **A**ssisted **T**ake**O**ff

A method of getting an airplane off the ground, first used
just after World War II, which utilizes one or more rocket
engines to boost the plane's power. These jato units are typically discarded after the airplane is fully airborne. The British
term for this process is ATO—**A**ssisted **T**ake**O**ff.

STOL
Short **T**ake**O**ffs and **L**andings

A type of aircraft specially designed in the '50s with high
lift devices and extra jets so that it could use the short runways
commonly found at a STOLport—an airport found in urban
areas where space is at a premium.

There's also the VTOL (**V**ertical **T**ake**O**ffs and **L**andings),
a class of airplane that includes the helicopter. The VTOL uses
a VTOLport or Vertiport.

In the '70s, when people were more aware of environmen-
tal issues, the RTOL (**R**educed **T**ake**O**ff and **L**andings) plane
was created. It used less than half the standard runway. Also in
the '70s came the QSTOL (**Q**uiet **S**hort **T**ake**O**ff and **L**andings),
built in response to concern about noise pollution.

WOE
Withdrawal **O**f **E**nthusiasm

You know how tired we passengers get of hearing that
same old "Welcome aboard" speech every time we fasten our

airplane seat belts? Hey, sometimes the pilots feel the same way about doing the spiel two or three times a day. They call it the WOE attitude.

CAVU
Ceiling **A**nd **V**isibility **U**nlimited

What every pilot hopes for—he or she can see more than 10,000 feet up and ten miles all around.

APEX
Advance **P**urchase **EX**cursion

A system of airfare discounting first used in 1971. You paid for your tickets three to six weeks early and promised not to cancel. In exchange for this early guaranteed money, the airline was willing to give you quite a break on the price.

FEAR
Failure-**E**ffect **A**nalysis **R**eport

The kind of memo that might be handed in after a flying student experienced BAT (**B**lind **A**pproach **T**raining).

RADIOWAVES

WILCO
will + comply

During World War II, radio operators had a standard set of codewords to facilitate communication. When one operator had finished sending a message, the second operator would answer, "Roger." This was the codeword standing for the letter "R." And "R" meant "received," which assured the first operator that his or her message had gotten through.

When the first operator heard "Roger," he or she would reply, "Roger Wilco," meaning, "I know you've gotten my message and I'm signing off."

Civilians appropriated much of the military language during the war and "Roger Wilco" was no exception. On the home front, it meant, "Yeah, I'll do it."

More recently, Roger Wilco has been used facetiously for

the name of the bumbling but nonetheless effective hero of a highly popular series of computer games called *Space Quest*.

REACT
Radio **E**mergency **A**ssociation **C**itizens **T**eams
A volunteer association of CB radio operators.

MARS
Military **A**ffiliate **R**adio **S**ystem
A network of amateur radio operators spread throughout the world that helps the military in emergency situations.

HAWAII

PIO
Press **I**nformation **O**fficer
Reporters assigned to cover fires in Hawaii wear hats with PIO printed on them. "Pio" means "to extinguish" in Hawaiian. A little in-joke that goes right by the tourists.

ALOHA
Aboriginal **L**ands **O**f **H**awaiian **A**ncestry
Now owned by Americans, Filipinos, Chinese, Japanese, etc., etc. The members of ALOHA work to regain their lost property.

ENVIRONMENTAL MATTERS

REJASING
REusing **J**unk **A**s **S**ometh**ING** else
An early word for recycling.

LITEK
LIght **TECH**nology Corporation (with a modernistic "K" for the "CH")
Imagine a light bulb that lasted ten years and, at the same time, used 70 percent less energy than a regular bulb. It was actually invented by an American physicist named Donald D.

Hollister. Litek is the name of his company, trademarked in 1976, that manufactures these fluorescent bulbs.

ADAPTS
Air **D**eployable **A**nti**P**ollution **T**ransfer **S**ystem

This is the system used in the mid '70s by the U.S. Coast Guard to clear up oil spills by pumping oil out of a stranded or damaged tanker into other vessels or into rubber tanks.

BASEBALL

ROSIE
Rooters **O**rganized to **S**timulate **I**nterest and **E**nthusiasm

An organization of women baseball fans in Cincinnati, the city of Pete Rose.

SABR ("Say-ber")
Society for **A**merican **B**aseball **R**esearch

Statistics are the soul of baseball talk. In 1971, L. Robert Davids created a group to measure and analyze baseball stats that has become so well known that in 1984 it generated its own noun: sabermetrics. SABR holds regular meetings and a convention of national scope. Its computer database must be a wonder to behold.

RBI ("Ribbie")
Run **B**atted **I**n

Though you'll more commonly hear RBI pronounced as an initialism, this common baseball statistic's nickname is "Ribbie." A player typically gets an RBI every time he hits the ball and a run is scored because of that hit. (There are some exceptions, but let's keep this nontechnical.) The slugging stars of the game can earn more than a hundred RBIs in a season. As in horse racing, only rarely does any competitor win the Triple Crown. In baseball, that consists of having the top batting average, the top number of home runs, and the top RBI, all in the same year. Carl Yastrzemski of the Boston Red Sox was the last Triple Crown winner in 1967.

WHIP
Walks and **H**its (divided by) **I**nnings **P**itched
One of the conjured-up statistics used by people playing fantasy baseball. Once you've picked your fantasy team (typically made up of actual players on many different real teams), you see how each of "your" players has done each week in the real games going on around the country. Your fantasy team's score is based on the performance of each of your players.

The WHIP is one way each of your pitchers' performances is measured. You take the number of walks and hits he has allowed the other team and divide that by the number of innings he has pitched. The better the pitcher, the lower his WHIP.

Slurve
slider + curve
The slurve is a pitch that curves more than the typical slider and is faster than the typical curve ball. However, the term has also been said to refer to a famous pitch of Don Drysdale's, which was supposedly one part slobber and two parts curve.

WUNY
Wait **U**ntil **N**ext **Y**ear
An end-of-the-season term.

Here's a handful of happy matings of names and the organizations they stand for.

CAGE
Convicts' **A**ssociation for a **G**ood **E**nvironment

FIB
Fishermen's **I**nformation **B**ureau

FIT
Fashion **I**nstitute of **T**echnology

AFIRE
Association of **F**undamentalist **I**nstitutions of **R**eligious **E**ducation

POND
Parents **O**f **N**ear **D**rowning

AURA
Association of **U**niversities for **R**esearch in **A**stronomy

EEL
English **E**lectric **L**imited

SHARE
Society to **H**elp **A**void **R**edundant **E**ffort

STRAYS
Society **T**o **R**escue **A**nimals **Y**ou've **S**urrendered

DOGMAD
Dissatisfied **O**wners of **G**eneral **M**otors **A**utomotive **D**iesels

BASS
Bass **A**nglers **S**portsman **S**ociety

BURP
Brewers **U**nited for **R**eal **P**otables

OARS
Outdoor and **A**quatic **R**ecreation **S**pecialists

SMASH
Santa **M**onica **A**lternative **S**chool **H**ouse

HISS
Herpetological **I**nformation **S**earch **S**ystems

TUBE
Terminating **U**nfair **B**roadcasting **E**xcesses

UNWRAP
UNited **W**e **R**esist **A**dditional **P**ackaging

WHIGLE
West **H**ollywood **I**nstitute of **G**ay and **L**esbian **E**ducation

WHOAA
Walking **H**orse **O**wners' **A**ssociation of **A**merica

Ready to hop all over the map and the timeline? Here's a true scattering of acronymic happenings.

RASHI
RAbbi **SH**lomo Yitzhaq**I**

The pen name of Jewish philosopher and linguist Solomon ben Isaac of Troyes. Living in medieval France, he founded a major school of Talmudic study whose explanations of the language and intent of the Bible and its learned commentaries are still studied today.

OEDIPUS
Oxford **E**nglish **D**ictionary—**I**ntegration **P**roofing and **U**pdating **S**ystem

Many word mavens would love to own their own copy of the *Oxford English Dictionary*—it's *the* authority on the history of any given word. One small problem. It's sixteen enormous volumes long. Some of us have broken down and bought a home version, but the two-book set is bigger than many bread boxes, plus you've literally got to use a magnifying glass to read the print.

Computer technology to the rescue. The *OED* has now been stored on three featherweight CDs and its editors have given this version the fond nickname of "Oedipus Lex."

CoBrA
Copenhagen, **Br**ussels, and **A**msterdam

An art movement that flourished in the aforementioned cities from 1948–1951. Karel Appel, Pierre Alechinsky, and Christian Dotrement were highly influential because their paintings expressed the postwar revolt against cerebral art and an emotional response to the horrors of World War II that was being felt by artists throughout the world. CoBrA style included violent brushwork, saturated color, folk art imagery, and intense emotionality, with ecstasy and horror being common themes.

FIDO
Freaks, **I**rregulars, **D**efects, **O**ddities

Numismatist Edward Wallace coined (ahem) this term in 1966 to refer to coins minted with an error. Since such coins are rarities, a fido can be worth a lot of money to an alert collector.

DASH
Downtown **A**rea **S**hort **H**op

A shuttle service in Los Angeles designed to lessen traffic congestion in the center of the city.

RESCUE
Referring **E**mergency **S**ervice for **C**onsumers' **U**ltimate **E**njoyment

The Service Plan of the Recreational Vehicle Dealers of America.

NECCO wafer
New **E**ngland **C**onfectionery **CO**mpany

When you were a kid, did you go for the roll of Necco wafers that came in all the colors of the pastel rainbow? (The flavors were orange, lemon, lime, clove, chocolate, cinnamon, wintergreen, and licorice.) Or did your purist soul direct you to the all-chocolate roll? Little did you know that you were participating in a tradition that started in 1847 when a young Bostonian named Oliver Chase invented the first American candy machine, a lozenge cutter. Chase and Company fed the American public their lozenges for over fifty years and then merged with two other candy companies to become the New England Confectionary Company in 1901. Necco was its trademark and it was stamped on their famous wafers, as it is today.

SNOT
Super **N**auseating **O**bnoxious **T**reat

Since Necco Wafers appeared in 1847, an awful lot of candies have appeared and disappeared in sweet shoppes, grocery stores, and, more recently, 7-11's. Manufacturers are constantly on the lookout for that new shape, flavor, or other twist that will tickle the fancy of our collective sweet tooth.

Kevin Sherman and Lori Basset of the How Can It Be So Sour Company predict that the new wave in candy is repulsiveness. And, believe it or not, their nose-shaped container, oozing a Jellolike sweet substance, is selling quite well. The target buyers, six to twelve year olds, can squeeze and lick green-apple, cherry, or Schnozzberry goo to their hearts' content (and to the gratifying grimaces of their elders).

CUSS
Continental, **U**nion, **S**hell, and **S**uperior
The name of a deep-sea oil-drilling ship owned by these four oil companies. Chances are they don't make a strike on every try.

OPTACON
OPtical-to-**TA**ctile-**CON**verter
Braille is a wonderful invention, but in everyday situations, a blind person is going to be confronted with conventionally printed material that hasn't been translated. The Optacon is an electronic device trademarked in 1970 that uses a small camera to take pictures of print and then converts that information into a pattern of vibrating pins which the blind user can read by touch.

TANDEM
Tibi **A**derit **N**umen **D**ivinum, **E**xpecta **M**odo
Translation from the Latin: God Will Help Thee—Only Wait. This was the motto of Elizabeth Ernestine Antonie, Duchess of Saxony (1681–1766).

EGAD
Electronic **GA**s **D**etector

POETS
Piss **O**ff **E**arly, **T**omorrow's **S**aturday
British for TGIF—**T**hank **G**od **I**t's **F**riday.

KYBO
Keep **Y**our **B**owels **O**pen
American slang from the mid-twentieth century that means, "Stay healthy."

CHAPTER 15

A Little Dictionary
of Portmanteaus

WHEN IS A WORD like a large satchel? When it carries the meaning of two different words within it. So said Lewis Carroll, master of wit and nonsense, in *Through the Looking Glass*. Well, actually he directed Humpty Dumpty to say it when Alice needs help understanding the first verse of "Jabberwocky." She asks what the odd word "slithy" means and Humpty explains that it combines the meanings of slimy and lithe. "Mimsy" turns out to mean miserable and flimsy. He offers her a useful image: "'You see, it's like a portmanteau—there are two meanings packed up into one word.'" The portmanteau itself is a large suitcase with two hinged compartments.

Some of Carroll's little suitcase words have actually entered common use. "Squawk," crafted from squall and squeak in the late nineteenth century, is still used today. So is "chortle," which he blended from chuckle and snort.

In the hundred-plus years since the inventor of Alice tailor-made a language for Wonderland, we English speakers have been following his lead with great enthusiasm. Journalists, plant and animal hybridizers, teenaged slang slingers, advertisers, and almost everyone else telescopes word pairs with abandon and, often, wit. We're so used to some of these blendings that we forget that "charbroil," for example, was manufactured from charcoal + broil or that a "cyborg" is the product of cybernetic + organism. And some portmanteaus, in fact, some of the most widely used informal ones, don't actually pack in two meanings but instead combine two words that mean close to the same thing ("Posilutely" from positive + absolutely, or "Humongous" from huge + tremendous). The effect is to stress the concept, to give it a sort of double whammy.

Another interesting portmanteau phenomenon is the creation of new word parts. "Workaholic" was created from work + alcoholic. Since then, the ending -aholic has been added to so many words (chocolate, food, book, etc., etc.) that it's moving toward becoming as acceptable a root as *graph* or *phobe*. Another example is -athon, taken originally from marathon. Seems like people are always participating in "jogathons" or "swimathons" these days.

This little dictionary contains approximately 200 portmanteaus. In addition, there are approximately 125 more portmanteaus to be found in various other chapters of the book. And this very minute there's probably another one being born in the fertile brain of a correspondent for *The New York Times* or the equally irreverent imagination of a rapping teenager.

*** A ***

Abuzak
abuse + Muzak
    Teen slang for elevator music.

Adhocracy
ad hoc + democracy
    Futurologist Alvin Toffler's term for a team created to manage any sort of a short-term project. The task force is disbanded as soon as the project is completed.

Advertorial
advertisement + editorial
    Instead of publicizing a product, this ad pitches a point of view.

Agitprop (1934)
agitation + propaganda
   The name of a department of the Russian Communist party. Many Russian towns had local branches responsible for producing propaganda. In the United States, the term is used to refer to a style of theater, common in the 1930s, that extolled the Communist way of life and encouraged workers to revolt.

Agrimation (1987)
agriculture + automation
   The use of robots for farming.

Alegar
ale + vinegar
   Vinegar that's made from ale.

Altazimuth (1860)
altitude + azimuth
   An astronomical instrument, commonly a telescope, mounted so that it can be used either vertically or horizontally. It was used to determine the position of a heavenly body. Invented by a Professor Airy.

Ambisextrous
ambidextrous + bisexual
   Slang term for bisexuality, using double-handedness to stress double-sexedness.

Amerasian
American + Asian
   Of mixed American and Asian descent. Originally used to describe children of Oriental women and American servicemen stationed in Japan and Korea. Patterned after Eurasian.

Amerind (1900)
American + Indian
   A term invented by early anthropologists for an individual of native American descent. The term includes those natives from Alaska as well as the lower forty-eight states.

Avionics (1949)
aviation + electronics
Coined by the magazine *Aviation Week* to refer to the application of electronics to aeronautics. Radar is an example.

*** B ***

Ballute
balloon + parachute
Parachute jumpers often have this small balloonlike device that helps keep them in position until the major chute opens.

Barococo
baroque + rococo
The fusion of two similar styles of art and architecture, which is likely to result in elaboration piled on excess ornamented with curlicues.

Beefalo (1974)
beef + buffalo
A crossbreed developed by D. C. Basolo, a rancher in California. (*Also see* Cattalo and Yakow.)

Beefish (1974)
beef + fish
Ground beef and fish mixed together and used for making burgers and other dishes requiring minced meat.

Bizotic
bizarre + exotic
Teen slang word for weird.

Bodacious (1845)
bold + audacious (also possibly from an earlier English word "boldacious")
U.S. dialect meaning complete, thorough, as in "She's bodacious unreasonable when you break a dish."
More recently, bodacious has become a popular slang term for astounding, as in: "What a bodacious babe!"

Bosox
Boston Red Sox
A nickname for this professional major league baseball team. (*Also see* Chisox.)

Boatel (1956)
boat + hotel (also spelled "botel")
Can mean a hotel on an island that can be reached only by boat or a hotel that caters to people on a boating holiday (usually found where boats dock). Can also be a ship that has the facilities of a hotel on board.

Bomphlet (1944)
bomb + pamphlet
During World War II, some of the Allied raids over enemy territory involved dropping propaganda leaflets instead of bombs. The term was coined by A. P. Herbert, a British author. He referred to the airmen involved as "bomphleteers."

Booboisie
boob + bourgeoisie
H. L. Mencken's derisive nickname for the American middle class.

Breathalyser (1960 trademark)
breath + analyse + -er
When you blow into the plastic bag of this device, your breath passes over a length of crystals. If they turn green, you're arrested for drunk driving.

Broccoflower
broccoli + cauliflower
A chartreuse-colored blend of the two vegetables.

Brunch
breakfast + lunch
One of the earliest blended words—from 1900 or thereabouts.

Buel
body + fuel
  Recent teen slang for voracious eating, as in "Let's go buel on some pizza."

Bulimarexia (1976)
bulimia + anorexia
  A psychological disorder characterized by alternate cycles of gorging and disgorging that is most commonly found among young women.

*** C ***

Cabatoe
cabbage + potato
  An actual plant, offered in the catalog of Lakeland Nurseries of Hanover, Pennsylvania, that grows potatoes under the ground and cabbage on the surface.

Cablecast (1968)
cablevision (cable + television) + telecast
  Television programming originating on cable channels— not taken from retransmission of commercial broadcast signals (noncable television).

Camcorder (1982)
camera + recorder
  A portable video camera with a built-in audio and video recorder.

Camporee
camp + jamboree
  Summer Boy Scout meeting.

Canalimony
canal + alimony
  Twenty-one million dollars in compensation paid to Colombia (former owner of Panama) by the United States in 1921 after the United States had encouraged Panamanian nationalists to revolt against Colombia and become a separate nation. (The United States had done so in order to secure the

right to build the Panama Canal, which Colombia had refused to grant.)

Canogganing
canoeing + tobogganing

An odd winter sport where people in canoes slide down snow-covered hills.

Caplet (1979)
capsule + tablet

After the Tylenol scare when someone put poison into painkilling capsules, Johnson & Johnson developed this coated tablet shaped like a capsule in order to protect its customers.

Carbeque
car + barbeque

When a car is beyond repair, the remains can be disposed of by using this machine which rotates the carcass over a fire.

Cattalo
cattle + buffalo

The first successful cross between these two animals was accomplished in the 1880s by a rancher in Texas.

Celebutante (1986)
celebrity + debutante

A young woman who becomes famous on her first or "debut" appearance in the media. A fairly recent example is Brigitte Nielsen, the twenty-two-year-old statuesque Danish model turned actress who married Sylvester Stallone and became the instant darling of the gossip magazines.

Celtuce
celery + lettuce

A vegetable bred from lettuce whose stalks taste like celery.

Chicagorilla
Chicago + gorilla

Slang for a gangster gunman.

Chicom
Chinese + Communist
A derogatory term from the 1950s. President Eisenhower liked this word.

Chimponaut
chimpanzee + astronaut
Experimental passengers sent into space.

Chisox
Chicago White Sox
A nickname for this American League baseball team.

Cigaroot
cigarette + cheroot
A facetious term for a cigarette. (A cheroot is a cigar square-cut at both ends.)

Civex (1978)
civilian + extraction
Nuclear wastes often contain plutonium, which can be used by terrorist groups to make nuclear weapons. Civex is a system that processes the wastes without producing plutonium.

Clamato Juice
clam + tomato (juices)

Clousy
cloudy + lousy
A weather judgment.

Cockapoo
cocker spaniel + poodle
A crossbreed.

Cockaterr
cocker spaniel + terrier
Another one.

Compuserve
computer + service
The largest current computerized information service in the United States. As a member, you can exchange computer

data files, shop, make airline reservations, find out the weather in southern Utah, leave messages for fellow subscribers, etc., etc.

Comsymp
Communist + sympathizer
    A synonym for a fellow traveler or a pinko rather than an actual member of the Communist party.

Confab
confer + confabulation
    Another oldie—from 1901. Until 1925, carnival people used it as a slang word for a talk. Now it's used generally.

Contrail (1945)
condensation + trail
    The visible trail of vapor left in the sky by airplanes, often in very cold weather.

Cowbot (1987)
cowboy + robot
    A mechanism designed to feed and milk a herd of dairy cows. It even cleans the machinery.

Cranapple juice
cranberry + apple (juices)
    There are many similar blends: Cranorange, Cranprune, Cranraspberry, Cranstrawberry, Crangrape and Cranblueberry.

Cremains
cremated + remains

Croodle
crouch + cuddle
    A word found in some Victorian novels.

Cybernation (1962)
cybernetics + automation
    The adaptation of equipment to computers so that factories, economic prediction, and even social analysis can be run

by computers. Term coined by Donald N. Michael, a communications expert.

Cyberpunk (1980s)
cybernetics + punk
   A leading-edge school of science fiction characterized by a bleak high-technological future and nihilistic or antisocial characters who often interface in primal ways with artificial intelligences.

*** D ***

Daddylac
daddy + cadillac
   Teen slang for an expensive car that parents buy for their child.

Dakoming
Dakota + Wyoming

Dancercise (1967 trademark—used generally in early 1980s)
dance + exercise
   High kicking, jumping, and jiving to music when used as physical exercise.

Dat
dog + cat
   A crossbreeding hoax.

Datamation (1963)
data + automation
   The processing of data automatically. Term used especially in industry and banking and is also the name of a well-known trade journal.

Datel (1967)
data + telex
   In England, the post office offers high-speed transmitting of data by computer.

Delmarvia (or DelMarVa)
Delaware + Maryland + Virginia
   The peninsula composed of parts of these three states.

Detectionary
detective + dictionary
   A reference for mystery buffs.

Dickel
dime + nickel

Diesohol (1978)
diesel + alcohol
   A blend used as a fuel in diesel engines.

Disastrophe (1976)
disaster + catastrophe

Dockaminium (or Dockanominium) (1984)
dock + condominium
   A condo unit that is sold with a berth for a boat. Commonly part of a complex that includes a boating clubhouse.

Dogolatry (1987)
dog + idolatry
   A term of social criticism coined by newspaper columnist Colman McCarthy. People who care more about pampering their pets than helping other people survive are guilty of this vice.

Dolphinarium (early 1970s)
dolphin + aquarium
   There's one in Pittsburgh and another in London.

Droned
drink + stoned
   Modern teen slang for being in a haze due to drugs or alcohol.

Droob
drip + boob
  Australian slang for someone slow and dull.

Dymaxion (1929)
dynamism + maximum + -ion
  A term coined by business associates of R. Buckminster
Fuller, which they called "a word-portrait" of him and his
work. It means to accomplish the most using the least. He
used the term for several of his inventions: the Dymaxion car,
the Dymaxion house, etc.

*** E ***

Ecotage (1972)
ecological + sabotage
  Acts committed by certain extremists in the conservation
movement who might pull down billboards or put sand in the
gas tanks of landmovers to stop developers from taking over
wild areas.

Educrat (1968)
educator + bureaucrat
  Someone high in the "edbiz."

Eroduction (1965)
erotic + production
  A Japanese sexploitation film that includes violence, particularly torture.

Eurailpass (1961)
European + railroad + pass
  A discount train ticket sold to tourists. By 1970, more
than 100,000 were sold yearly.

Exercycle (1967 trademark)
exercise + bicycle

*** F ***

Fantabulous
fantastic + fabulous

Freezoree
freeze + jamboree
  Winter Boy Scout meeting.

Frogurt
frozen yogurt

Fuelish (1975)
fuel + foolish
  Using more fuel than necessary—an energy crisis term.

*** G ***

Gasid (indigestion)
gas + acid indigestion
  That burning sensation.

Gasohol (1974 trademark)
gasoline + alcohol
  Used as fuel in automobiles. (*Also see* Diesohol.)

Gastroporn (1986)
gastronomy + pornography
  A specialized baroque language used to titillate the reader's taste buds. It adorns the menus of fancy restaurants. Similar language coupled with lush photographs often accompanies recipes in gourmet cookbooks and magazines. An example: ". . . a sumptuous plateful of honey-and-orange lacquered duck studded with coarsely crushed spices and accompanied by a prune puree happily laced with shredded lime zest."

Gayola
gay + payola
  The blackmail money paid by homosexuals who haven't come out and are threatened with exposure to the media.

Geep (1963)
goat + sheep (also called a Shoat)
  The nonviable fetus of a female goat impregnated by a ram.

Gestapaches (1944)
Gestapo + Apaches
   In World War II, French collaborators (often ex-cons) who tracked down and turned over to the Gestapo many Allied officers who had parachuted into France. The term was used during war-criminal trials where many of these cutthroats were convicted.

Girlcott (1963)
girl + boycott
   A boycott mounted against an organization that has shown prejudice toward women.

Guesstimate (sometimes spelled Guestimate)
guess + estimate
   Can mean an estimate made without enough data or arrived at solely by guessing.

*** H ***

Hairologist (1973)
hair + cosmetologist
   Found in very upscale hair salons, this person advises the customer on the healthiest alternative in hair treatment.

Handtector (1972)
hand + detector
   When hijacking became common, airport security came to include electronic screening using this hand-held metal detector.

Happenstantial (1958)
Happenstance (itself a blend of happen + circumstance) + circumstantial
   Accidental.

Hashbury (1960s)
Haight + Ashbury
   Nickname for the hippie district of San Francisco. Also reflects the shortened name for the drug hashish—hash—which was popular during this period.

Helihop (1966)
helicopter + hop
>To travel a short way using a helicopter.

Heliport
helicopter + port

Heliskiing (1976)
helicopter + skiing
>To ski mountains after reaching them by helicopter.

Himbo (1988)
him + bimbo
>An extravagantly good-looking man who has neither intelligence nor character. A slang term invented by the media for the male version of a bimbo.

Hozey (1920s)
honey + floozy
>A lady of light reputation.

*** I ***

Imeldific (1988)
Imelda + terrific
>Actually coined by the shoe-stockpiling wife of Philippine President Ferdinand Marcos. *The Boston Globe* quotes her as saying, "I was born ostentatious. They will list my name in the dictionary someday. They will use 'Imeldific' to mean ostentatious extravagance."

Infanticipatory
infant + anticipatory
>A blend meaning pregnant coined jokingly by Walter Winchell.

Instamatic (1964 trademark)
instant + automatic
>The Eastman-Kodak camera that was designed to be picked up and snapped—no focusing.

Interrobang (1962)
interrogation point (a question mark) + bang (printers'
slang for an exclamation point)

A mark of punctuation combining the "?" and the "!" It
was invented by Martin K. Spector and first used in the late
1960s to express a question and an exclamation at the same
time. Example: Who'd a thunk it?"

*** J ***

Jackalope
jackrabbit + antelope

Pictures of this supposed hybrid, typically showing a rab-
bit with antlers, can still be found sometimes on postcards in
the Southwest.

Jamoke (1946)
java + mocha

Post–World War II slang for the kind of coffee served in
the armed forces—strong and black.

Jargonaut (1963)
jargon + astronaut

A person addicted to using jargon. The blend is probably
influenced by the word "argot" (meaning lingo).

Jazzercise (1977 trademark)
jazz + exercise

Modeled on dancercise, a similar exercise-to-music program of the '60s. Jazzercise was one of many such programs
popular in the '80s.

Juco (1987)
junior + college

Juco sports figures are players in their first two years of
college.

*** L ***

Laurasia
Laurentians (a term for the mountains of North America)
+ Eurasia

A supercontinent made up of Asia, Europe, and North
America that scientists believe existed some sixty million
years ago.

Leopon (1967)
leopard + lion
    The result of the mating of a lioness and a leopard.

Liger (1988)
lion + tiger
    The enormous offspring of a male lion and a female tiger.
In the wild, natural aversion between species prevents such
crossbreedings but circus animal trainers, always in the market for marvels, raise different cat species together in order to
encourage them to mate. Zoos object to creating such "junk
animals" from endangered species instead of preserving pure
populations. (*Also see* Tiglon and Tili.)

Limequat
lime + kumquat
    A hybrid.

*** M ***

Macon (1940s)
mutton + bacon
    Bacon made from mutton instead of pork. Used in World
War II.

Maglev (1968)
magnetic + levitation
    A train that uses magnetic force to lift above the track.
This reduces friction so much that the train can move more
than two hundred miles an hour using very little fuel.

Mailgram (1970 trademark)
mail + telegram
    A letter sent electronically by the U.S. Postal Service and
delivered by a regular mail carrier.

Mediamorphosis (1971)
media + metamorphosis
    When the media twist the facts.

Medicaid (1966)
medical + aid
    Government program to provide hospital care for the
poor.

Medicare (1962)
medical + care
   Government health insurance for the disabled and elderly.

Meld (1939)
melt + weld (or perhaps from English dialect word "melder")
   To merge or blend.

Mellotron (1968)
mellow + electronic
   A musical instrument used in England that can produce the sounds of the orchestra. A computer programs its electronic output.

Migronaut (1970)
migrant + astronaut
   People fleeing their land who have to keep moving from country to country because no government will allow them to stay.

Mocktail
mock + cocktail
   A Shirley Temple, for instance.

Moondoggle
moon + boondoggle
   A flimsy project that uses up a lot of money.

Moped (1952)
motor + pedal
   A vehicle with two wheels and two options for go-power: pedaling and motoring. Originally a Swedish word that was taken up in England in 1956. The vehicle itself generated a legal controversy regarding whether minors should be licensed to use it.

Motel (1925)
motor + hotel

*** N ***

Neorican (formerly Nuyorican) (1972)
New Yorker + Puerto Rican
A New Yorker from Puerto Rico.

Newt
new + recruit
Used in the army and the factory during World War II.

*** O ***

Octopush (1970)
octopus + push
British form of hockey played in water where the ball is propelled along the bottom of the pool.

Oilberg (1977)
oil + iceberg
The major part of an oil spill is below the surface, much like that of an iceberg. Hence the name.

Orature (1981)
oral + literature
A name for the literature of a culture that does not commit its stories and poetry to paper.

Oxbridge
Oxford + Cambridge
The equivalent in England to our Ivy League schools. Novelist Virginia Woolf used the term in her 1929 lecture series later published as *A Room of One's Own*. Oxbridge was coined eighty years earlier by novelist William Thackeray as a fictional name for a university.

*** P ***

Parafoil (1967)
parachute + airfoil
A parachute developed by the navy for greater safety that glides down through the air rather than simply falling vertically.

Parakiting (1970)
parachute + kite + "ing"
Sometimes called Parasailing, the sport of sailing through the air with a parachute while being towed by a motor boat or other motorized vehicle.

Paralympics (1965)
paraplegic + Olympics
An international sports event for differently abled people. In 1976, more than four hundred athletes from fifty-two countries attended the competition.

Paratrooper (1943)
parachute + trooper
Soldiers dropped onto the battlefields of World War II from parachutes.

Permafrost (1943)
permanent + frost
Subsoil that remains below 0 degrees centigrade throughout the year, typically found in arctic regions.

Polyglass (1968)
polyester + fiberglass
A material for making automobile tires that gives better traction and longer life for the tread.

Populuxe
popular + luxury
Design critic Thomas Hine coined this term to describe what he considered the melding of vulgar design and conspicuous consumption that characterized the popular taste of the decade 1955–1965.

Pornotopia
pornograpic + utopia
A landscape that is perfect for activities of a pornographic nature. (No stinging insects?)

Pregaphone (late '80s)
pregnant + telephone
Pressing this miniature megaphone to her stomach, an expectant mother can speak to her fetus. Even fathers can use it.

Prissy (1895)
probably from prim + sissy
Prudish and priggish.

Psychedelicatessen (1966)
psychedelic + delicatessen
Synonymous with head shop.

*** Q ***

Quackupuncture (1973)
quack + acupuncture
Dishonest practice of the pinprick science.

*** R ***

Racon
radar + beacon
In World War II, stations functioning similarly to lighthouses but using radar instead of light.

Repunit (1970)
repeating + unit
A number with one or more of the same integers. Examples: 11, 222, 3333.

Rotovator (1970 British trademark)
rotary + cultivator
The English version of the Rototiller, a machine that breaks up soil.

Ruckus (1890)
ruction (an insurrection) + rumpus (an uproar)
Originated in America.

*** S ***

Samink (1972)
sable + mink
    Mink breeders have long sought to create a mutated mink with the qualities of sable, since sable is worth far more money.

Scrapnel (1972)
scrap + shrapnel
    The small pieces of metal contained in a homemade bomb that scatter in the explosion.

Scrowsy (1930)
screwy + lousy
    Student slang for contemptible or absurd.

Sexpionage (1976)
sex + espionage
    Coined by British journalist David Lewis to refer to a particular form of intelligence gathering.

Sexploitation (1941 and revived 1966)
sex + exploitation
    A way of boosting sales in the arts, especially in movies.

Shunpike (1963)
shun + turnpike
    To take a trip by car with the purpose of enjoying the scenery. Thus freeways and their ilk are avoided.

Skyjack (1961)
sky + hijack

Simulcast (1948)
simultaneous + broadcast
    Originally meant to broadcast by radio and TV at the same time. Its first use was in sports reporting. Now also means to transmit a TV program on more than one channel at the same time.

Skort
skirt + short

Skurfing (early '60s)
skating + surfing
   Synonym for skateboarding.

Slimnastics (1967)
slim + gymnastics
   An exercise program that helps with weight loss.

Slurb
slum + suburb
   The area just outside a large city that is filled with used-car lots, government and other cheap housing, and is interspersed with gas stations.

Smaze (1953)
smoke + haze
   Another word for smog.

Smice
smoke + ice

Smog (1905)
smoke + fog
   Coined by Dr. H. A. des Voeux, honorary treasurer of the Coal Smoke Abatement Society during a speech he gave at a meeting of the Public Health Congress in London.

Smust
smoke + dust

Snofari (1970)
snow + safari
   Traveling through a snowy region on a bobsledlike contraption with skis in front and tank tracks in back.

Snurfing (1970)
snow + surfing
   Sailing over the snow while standing sideways on a special board and holding on to a safety line.

Spansule
span + capsule
   The technical name for the medicinal capsule filled with "tiny time pills" that releases small amounts of a drug continuously over a period of hours.

Splanch (1961)
split level + ranch
   A house design combining both architectural styles.

Spork (1976)
spoon + fork
   A single plastic utensil with the bowl of a spoon and a short version of the tines of a fork on the tip.

Sprog
spawn + frog
   British air force slang during World War II for a very green recruit.

Squiggle
squirm + wiggle
   A scribble.

Staplepuncture (1974)
staple + acupuncture
   A form of acupuncture used for aiding dieters. Staples are inserted into certain parts of the outer ear where it is claimed the obesity nerve endings lie. The dieter can twist the staples whenever the urge to overeat threatens.

Stoked (late '80s)
stunned + ·choked (or perhaps derived from the phrase "stoked up")
   Teen slang for thrilled.

Swacket
sweater + jacket
A term used in the fashion industry when referring to a sweater that buttons like a jacket.

Sweave
swerve + weave
Current teen slang for the inability to walk in a straight line.

*** T ***

Tangelo (1904)
tangerine + pomelo
A hybrid fruit created from the tangerine crossed with a type of grapefruit called a pomelo or shaddock.

Tangemon
tangerine + lemon
A hybrid of the two fruits.

Tarmac (1903 trademark)
tar + macadam
A material combining crushed rock and tar that is used to pave roads. Since it is often used at airports, a late '80s journalistic coinage spoke of politicians or diplomats who were constantly hopping on a jet as "tarmacking."

Telex (1932)
teleprinter + exchange
Belonging to the telex exchange means one can send a printed message (using public telephone lines) to another printer which prints out the message for the receiver.

Tensegrity (1959)
tensional + integrity
R. Buckminster Fuller coined this term for a principle of construction that he used in creating the geodesic dome.

Terrorilla (1980s)
terrorism + guerrilla
The style of warfare waged by terrorists and guerrilla fighters in southern Lebanon. The word was created by the Israeli forces experiencing this opposition.

Tiglon (1927)
tiger + lion
   The offspring of a male tiger and a female lion. (*Also see* Liger.)

Tili
tiglon + liger
   The offspring of two hybrid animals, the liger coming from a female tiger crossed with a male lion and the tiglon coming from a male tiger crossed with a female lion. (*Also see* Liger.)

Tinner (since 1900)
tea + dinner
   British slang.

Toreador
torero + matador
   Coined by composer Georges Bizet for his opera *Carmen*.

Transistor (1948)
transfer + resistor
   An electronic device that transfers an electrical signal across a resistor, which amplifies the signal.

Trog
trek + slog (probably)
   Originally used in the army to describe walking wearily and picked up by the civilian world in the '70s.

Tudorbethan
Tudor + Elizabethan
   A style of furniture common in sixteenth- and seventeenth-century England, which included large dignified forms in wood elaborately carved.

Tyco
Tylenol + Codeine
   A pharmacy term.

*** U ***

Urgicenter (1987)
urgent (care) + center
 A medical clinic that operates on a walk-in, profit-making basis. It's often found in a mall or among stores. Since it is not set up to provide long-term care, only fairly minor medical problems like flu or sprained muscles can be treated. Other nicknames: Doc-in-a-Box, McDoctor, Surgicenter.

*** V ***

Videots
video + idiots
 Coined in the same spirit as "boob tube."

Vodkatini (1955)
vodka + martini
 A martini made with vodka rather than gin.

Vog (1984)
volcanic + fog
 The Hawaiian version of smog, caused from continuous venting of gases from active volcanoes.

Vomatose
vomit + comatose
 Current teen slang for disgusting.

*** W ***

Waitron (1980)
waiter/waitress + neutron
 A jokey genderless name for the person who brings you your espresso.

Wargasm
war + orgasm
 Instantaneous and total war.

Winge (sometimes spelled Whinge) (late '70s)
whine + cringe
 Originally from Australia, meaning to whiningly make excuses.

Winterim (1972)
winter + interim
   A school and sport term describing the winter period between sessions.

Wodge (sometimes spelled Wadge)
wad + wedge
   A British word in use since 1850. It means a lump or a
slice.

*** Y ***

Yakow (1975)
yak + cow
   A crossbreed developed in England similar to the beefalo
but better adapted to wet, cool, higher altitudes.

*** Z ***

Zedonk (1971)
zebra + donkey
   A rare crossbreed from the mating of a male zebra and a
female donkey.

CHAPTER 16

How Clever Can You Get?

IF YOU'VE EVER TRIED to create a witty, apt, or telling acronym, you know how hard it is to produce even a four or five letter word that stands for a sensible phrase. How much harder it must be to assemble a six or seven or eight or even nine letter acronym—especially if you want it to be entertaining and instructive at the same time! In this chapter, we salute some outstanding acronyms crafted by creative hard-playing souls who kept fiddling and noodling, substituting and searching, until at last they'd made the perfect letter-word-phrase match.

Famous name acronyms are some of the hardest to generate. When you want PLATO to be your acronym, PLOTO or PLATA simply won't do. The Greeks, both mythological and real, dominate this field.

ARISTOTLE
Annual **R**eview of **I**nformation and **S**ymposium on the **T**echnology **O**f **T**raining and **L**earning and **E**ducation
OK—maybe not the most graceful way of expressing the idea (three "ands"), but NINE letters?!

SOCRATES
System for **O**rganizing **C**ontent to **R**eview **A**nd **T**each **E**ducational **S**ubjects
Actually, chatty walks were more Socrates' style than a systematic curriculum. Maybe he would have done better to

plan where some of his probing questions were going to lead. Look what happened to him.

PLATO
Programmed **L**ogic for **A**utomatic **T**eaching **O**perations
A 1963 computer-based individual system of instruction.
and
The PLATO Society
Perpetual **L**earning **A**nd **T**eaching **O**rganization
The association holds ongoing study-discussion groups that explore any subject the members have chosen.

SAPPHO
Scientific **A**ctivity **P**redictor with **H**euristic **O**rigins
In other words, a hypothesis-testing program. From Sussex University in England. (The poetess wouldn't have objected to one less *p*. Poetic license, you know.)

EUCLID
Experimental **U**se **C**omputer, **L**ondon **I**ntegrated **D**isplay
An early British system of air traffic control.

CLEOPATRA
Comprehensive **L**anguage for **E**legant **OP**erating System
And **TRA**nslator Design
Another niner, though something less than perfect. The lady evoked, however, makes up for the stretch.

ARTEMIS
Automatic **R**etrieval of **T**ext Through **E**uropean
Multipurpose **I**nformation **S**ystems

ADONIS
Automatic **D**igital **ON**-line **I**nstrumentation **S**ystem
And a handsome system it is.

PROTEUS
Project to **R**esearch **O**bjects, **T**heories, **E**xtraterrestrial and
Unusual **S**ights
The Greek sea god who could assume any shape is a good choice for this very general project.

PANTHEON
Public **A**ccess by **N**ew **T**echnology to **H**ighly **E**laborate **On**-line **N**etworks

SOLOMON
Simultaneous **O**peration **L**inked **O**rdinal **MO**dular Network

PATRICIA
Practical **A**lgorithm **T**o **R**etrieve **I**nformation **C**oded **I**n **A**lphanumeric

Finally—a plain old ordinary twentieth-century person among this exalted bunch. The program is used in British library science.

IACOCCA
I Am **C**hairman **O**f the **C**hrysler **C**orporation of **A**merica

One of your authors' favorite acronyms from the many thousands we've perused. Like all works of genius, grand and small, it seems obvious, even inevitable, now that it stands before us. But how did they ever come up with it??

Many information systems created by programming teams have powerful, aggressive titles. Perhaps there's something about creating whole algorithmic worlds for a living that stimulates conquering hero fantasies.

ASSASSIN
Agricultural **S**ystem for **S**torage **A**nd **S**ubsequent **S**election of **IN**formation

Belongs to Imperial Chemical Industries from England. There's also MIDAS—**M**edical **I**nformation **D**issemination **Us**ing **AS**assin.

AIRLORDS
AIRlines **L**oad **O**ptimization **R**ecording and **D**isplay **S**ystem

STARFIRE
System **T**o **A**ccumulate and **R**etrieve **F**inancial **I**nformation with **R**andom **E**xtraction

EMPIRES
Excerpta Medica Physicians Information Retrieval and
Education Service

CROSSBOW
Computerized Retrieval of Organic Structures Based On
Wiswesser
From the United Kingdom.

CAPTAINS
Character And Pattern Telephone Access Information
Network System

Scientists are sometimes accused of having a limited
sense of humor, but the following acronyms undercut that
cliché.

MARTINI
Massive Analog Recording Technical Instrumentation for
Nebulous Indications
Manufactured by Hewlett Packard.

SCREAMS
Society to Create Rapprochement Among Electrical,
Aeronautical, and Mechanical Engineers

MANIAC
Mathematical Analyzer, Numerical Integrator, And
Computer

CHAOTIC
Computer-Human-Assisted Organization of a Technical
Information Center

COSA NOSTRA
Computer-Oriented System And Newly Organized Storage-
To-Retrieval Apparatus
A sort of all-in-the-family system.

Librarians are another group whose frolic potential has
clearly been underestimated.

SCORPIO
Subject-**C**ontent **O**riented **R**etrieval for **P**rocessing
Information **O**n-line
From the Library of Congress.

CATCALL
Completely **A**utomated **T**echnique for **C**ataloging and
Acquisition of **L**iterature for **L**ibraries

COCTAILS
Chelle **O**'**C**onnell's **T**otally **A**utomated **I**nterlibrary **L**oan
Statistics
From the Health Sciences Library at the State University
of New York at Buffalo. (Maybe the missing "k" is in the
martini pitcher.)

SWIFT LASS
Signal **W**ord **I**ndex of **F**ield and **T**itle—**L**iterature **A**bstract
Specialized **S**earch
and
SWIFT SIR
Signal **W**ord **I**ndex of **F**ield and **T**itle—**S**cientific
Information **R**etrieval

As for those inventive acronym assemblers who can not
only produce five or more letter terms but also have those
terms cleverly mirror the words the acronym stands for, we
can only stand in awe.

BROILER
Biopedagogical **R**esearch **O**rganization on **I**ntensive
Learning **E**nvironment **R**eactions
Do we learn better when the heat's turned up?

PARDON
Pastor's **A**nonymous **R**ecovery-**D**irected **O**rder for **N**ewness
A rehabilitation program for troubled clergymen.

CHAOS
Consortium for the **H**astening of the **A**nnihilation of **O**rganized **S**ociety

ROOSTER
Rural **O**utcry **O**ver **S**exist **T**actics to **E**xterminate **R**oosters
　　A political action group from the north valley of Los Angeles that agitates against a law allowing hens, but not roosters, to be kept in the backyard.

INFANTS
INterested **F**uture **A**ttorneys **N**egotiating for **T**ot **S**afety
　　"Let's do lunch—you bring the Pampers."

BORN FREE
Build **O**ptions, **R**eassess **N**orms, **F**ree **R**oles Through **E**ducational **E**quity

PEQUOD
Pacific **EQU**atorial **O**cean **D**ynamics
　　Let's hope a strikingly oversized and vengeful white whale isn't after this oceangoing group.

WHIMSY
Western **H**umor and **I**rony **M**embership, **S**erial **Y**earbook
　　A publication from Tempe, Arizona.

　　And the last group is simply astonishingly long and fluent at the same time.

AUDACIOUS
AUtomatic **D**irect **AC**cess to **I**nformation with **O**n-line **U**DC **S**ystem

CLASSMATE
Computer **L**anguage to **A**id and **S**timulate **S**cientific, **M**athematical **A**nd **T**echnical **E**ducation

MASQUERADE
Marathon's **A**utomatic **S**ystem for **QUER**y **A**nd **D**ocument **E**ntry

CONSCIENCE
Committee **O**n **N**ational **S**tudent **C**itizenship **I**n **E**very **N**ational **C**ase of **E**mergency

CHAPTER 17

Did They Realize?

Suppose you are a founding member of a national organization of, let's say, teachers. One of your first orders of business is to pick a name. The debate is on. Shall the name be catchy, dignified, or simply informative? After much consideration, a simple title is chosen: National Union of Teachers. Years pass. At first, the organization is a real force for change and then it ossifies into an entrenched and respected member of the Establishment. Then one day, some frustrated member of a more radical group of teachers or a journalist with a jaundiced eye refers to your august body as a bunch of NUTs. Omigod, the leaders mutter at each other. How could we have ever picked such an embarrassing name? However did we miss the denigrating acronym? But it's far too late to change the name now. The Union is too well known. The ruckus, after all, will die down. After everyone has had a chuckle at N.U.T.'s expense.

Although the story you have just read is fiction, the British organization National Union of Teachers and its initialism NUT are absolutely real. Your indefatigable acronym research team (ART) has been amazed at how many truly funny, insulting, bawdy, vulgar, or otherwise inappropriate acronyms can be made from the initials of seemingly straightforward names. The burning question is: Did they do it on purpose?

After many rounds of thought, we return to our first instinctive response—nope. Why would people deliberately insult themselves? Belittle something they believe in? As you snicker through the list that follows, see if you agree.

SAP
Society for **A**merican **P**hilosophy
   You know what they say about deep thinkers with their heads in the clouds?

ACHE
Alabama **C**ommission on **H**igher **E**ducation
   When the state university's test scores call for three Excedrins?

AHA
American **H**istorical **A**ssociation
   Kind of cute, actually, but not very dignified.

NIT
National **I**ntelligence **T**est

ALARM
Assessment of **L**anguage **A**nd **R**eading **M**aturity
   We'd heard that reading scores were getting lower and certainly this is cause for alarm, but actually calling a reading test "Alarm" might be a bit of an overreaction.

DRIFT
Diagnostic **R**etrieval **I**nformation **F**or **T**eachers
   Maybe it's designed to make retrieval difficult?

SLUTS
School of **L**ibrarianship **U**rban **T**ransportation **S**ystem
   From the British Columbia University in Canada. Really.

BOG
Boston **O**pera **G**roup
   If you know anyone who's tried to finance ventures in high art, you know how these productions suck down money like hungry swamps.

LAG
London **A**musement **G**uide
  Pub crawling isn't the half of it.

NAG
Naval **A**dvisory **G**roup
  A guy can't even scrub down a deck without a bunch of jokers getting in the act.

ASS
Army **S**pecial **S**taff

BADS
British **A**ssociation of **D**ermatology and **S**yphilology

PAIN
Pan-**A**merican **I**nstitute of **N**eurology

PROM
Premature (or **P**rolonged) **R**upture **O**f **M**embranes
    From Gynecology

ROT
Remedial **O**ccupational **T**herapy
  Maybe basketweaving can be deleterious to your mental health.

EATM
Exotic **A**nimal **T**raining **M**anagement
  A college program at Moorpark College in California. There are classes in Veterinarian Procedures (EATM 24A), Exotic Animal Health and Safety (EATM 2) and Exotic Animal Nutrition (EATM 3).

CACA
Canadian **A**gricultural **C**hemicals **A**ssociation
  Think of driving by freshly fertilized fields in the hot summer sun.

USDRIP
Upper San Diego River Improvement Project
An unfortunate acronym for the development of a new sewage plant.

PEE
Pressure Environment Equipment
When you gotta go, you gotta go.

BARRF
Bay Area Resource Recovery Facility
Think of the rich odor of your neighborhood recycling center during the third week of a heat wave.

LUST
Leaking Underground Storage Tank
An Environmental Chemistry term. Implosion comes in many forms.

BAR
Bureau of Automotive Repair
Bodywork is thirsty business.

MAP
Missed Approach Procedure
As in, when all else fails, read the directions.

LOST
Law Of the Sea Treaty

ICY
International Cooperation Year (1965)

NAPS
National Alliance of Postal Supervisors
Makes a surprising amount of sense, yes?

WADE
World Association of Document Examiners
And the waves of paperwork never stop coming.

NASSTIE
National Association of State Supervisors of Trade and Industrial Education

RUIN
Regional Urban Information Network
    From Washington, D.C.

ERRS
Environmental Response and Referral Service

CRIMP
Cultural Resources Implementation Monitoring Plan
    Ever tried to run a program with bureaucrats "monitoring" your every move?

SCAG
Southern California Association of Governments
    OK, it's hard running the south half of the sunshine (and moonbeam) state. But shooting up isn't going to solve the inner cities' crisis and the budget crisis and the smog crisis and the . . .

SCAM
Southern California Auto Mart
    This one, according to Oscar Aldridge, the manager who runs the lot, was designed deliberately to get attention. He reported that his clients trusted him so he could have some fun. Mr. Aldridge particularly enjoyed picking up the phone and answering in the affirmative when a caller asked, "Are you SCAM motors?"

CHAPTER 18

Oddities, Records, and Other Irresistible Miscellanea

BEFORE OUR TOUR of the kaleidoscopic country of Acronymia comes to an end, there are a few curiosities to investigate. First let's drop in on the acronyms about acronyms—those words engaged in contemplating their own navels. Then we should whip out our rulers and measure a few acronym giants. Let's also call on those aristocrats we call the "true" acronyms as well as those pretenders, the folk acronyms, and their cousins, the German quasi-acros. Finally we might join in a rousing round or two of the Acronym Game.

ACRONYMS ABOUT ACRONYMS

There are very few things in this world that people don't have an attitude about. Wars have been fought, families have split irrevocably, whole careers have been made on such seemingly neutral issues as the size of a pin's head, Mama's old casserole recipe, or a three-penny savings on a bar of soap. So it should come as no surprise that acronyms have attracted both supporters and detractors. And both sides have expressed themselves, not surprisingly, in acronyms.

First the "yes" votes:

ACRONYMS
Acceptable **C**ontractions of **R**andomly **O**rganized **N**ames **Y**ielding **M**eritorious **S**pontaneity

BEAR HUG
Basic **E**xtended **AcR**onym **H**uman **U**sers **G**uide

FASGROLIA
FASt-**GRO**wing **L**anguage of **I**nitialisms and **A**cronyms
     Coined by *Time* magazine.

     Now the "nays":

ACRONYM
A Contrived **R**eduction **O**f **N**omenclature **Y**ielding **M**nemonics
     and
Acronyms **C**an **R**eally **O**bsess **N**eurotic **Y**oung **M**en

ACORN
ACronym-**OR**iented **N**ut

APPALLING
Acronym **P**roduction, **P**articularly **A**t **L**avish **L**evel, **I**s **N**o **G**ood
     Invented by *New York Times* editor Theodore M. Bernstein.

CHAOS
Committee for **H**alting **A**cronymic **O**bliteration of **S**ense

CRAP
Committee to **R**esist **A**cronym **P**roliferation

SEA
Society for the **E**limination of **A**cronyms

     Plus there are a couple of mild-mannered ones:

AIM
Acronyms **I**n **M**oderation

ACRONYM
Allied **C**itizens **R**epresenting **O**ther **N**ew **Y**ork **M**inorities

The Giants

The longest pure acronym in English is SWIFT-ANSWER (**S**pecial **W**ord **I**ndexed **F**ull **T**ext **A**lpha **N**umeric **S**torage **W**ith **E**asy **R**etrieval). Note that every one of the eleven letters in the acronym corresponds to a whole word in the phrase. Note also that there are no words in the phrase (not even tiny ones like "the" or "of") whose first letter isn't in the acronym. Kudos to the place where library science and computers meet.

Computers take second place in the pure acronym sweep-stakes with ten-letter COSA NOSTRA (**C**omputer-**O**riented **S**ystem **A**nd **N**ewly **O**rganized **S**torage-**T**o-**R**etrieval **A**pparatus). Coming in third is the slightly less pure but rather flowing CONSCIENCE (**C**ommittee **O**n **N**ational **S**tudent **C**itizenship **I**n **E**very **N**ational **C**ase of **E**mergency). Only the "of" kept it out of a tie for second place.

Once we relax our standards of purity, the U.S. Navy utterly dominates the race. The longest acronym in the English language stretches for twenty-six letters. It's so long that even the acronym has its own abbreviation. COMSUBCOM-NELMCOMHEDSUPPACT stands for **COM**mand, **SUB**ordinate **COM**mand, U.S. **N**aval Forces **E**astern At**L**antic and **M**editerranean, **COM**mander **HE**a**D**quarters **SUPP**ort **ACT**ivities. People in a hurry use CSCN/CHSA.

The next five longest acronyms are also products of the navy's peculiar take on abbreviation. Weighing in at twenty-three letters is NAVELECSYSCOMCENLANTDIV, short (?!) for **NAV**al **ELEC**tronics **SYS**tems **COM**mand, **CEN**tral At-**LANT**ic **DIV**ision. Rather than weigh you down with the next four, we'll just say that they are twenty-one, twenty, nineteen, and seventeen letters long respectively and each one is just as clever and effervescent as the two winners. The navy is apparently wedded to this style of telescoping terms—there are over five hundred such acronyms in existence.

Another prize-winning category is the acronym that is used to stand for the most different phrases. Requirements to enter the contest:

The acronym is at least three letters long.

The acronym is a real word.

At least two of the words from the phrase that's abbreviated by the acronym contribute to the acronym.

The acronym appears in *the* reference book for shortened words, *Acronyms, Initialisms and Abbreviations*, a Gale publication, 1992 edition.

And the winner is ARC, with one hundred and thirty-two different abbreviated meanings, everything from **A**ids-**R**elated **C**omplex to the **A**merican **R**ed **C**ross to **A**irborne **R**adio Control. Why is ARC so popular? First, the "A" is used in many geographic words, like "American," "Australian," "Atlantic," "Asian," etc. Second, the "C" is often the first letter of words that mean "group": Committee, Council, Corporation, Company, Coalition, Commission, etc. ARCs practically create themselves. Try a few yourself. Start with a geographic term for "A," add an "R" word, and end with one of the "C" group words. How about **A**ustralian **R**ugby **C**ommission? Or **A**tlantic **R**ealty **C**orporation? Or **A**merican **R**eptile **C**oalition? (How do you keep those alligators down in the swamp after they've seen New York?)

Returning to reality, the second most commonly used acronym is ACT. The one hundred and nineteen abbreviated meanings include everything from **A**merican **C**ouncil for **T**urfgrass to **A**lliance for **C**annabis **T**herapeutics. In third place is ACE with one hundred and five. There's **A**merican **C**oaster **E**nthusiasts, **A**ctive **C**orps of **E**xecutives, and **A**mateur **C**artoonist **E**xtraordinary, which is an award given by the National Cartoonists Society.

Just for the record, here are the rest of the top ten acronyms: CAP—104, tied with ASP—104, MAP—96, AIM—88, CAT—85, SPA—82, and SIS—78.

"TRUE" ACRONYMS

Of all the teeming thousands of acronyms (more than 100,000 by one estimate, and growing even as we speak), only fourteen have earned their own dictionary entry. Not surprisingly, they are some of the oldest acronyms around. And with two exceptions, these aristos come from science and technology. (Many have been discussed in earlier chapters.)

1. RADAR (1941) (**RA**dio **D**etecting **A**nd **R**anging)

2. SOFAR (1946) (**SO**und **F**ixing **A**nd **R**anging)—A system for locating an underwater explosion.

3. SONAR (1945) (**SO**und **N**avigation **A**nd **R**anging)

4. LORAN (1932) (**LO**ng **RA**nge **N**avigation)—Used by airplanes to determine their geographic position.

5. LASER (1957) (**L**ight **A**mplification by **S**timulated **E**mission of **R**adiation)

6. MASER (1955) (**M**icrowave **A**mplification by **S**timulated **E**mission of **R**adiation)

7. REM (1947) (**R**oentgen **E**quivalent **M**an)

8. REP (1947) (**R**oentgen **E**quivalent **P**hysical)—Similar to REM in that it measures the amount of radiation absorbed by a living being. REMs measure the damage caused by radiation and REPs measure the amount of energy that the radiation causes the living tissues to develop.

9. ALNICO (1935) (**AL**uminum, **NI**ckel and **CO**balt)—A powerful permanent-magnet alloy.

10. JATO (1947) (**J**et-**A**ssisted **T**ake**O**ff)

11. SCUBA (1952) (**S**elf-**C**ontained **U**nderwater **B**reathing **A**pparatus)

12. TOKAMAK (1965) (**TO**roidskaya **KA**mera **MA**gnet-iches**Ka**ya)—A machine used to create controlled thermonuclear power. Its Russian name means "Toroidal Magnetic Chamber."

13. SNAFU (1940) (**S**ituation **N**ormal, **A**ll **F**ouled [*sic*] **U**p)

14. GESTAPO (1934) (**GE**heime **STA**ats**PO**lizei)—German for "Secret State Police." (For a fuller discussion, see page 275.)

(For a fuller discussion, see page 275.)

FOLK ACRONYMS

Acronyms are such delightful critters that some people see them everywhere, even when they're not really there. Take the name for the first popular car—Ford. Though there's no question that the car was named for Henry Ford, its creator, some wags claim that FORD stands for **F**ound **O**n the **R**oad **D**ead.

That one's easy to debunk (and enjoy), but some words have been given mythological acronymic ancestry so convincingly that linguists put a good deal of work into proving otherwise. And sometimes their efforts are not totally convincing because the actual origin of the disputed word is obscure. The following words have been given "folk etymologies," as linguists call the charming if incorrect word histories we folk devise.

Cabal
(**C**lifford, **A**rlington, **B**uckingham, **A**shley, and **L**auderdale)
First the folktale origin of the word. In 1672, during the reign of Charles II of England, the English surreptitiously signed an alliance with the powerful and devious Louis XIV of France, which led directly to a war with Holland, a supposed English ally. The five above-mentioned men were members of Charles's junto of the King's Privy Council, a powerful group of advisers much like our president's cabinet.

They apparently connived with their own boss's arch rival Louis and managed to get the treaty signed without Parliament okaying the move. Perhaps their conspiracy was aided by Charles's tendency to dally overmuch with the ladies. (His father had been beheaded by his subjects and the son was committed to keeping a low profile so as to have any profile at all.)

When the five conspirators were linked in a widely read political pamphlet, the word "cabal," with its coincidental fit with the men's names, became an extremely popular topic of conversation in the coffeehouses of London. People came to believe it was true and even today you'll hear the story told as if it were gospel.

However, "cabal" appears in print in England half a century before Charles II's reign. It meant basically what it means today—a group of people secretly united to bring about some major change or overthrow. "Cabal" can be traced all the way back to the Hebrew word "qibbel" meaning "he received." In the form "qabbalah" it came to refer to the doctrines received by the Jewish people from Moses and handed down century by century. (The mystical tradition of the Cabala, which is an occult interpretation of the Old Testament, is named from this same early root.)

As "cabbala" in medieval Latin, it took on an aura of secrecy and magic as did many old, non-Christian religions during the Middle Ages. So it entered French as "cabale," meaning much as it does today, without the political overtones. And the French gave it to us.

Cop
Constable **O**n **P**atrol

Call a policeman a "cop" to his face and you'll get anything from a glare to a frown to an extra fine on your traffic ticket. Why? Because of the real origin of the word. In eighteenth-century England, thieves "copped" other people's goods. How did an underworld cant word for stealing get associated with the opposition? The thieves themselves turned it into a slang word in the mid-nineteenth century to describe the police apprehending a robber. Soon after, the "er" was added, and a policeman became a "copper."

At this point, several folk etymologies turned up to explain why the bobby on the corner was called by the name of a reddish metal. C.O.P. was said to stand variously for "**C**onstable **O**n **P**atrol," "**C**onstabulary **O**f **P**olice", and "**C**hief **O**f **P**olice." A police officer would supposedly sign a report with his name followed by C.O.P.

There was also some talk about "copper" referring to the copper buttons on police uniforms or even the star-shaped copper badges that some officers wore. But actually the origin is an ancient one. In the Latin of early Rome, "capere" meant "to capture." As an offspring of Latin, French took the word in the form "cap" and brought it to England in the eleventh century when the Norman French captured (ahem) the island.

Some of the early thievish cant flavor has remained with our current word—note such phrases as "cop a plea." J. Edgar Hoover reportedly detested the word and railed against it for many years.

Mafia

Morte **A**i **F**rancesi **I**talia **A**gogna (Death to the French! Italy Lives!)

or

Movimento **A**nti **F**rancesi **I**taliano **A**zione (Italian Movement Against the French)

or

Morte **A**lla **F**rancia **I**talia **A**nelo (Death to France Is the Cry of Italy)

Clearly people have been hard at work trying to make "Mafia" stand for the strong anti-Napoleon sentiment prevalent in Italy in the 1860s. Unfortunately, the existence of three different phrases pretty much proves that Mafia must have a different origin.

It's actually taken from an Arabic word, "mahyah," meaning "boastful." In Sicily, it took on the added meanings of "lawless" and "bold," which in that time and place were both considered good qualities to have.

Why did the citizens admire lawbreakers? Apparently the rulers of Sicily in the eighteenth and nineteenth centuries were a corrupt and despotic bunch and foreigners to boot. Sicilian landowners, who were typically living far from their holdings, hired their own small armies or "mafie" to protect the properties from bandits.

By 1900, these private armies had formed loose confederations or "families" that had taken control over most of the land and the wealth it produced. Landowners paid protection money and never asked for help from the legal authorities under threat of terrible reprisal by the Mafia clans.

Emigration by members of these families led to similar organizations in other parts of the world. "Mafia" turns up in American print around 1860 and by the end of the century, the offshoot criminal syndicate was quite active in this country.

News

North, **E**ast, **W**est, **S**outh

No one knows for certain where this idea originated. One reasonable theory is that a group of newspapers that called themselves "The Globe" had the four cardinal directions printed on their mastheads along with a drawing of a globe.

Another clue comes from an old children's rhyme from England:

News is conveyed by letter, word, or mouth
And comes to us from North, East, West and South.

Wherever the folk etymology comes from, it is perhaps the most popular of all such tales. The true story isn't half as charming.

"News" comes from the Greek "neos" meaning "new" which led to the Latin "nova" which in turn led to the French "noveles" which came over to England in 1066 with William the Conqueror and became the English word "new." "News" is simply a story that is new to the hearer.

Posh
Port **O**utward, **S**tarboard **H**ome

This is one of those stories that should be true but, as they say in *Webster's Word Histories*, "the story won't float."

When India was the "jewel in the crown" of the British Empire, English civil servants did much traveling to and from the colony. Going out to India, they would typically travel on a ship from the Peninsular and Oriental Steam Navigation Company, which was the major steam-packet service in the second half of the nineteenth century. The P&O took passengers (and mail) through the Suez Canal and the Red Sea and the route was often a very hot one.

Old India hands knew that the port side of the ship got morning sun and then cooled the rest of the day. The starboard side got sun in the afternoon and thus was still hot when it was time to turn in for the night. Therefore the port-side cabins were a smart choice, particularly because they also were on the sheltered or lee side of the ship so that passengers going in or out of their cabins would be protected from the weather.

The same steam packet carried passengers back to England and knowledgeable travelers insisted on cabins on the opposite, starboard side for this trip because everything was turned around for the return passage.

The more desirable cabins came to be the most costly and only upper-class passengers could afford them. The tickets of the wealthy were stamped POSH in large letters. "Posh" then moved from the P&O into general usage as a word meaning "elegant and fashionable."

This story is so much fun that the P&O even used it in its advertisements during the 1960s. Unfortunately, it has a couple of holes.

First of all, the P&O itself has no record of ever stamping POSH on tickets or ever referring to any accommodations, expensive or otherwise, with this acronym. And second, though the heat/shade differential may be true, the windy/ sheltered one isn't. The monsoon winds change depending on the season.

So where does "posh" really come from? It's not certain. There's a British Gypsy word for a coin, "posh-houri," that means "half pence," and "posh-kooroona" means "half crown." Apparently this prefix was taken into thieves' slang to mean "money." There's also a British slang word "posh" meaning "a dandy."

Whatever its origin, its first recorded use in print is in 1918 when humorist P. G. Wodehouse used the word with its current meaning.

Snob
Sine **NOB**ilitate
This is another word with mysterious origins. There are two separate stories of acronymic ancestry, neither apparently true. The first involves freshmen enrollment procedures at Oxford University. It seems that any student who wasn't of noble birth was required to write "sine nobilitate" after his name on college forms. This came to be abbreviated "s. nob." Since most university students were of blue blood, the few commoners who chose to mingle with noblemen were seen as aping their betters, thus acting like "snobs."

In the second, very similar story, the university is changed to Cambridge and the abbreviation to "sinc. nob." which later coalesces into "snob."

The *OED* says that the word is "of obscure origin." The earliest mention reported is in 1781, where a "snob" is a cobbler's apprentice. (This name is still used for a cobbler in some English dialects.) In 1796 the word turns up in Cambridge

University slang, referring to any townsperson not a student. But it dies out. In the mid-1800s, it appears again in print, this time describing anyone from the lower or middle classes. Soon novelist William Thackeray, early in his career, uses the word for someone without good taste and, ten years later, uses it for someone who tries to imitate wealthy people in a crude way. By the turn of the century, "snob" is being used as we use it today.

Tip
To Insure Promptness

There is a story about the coffeehouses of London during the middle years of the eighteenth century when learned and oratorical men such as Dr. Samuel Johnson would argue the issues of the time for hours on end. It was said to be the custom to toss a few coins into a box near the entrance when one first arrived. The box was labeled "To Insure Promptness," or T.I.P. for short. This of course is different from our current style of tipping, which occurs at the end of the meal rather than at the beginning.

Once again we seem to have a myth on our hands. Nowhere in the writing of the times is this box mentioned, not even in Dr. Johnson's *Dictionary* nor in his biographer James Boswell's works. However, that is not to say that we know for certain where the word "tip" does originate.

The first time it appears in print, in the early seventeenth century, it is used as thieves' slang and means "to give." A century later, it has come to mean "to give a small present of money." Possibly it's from "stipend," which is a small payment. Or perhaps it's from "tipple," which means "to drink" and might have led to giving the bartender a "tip." What does seem clear is that it is not an acronym.

Azusa
A to Z in the USA

Azusa is a town near Los Angeles and the story goes that the odd name was deliberately created by its founding fathers around the turn of the century. They hoped to suggest that Azusa had everything anyone could want. According to the city clerk of Azusa, Adolf Solis, this story isn't at all true.

"Azusa" is a modern pronunciation of the original Shoshone name for the Indian village that once stood where part of the city is today. The word: Asuksa-gna. It is pronounced "a-sook-SAHG-nah." Kind of pretty, if a bit long for folks who call Los Angeles L.A. So why the myth? Well, Asuksa-gna in Shoshone means "Skunk Hill." It seems there were quite a few of the little stinkers living near the village. And there still are, says Mr. Solis, a fourth-generation Azusa resident.

JEEP or Jeep
G. ("Gee") + **P.** ("Pee")

This word is an anomaly in more ways than one. First of all, there are two perfectly good origins for it, one of which is acronymic. Second, it earned its place in the dictionary (that is, became a true word) almost immediately after it appeared in print. Words typically take decades from first use to dictionary inclusion.

The acronymic story goes like this: The army's initials for this new kind of vehicle, first made in 1939, were G.P., standing for "General Purpose." "Jeep" was a quick way of saying the initials, much as the initialism for vice president, "V.P.," became "Veep."

The rest of America first heard the acronym "Jeep" on February 22, 1941, when the amazingly versatile vehicle was exhibited in Washington, D.C. Everyone read how this little vehicle actually climbed the long flight of stairs of the Capitol building. There was even a photograph.

The nonacronymic version goes like this: One of the most popular comic strips of the '30s and '40s was E. C. Seger's *Thimble Theater* starring Popeye the Sailor Man and his girlfriend Olive Oyl. In March of 1936, Olive gets a gift, a small animal called Eugene the Jeep, that has magical powers—he can foretell the future, travel through time, and always tells the truth when asked a question. Eugene also makes a peeping noise that's written, "Jeep, jeep." The stair-climbing vehicle, being small and seemingly magical, is named after Eugene.

So what's the truth? In all likelihood, the name of the car comes from a combination of the two histories. Does that make "Jeep" an acronebbish?

Gorp

Good **O**ld **R**aisins and **P**eanuts

or

Granola, **O**ats, **R**aisins, **P**eanuts

Why do we call that high-energy handful of nuts, dried fruit, cereal, and chocolate that we munch during a hiking break "gorp"? No one really knows for certain, but there're sure a lot of theories. It doesn't look very promising for the acronymic ones, however. The slang term appeared in print in 1972, and was used for some time before that. There is an earlier slang verb "gorp" that meant "to eat greedily" but it too has an unknown origin.

Other suggestions: It's a blend of "gulp" and "snort" or it's one of the short words beginning with "g" that have to do with eating like "gulp" and "gorge" and "gob."

You VILL Call Me Acronym

The German language has an interesting habit. In a phrase like "chocolate chip cookie," where the separate words put together refer to a single entity, a German might say "chocolatechipcookie." This sort of pushed-together word is a product of a common German language practice called agglutination. Four of the most common World War II words that our language acquired from Germany are shortenings of agglutinate German words.

The best known one is "Nazi." It is an acronymic-like shortening of agglutinate "**NA**tionalso**ZI**alist," part of the name of the National Socialist German Workers' Party. There's also "Gestapo," short for "**GE**heime **STA**ats**PO**lizei," meaning "Secret State Police." And the German dive bomber used early in the war was called a "Stuka," standing for "**STU**r-z**KA**mpfflugzeug," which translates as "dive fighter."

Finally there's the word for antiaircraft fire, "flak," short for "**FL**ieger**A**bwehr**K**anone" or "aviator defense guns." This word has widened in meaning. By the end of World War II, it was soldier-slang for any barrage of words. In the '50s, it came to mean any kind of nagging or criticism, as it still does today.

THE ACRONYM GAME

Some call them bacronyms, some say they're retronyms, and some say that, when we create them, we are acronaming. Whatever you call the gentle art of creating acronyms, it's one of life's small but sustaining pleasures.

Hard as it is to believe, there are those curmudgeons who rail against what they call the "dishonesty" in starting with the acronym and finding a phrase to match it. (These are probably the same folks who claim the piano is a phony, tricked-up version of the noble harpsichord.) They frown on such practices as a group working to aid the homeless calling themselves HOPE and then devising a phrase like "**H**elp **O**ffered to **P**eople **E**verywhere" as the name of their organization.

We not only applaud such acronaming, we invite you, the reader, to join in the fun. Journalists play the acronym game quite frequently, coining terms to capture the latest developments. In fact, linguists have a term for these invented words in the news. If a journalistic acronym or portmanteau is used only a few times before it disappears from usage, it's called a "nonce" word. Several of the more recent terms we've presented in this book, particularly in the chapter on politics, may very well be nonce words—"Billary Clinton," for example, or "guestages."

While we wait to see which coinages become widely used and which are ephemeral as dragonflies, we can play the acronym game ourselves. The trick is to make the phrase you invent match its acronym both mechanically and thematically. The mechanical ideal is to have every word in the phrase match a single letter in the acronym. The thematic ideal is to have the phrase both mirror and comment upon the meaning of the acronym.

For your inspiration and delight, here are some wonderfully successful reacronyms. The first group is from a true artist of acronaming, Reverend Isidore Myers, in his 1915 *Acrostic Dictionary*.

LEGISLATURE
Laws **E**nacted, **G**enerally **I**n **S**incerity; **L**ater **A**mended;
Then **U**sually **R**epealed **E**ntirely

GOSSIP
Goes **O**n **S**preading **S**landerous **I**nsinuations **P**leasantly

FICTIONS
Forgivable **I**nventions **C**reated **T**o **I**mpress **O**ne's **N**agging **S**pouse

A second group is from the talented readers of William Safire's weekly column in *The Washington Post*. He had asked them to help out President Reagan who hated the nickname "Star Wars" that the press had given his strategic defense system. Here are some alternatives Safire received:

GIPPER
Governmental **I**nter**P**lanetary **P**rogram for **E**ffective **R**esponse

BONZO
Ballistic **O**ffense **N**eutralization **ZO**ne

RAYGUNS
Research **A**imed at **Y**ielding **G**reater **U**niversal **N**uclear **S**ecurity (to be called, of course, Ronald's Rayguns)

FLIMFLAM
Fly **L**ittle **I**ntergalactic **M**issiles **F**or **L**ove **A**nd **M**oney

So go for it, gang. Your authors have had several sessions of combing through the dictionary looking for the *mot juste* that will change our acronym from mundane to marvelous. It's a good transition between *Scrabble* and the Dictionary Game on those long winter nights.

And who knows? You might end up with an actual nonce word on your hands if your creation ever sees print. Or even an official acronym that might turn up in the next edition of *Acronym Soup*.

A Note to the Reader

Acronym Soup is not finished cooking. Even as we write these words, someone, somewhere is inventing an acronym. And it may just be funny enough or expressive enough or even caustic enough to belong in this book. In order to keep you up to date on the cream of the crop, we plan to write a second edition of *Acronym Soup*, and to do that, we need your help.

Have you noticed there are many acronyms from Southern California in this book? That's because some of the best acronyms around are the names of local organizations. Since we live in Los Angeles, we've had access to local papers, ads, signs, radio stations, etc., where the L.A. acronyms lurk. Wherever you live, you too encounter your own local acronyms.

If you hear one or two or ten acronyms, local or not, that really impress you, could you send them along to us? If you can tell us where you found them and/or a little bit about them, we would be very grateful.

Should your acronym appear in the next edition of the book, we will, of course, mention your name right beside it. After all, if you've done the legwork, you should get the credit.

Happy Hunting!

Gilda and Phil Feldman
Box 24815
Los Angeles, CA 90024

Bibliography

SINCE THIS BOOK covers a wide range of topics, hundreds of sources were consulted. While essential to chasing down elusive acronyms, the particular volume number of a decades-old magazine would probably be of little interest to you, gentle reader.

However, you might be intrigued by our major sources for acronyms, in case you'd like to do a little acronym-chasing yourself. We also include a list of books we consulted by some of the best-known writers in the field of language appreciation. We found these particular volumes both informative and fun. Finally, we couldn't resist listing a handful of the richest books we discovered that explore the language of a particular subject.

Enjoy!

MAJOR SOURCES OF ACRONYMS

Barnhart, Clarence L., Sol Steinmetz, and Robert K. Barnhart. *The Barnhart Dictionary of New English Since 1963.* New York: Harper & Row, 1973.

———. *The Second Barnhart Dictionary of New English.* New York: Harper & Row, 1980.

Barnhart, Robert K., and Sol Steinmetz with Clarence L. Barnhart. *Third Barnhart Dictionary of New English*. New York: H. W. Wilson, 1990.

Burek, Deborah M., ed. *Encyclopedia of Associations*. 26th ed. Detroit: Gale Research Inc., 1991.

Crowley, Ellen, ed. *Acronyms, Initialisms and Abbreviations Dictionary, Vol. I, Parts 1–3*. Detroit: Gale Research Inc., 1992.

De Sola, Ralph. *Abbreviations Dictionary*. New York: Meredith Press, 1967.

———. *Abbreviations Dictionary*. New York: Elsevier, 1981.

———. *Abbreviations Dictionary*. Boca Raton, Fla.: CRC Press, 1992.

Lemay, Harold, Sid Lerner, and Marian Taylor. *The Facts on File Dictionary of New Words*. New York: Facts on File, 1988.

Soukhanov, Anna. "Word Watch." *The Atlantic* (January 1987 through April 1991).

Tulloch, Sara. *The Oxford Dictionary of New Words*. Oxford and New York: Oxford University Press, 1991.

BOOKS APPRECIATING LANGUAGE

Brandreth, Gyles. *The Joy of Lex*. New York: William Morrow and Company, 1983.

Bremner, John B. *Words on Words*. New York: Columbia University Press, 1980.

Ciardi, John. *A Browser's Dictionary and Native's Guide to the Unknown American Language*. New York: Harper & Row, 1980.

———. *A Second Browser's Dictionary and Native's Guide to the Unknown American Language*. New York: Harper & Row, 1983.

———. *Good Words to You*. New York: Harper & Row, 1987.

Dickson, Paul. *Names*. New York: Delacorte Press, 1986.

———. *Slang!* New York: Pocket Books, 1990.

———. *Dickson's Word Treasury*. New York: John Wiley & Sons, Inc., 1992.

Funk, Wilfred. *Word Origins and Their Romantic Stories*. New York: Bell Publishing Co., 1978.

Hellweg, Paul. *The Insomniac's Dictionary*. New York: Facts on File, 1986.

Homer, Joel. *Jargon*. New York: Times Books, 1979.

Lederer, Richard. *Crazy English*. New York: Pocket Books, 1989.

———. *The Miracle of Language*. New York: Pocket Books, 1991.

Morris, William, and Mary Morris. *The Morris Dictionary of Word and Phrase Origins, Vol. I*. New York: Harper & Row, 1962.

———. *The Morris Dictionary of Word and Phrase Origins, Vol. II*. New York: Harper & Row, 1967.

———. *The Morris Dictionary of Word and Phrase Origins*. New York: Harper & Row, 1977.

Safire, William. *I Stand Corrected*. New York: New York Times Books, 1984.

———. *Take My Word for It*. New York: New York Times Books, 1986.

———. *Language Maven Strikes Again*. New York: Doubleday, 1990.

Spears, Richard. *Slang and Euphemism*. New York: New American Library, 1982.

Wentworth, Harold, and Stuart Berg Flexner. *Dictionary of American Slang*. New York: Crowell, 1975.

WORDS FROM A SPECIFIC FIELD

Armstrong, Richard B. *The Movie List Book*. Jefferson, N.C.: McFarland & Company, 1990.

Becket, Henry S. A. *The Dictionary of Espionage*. New York: Stein & Day, 1985.

Brennan, Richard P. *Dictionary of Scientific Literacy*. New York: Wiley, 1992.

Brown, Les. *Les Brown's Encyclopedia of Television*. New York: New York Zoetrope, 1982.

Flexner, Stuart Berg. *I Hear America Talking*. New York: Van Nostrand Reinhold, 1976.

Konner, Melvin. *Becoming a Doctor*. New York: Viking, 1987.

McAleer, Neil. *The Omni Space Almanac*. New York: World Almanac, 1987.

Pessin, Allen H. *More Words of Wall Street*. Homewood, Ill.: Dow Jones—Irwin, 1986.

Raymond, Eric S., assisted by Guy L. Steele, Jr. *The New Hacker's Dictionary*. Cambridge, Mass.: The MIT Press, 1991.

Reinberg, Linda. *In the Field*. New York: Facts on File, 1991.

Taylor, A. Marjorie. *The Language of World War II*. New York: H. W. Wilson Company, 1948.

Appendix

Would you like to contact any of the organizations we've mentioned in this book? Save a wild horse? Educate your kids about drugs? Straighten out the legal system? Just in case, we're including this list of the most current addresses we could find for many of the acronymically named groups we've discussed. If our information is out of date, try the Encyclopedia of Associations at your local library.

ACORN
1024 Elysian Fields Avenue
New Orleans, LA 70117

ASH
2013 H Street N.W.
Washington, D.C. 20006

ACTION
8601 Georgia Avenue #500
Silver Spring, MD 20910

BACH
P.O. Box #71093
Los Angeles, CA 90071

ADAM
1008 White Oak
Arlington Heights, IL 66005

BLOOP
P.O. Box #1945
Iowa City, IA 52244

AIM
710 Clayton Street #1
San Francisco, CA 94117

BOLD
P.O. Box #6
Aspen, CO 81612

CANDLES
3393 Silsby Road
Cleveland, OH 44118-2936

CARE
660 First Avenue
New York, NY 10016

CORPUS
P.O. Box #2649
Chicago, IL 60690

CUB
2000 Walker Street
Des Moines, IA 50317

DARE America
P.O. Box #2090
Los Angeles, CA 90051

ENCORE
860 South 19th Street
Richmond, CA 94804

EPIC
P.O. Box #397
Garberville, CA 95440

EXPOSE
P.O. Box #11191
Alexandria, VA 22312

GAP
25 E Street N.W., Suite 700
Washington, D.C. 20001

GASP (smoking)
P.O. Box #632
College Park, MD 20740

GASP (environment)
10984 Ridge Road
Nevada City, NV 95959

HALT
1319 F Street N.W., Suite 300
Washington, D.C. 20004

JACGUAR
P.O. Box #02101
Brooklyn, NY 11202

Kids F.A.C.E.
P.O. Box #158254
Nashville, TN 37215

LADIES
P.O. Box #2974
Beverly Hills, CA 90213

LASER
P.O. Box #721
Bountiful, UT 84010

LAW
48 Shattuck Square, Suite 70
Berkeley, CA 94704

LIFE
310 N. Fairfax, 2nd floor
Los Angeles, CA 90036

LOW
P.O. Box #1355
Poplar Bluffs, MO 63901-1355

MADD
669 Airport Freeway, Suite 310
Hurst, TX 76053

NOCIRC
P.O. Box #2512
San Anselmo, CA 94960

NORML
2001 S Street N.W. #640
Washington, D.C. 20009

NOT SAFE
P.O. Box #5743 EA
Montecito, CA 93150

NOW
1000 16th Street N.W., Suite 700
Washington, D.C. 20036

OWL
730 11th Street N.W., Suite #300
Washington, D.C. 20001

PRIDE
71 Plaza Court
Groton, CT 06340

PURE
RR 1
Alden, IA 50066

ROMP
27211 Lasher Road #208
Southfield, MI 48034

SADD
P.O. Box #800
Marboro, MA 01752

SAFE (formerly)
(current name) Wildlife Preservation Trust International
34th Street and Girard Avenue
Philadelphia, PA 19104

SCROOGE
1447 Westwood Road
Charlottesville, VA 22901

SIECUS
130 West 42nd Street
New York, NY 10036

SPERMFLOW
P.O. Box #712
Cascade, CO 80809

TRIM
P.O. Box #8040
Appleton, WI 54913

VISTA
806 Connecticut Avenue, Room 1000
Washington, D.C. 20525

VOCAL
P.O. Box #1314
Orange, CA 95662

VOICES
P.O. Box #148309
Chicago, IL 60614

WAR
P.O. Box #65
Fallbrook, CA 92028

WARN
P.O. Box #423
Rosebud, SD 57570

WHOA!
P.O. Box #555
Reno, NV 89504

WIFE
c/o Cecile Starr
50 West 96th Street
New York, NY 10025

WISE
1527 4th Street
Santa Monica, CA 90401

YES
706 Frederick Street
Santa Cruz, CA 95062

Index

First page number for entry indicates location of principal discussion.

289